ACTIVATE
SUCCESS

Tips, Tools, & Insights
To Be A Leader In Your Niche

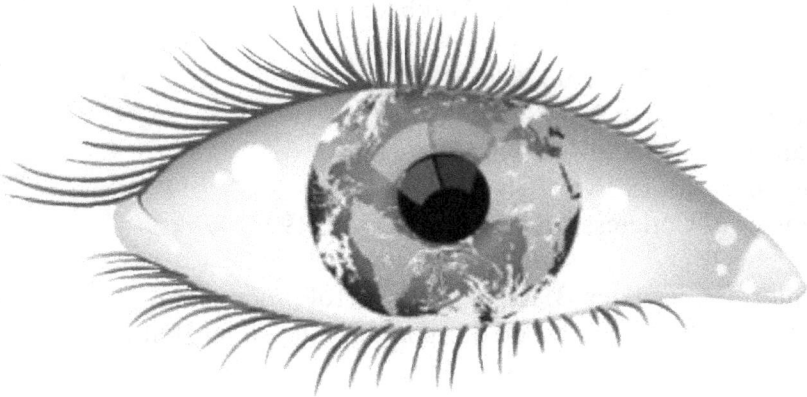

Sujata Ives, PhD
Sandra J. Horton, MA

www.activate-success.com
Print, E-book, Audible, and Workbook

eBook ISBN: 978-1-962570-71-8
Paperback ISBN: 978-1-962570-72-5
Hardcover ISBN: 978-1-962570-74-9
Ingram Spark ISBN: 978-1-962570-73-2
Library of Congress Control Number: 2024905757

Editor: Dr. Jeannine B. Bennett, VisionToPurpose.com
Publisher: Becky Norwood of Spotlight Publishing House

SPOTLIGHT
PUBLISHING HOUSE
Goodyear, Arizona

Endorsements

The world pandemic brought to light that people have numerous choices in their life.

Work life has thrown companies into a state of flux, change, and choice. It is a challenging time in history and so we must capitalize this context to create new definitions for leadership.

When I heard that two female leaders were publishing a book on leadership, I wanted to lend my support to the perspective. They bring a novel standpoint that addresses expectations for self-leading and leading others through specific essential questions of life.

As you read this book, you will begin to gain an understanding of how you can navigate through a myriad of contexts. This means that there is an individual responsibility that is at the forefront of your life for awareness, acceptance, behavior, and action.

The authors openly share their life growth through their experiences. In reading how their lives were shaped through lifespan development and work influences, I hope you will utilize their tips, tools, and insights for decision-making.

You will see that this book is intentionally designed to assist you through self-discovery, change, and impact that can lead to a positive change and supports continuous learning.

I wish the authors great success.

—Shawn E. Boynes, Chief Executive Officer,
American Counseling Association
www.counseling.org

Activate Success has the power to change lives, transform people, and shift journeys to a more positive place. I have known Sandra for many years, and she is a friend and colleague. She and Sujata have been making a positive difference on this planet for many years and they both continue to work hard to make this world a better place for us to coexist.

The same values that I represent in my book, "The Moral Compass," are the same values that these ladies hold dear to transforming the potential that resides in all of us. It is through self-discovery and growth that you can rise into the 2.0 of yourself.

There have been incredible leaders, male and female, throughout history that have had a strong moral compass rooted in integrity and compassion. My goals are the same in that we must stand up for something greater than ourselves so we can leave a legacy and impact this world. Not many females write about leadership so this is a great chance to have a perspective that can embrace integrity-driven success, so use their tips and tools and start integrating them in the work you do.

—**Moe Rock**, CEO, Los Angeles Tribune,
Author of "The Moral Compass"

For anyone seeking success in the workplace, this book is a must-read. It provides actionable insights into strategic thinking, effective communication, and fostering a positive organizational culture. By promoting continuous learning and emphasizing strong leadership qualities, *"Activate Success"* becomes a valuable companion on the journey to personal and professional fulfillment."

—Marty Apodaca, MA, LPCC, CCC, NCC
(He/Him/His)
Manager of Career Counseling, UNM Office of Career Services
President 2024-2025: National Career Development Association
Past President: New Mexico Career Development Association

Based on 50 years of work in the career development field, I feel this book on leadership is exciting in that it is written by two women who have combined their expertise to greatly help you.

—Dr. Marilyn Maze, Executive Director, Asia Pacific Career Development Association | 2016 Presidential Award Recipient, | National Career Development Association | 2010 Lifetime Achievement Award from the Maryland Career Development Association

"Activate Success: Tips, Tools & Insights To Be A Leader In Your Niche" is a must-read book! Not only does it deliver on its promises, but it is co-authored by two incredible heart governed leaders. Dr. Sujata Ives and Sandra J. Horton help global leaders get better at what they do. These powerful leader authors have packed this book with relevant content, tips, tools, neuro-tools, insights, and 27 positive success activators. These activators, when applied, help you create and sustain powerful momentum for self-discovery and transformation.

This amazing book provides crucial perspectives to develop awareness of your resourcefulness and leadership potential. It delves further in helping you develop the clarity needed as a leader to navigate troubled waters, overcome barriers to communication issues, and offer solutions to reach collaborative choices that benefit all. That's really smart and needed today. You benefit from reading 'Activate Success' because it helps you do that and more. The authors provide you with proven strategies to help you achieve higher performance and enjoy the process of continuous positive improvement. Buy the book. Study the book. Apply what you learn, and you'll excel in business and in your personal life. A must read!

Sujata and Sandra are two of my favorite leaders and authors whose united purpose is to help leaders around the globe. I love them both and their important work.

Visit: www.rexsikes.com for life-changing transformational tools & programs!

—**Rex Sikes,** "LIFE ON YOUR TERMS: Live the Life You Want" by Rex Steven Sikes

Two extremely bright, resilient, and capable leaders have gotten together to inspire this world through their intellect, knowledge, wisdom, and ideas.

They communicate empathetically on multiple levels to a wide variation of audiences across cultures and socio-economic spectrums. They had the great idea to put their heads together into actionable steps to improve the lives of others.

—**Robert Ian Bonnick,** Business Growth Strategist in Indonesia | Creating Valuable Dynamic Businesses for Domestic & Int'l Organizations in Indonesia, | Founder SpeakuP Monday-Destination Indonesia | #1 Talk Show for Entrepreneurs & Social Impact (400+ep), | Founder Institute Mentor Co-Creating Valuable Dynamic Businesses for Domestic & Int'l Organizations

It is my pleasure to recommend *"Activate Success"*. This book is a gift that has passion and heart with a strong emphasis on cognition and inspiration. The authors have written a book that is easy to understand and one that can be picked up for everyday life and organizational management. They have brought their empowering initiatives to harness the human potential in this world.

—**Senela Jayasuriya,** Top 10 International Women Speakers Leadership & People Driven Innovation Consultant, | Executive Leadership Coach, Advisory Board Member, | Top 10 International Women Speakers

Dedication and Thanks

This book is dedicated to everyone who works and are devoted to creating industrious and peaceable workplaces.

From Sujata

Expressing unconditional love and appreciation to my devoted husband, Robert Ives, PhD, and my accomplished daughters, Raven Collins JD, and Bryten Ives MS. My darling son-in-law, Evan Collins PhD, and my splendid soon to be son-in-law Jeffrey Sjogren JD. To Mary and Leight Collins, much love always. To Pam and Wade, grateful appreciation for our divine blessings! Thank you, all, for your support and love. I would be remiss if I did not mention the astonishing love I feel for the dogs in our lives: Orion, Khaleesi, and Broonie.

From Sandra

Greatest gratitude and unconditional love to my amazing husband, Gary Horton, who has been my rock, biggest cheerleader, and avid earlier editor. To my incredible children; son Matthew Zenk (Delane), and Nicole Tomkins; along with my exceptional adult stepchildren, step daughter Lizzie Pennock (Cody); Jennifer (Keegan) Fish; Stephen (Emily) Horton; and Kaitlyn (Liam) Brett. My amazing grandchildren Charlotte & Alexandra Fish; Levi, Emerson Brett, and with a soon to arrive newest 5th granddaughter. I feel so blessed, grateful, and honored to be your Mom, friend, and GMA. My absolute love to you all and may we continue to build our strong family bonds based upon acceptance, faith, and authentic connection.

For me, my true desire is to leave a legacy gift for my children and grandchildren. My wish is that with every word I have written may it touch their hearts, inspire their minds, and activate success within to follow their dreams.

"

And the people stayed home.
And read books, and listened, and rested,
and exercised, and made art, and played games,
and learned new ways of being and were still.

And listened more deeply.

Some meditated, some prayed, some danced.

Some met their shadows.

And the people began to think differently.

And the people healed.

And, in the absence of people living
in ignorant, dangerous, mindless,
and heartless ways, the earth began to heal.

And when the danger passed, and the people joined
together again, they grieved their losses, and
made new choices, and dreamed new images, and
created new ways to live and heal the earth fully,
as they had been healed.

~Kitty O'Meara~

"

Foreword

Based on 50 years of work in the career development field, I feel this book on leadership is exciting in that it is written by two women who have combined their expertise to greatly help you.

Their approach through a new leadership model is refreshing and thought-provoking. They ask us to focus on our feelings and values to become conscious leaders. This is a departure from traditional books that I have read on leadership that urge us to mold ourselves into a predetermined model of what society thinks a leader should be.

Leaders need to up-skill their behaviors through self-discovery. This kind of approach will be much more long-lasting compared to traditional methods, because self-understanding leads to change and impact. I believe that this book will help people to grow as leaders in their own unique ways.

As you read this book, take the time to explore your needs and motives. It would be possible to just whip through this book, enjoying the wisdom, smiling in recognition at the stories told by the authors, and happily acknowledging the insights. However, the most value will be gained if you move slowly through the book. Ponder each concept as it applies to your own experiences. Complete the self-exploration activities so that you can gain a deep understanding of yourself.

Ideally, find a colleague to read this book with you, so you can go through the discovery process together. It can be very helpful to discuss your insights with others because others can see eccentricities in us that we cannot see in ourselves.

I believe the approach to leadership that this book takes is far more fruitful than the more traditional approaches. It is helpful to understand the principles of leadership. Correspondingly, knowing how you (personally) have experienced the leadership of others can provide rich insight into how those you hope to lead are feeling and also what they may need from you, as their leader.

Most of those we hope to lead need understanding and support from their leaders. If you can provide that as well as wise direction, you will find yourself leading a healthy team.

Marilyn Maze, PhD
Executive Director
Asia Pacific Career Development Association
Recipient, NCDA Presidential Award

Preface

In the wake of the consequences of an unprecedented global pandemic crisis, war, and turmoil, we are thrilled to present ***Activate Success: Tips, Tools, and Insights to Be A Leader In Your Niche.*** This book equips you with our three-pillar model that involves ***Self-Discovery, Change Readiness, and Sustainable Impact.*** You can use this model to help yourself navigate through the complexities of work and life.

The sheer enormity of a global crisis shook the world of work to its core, and we instantly knew that the world would never be the same again. People lost family members, friends, and neighbors as the crisis ensued, swiftly budding into havoc that grew to mayhem and confusion. People quietly began leaving their jobs in hoards and this led to the 'The Great Resignation'. Workplace jargon changed and expanded into a new language that required different procedures, organizational practices, systems operations, human resource applications, AI, and different innovations.

Agile business practices were desperately needed at the three levels of individual, team, and organization. The workplace was evolving rapidly, and the workplace could not keep up. Many leaders were hoping that things would return back to normal with expeditious healthcare.

As expert leaders, we never assumed that things would return to the old ways. Why? Because crisis, war, and turmoil changes people. In our quest to understand how we could use historical events to adapt to a radical change, we observed that employees were yearning for *empathy*, never prioritized in workplaces before. They needed the creation of something new that could keep up with a new set of values that replaced the old ones with *empathy, psychological safety, and wellness.*

We witnessed extreme shifts in workplace retention, as droves of individuals made the decision to enter into a new reality at home to stay with children, aging parents, and pets. The world crisis highlighted the emergence of a *future employee*, where belongingness, connection, and engagement emerged as requirements for the creation of a new workplace.

Activate Success will assist you to easily identify what you *value* most and especially during transition times, so you can better rethink the way to success for your future. We know that your spirit, soul, and intuition have also entered the new workplace. We know that you are thinking about creating something existentially greater than yourself as you bring your new values into the workplace.

You have been conditioned by the old nature of the business world, which was to outwit, outplay, outlast – as the game of "Survivor" aptly displays. Some have compared the business arena to a jungle, where visuals of hungry animals, obstructed paths, and a hunt for survival become everyday rituals. Visuals that are not encouraging, by any means. We are not certain that pioneer leaders intended for things to go in that direction, but what we can share with you through our experiences is that some people have drastically misinterpreted some toxic behaviors as 'normal professional business practices'.

We encourage you to take a deep dive into creating a pleasing workplace for the future, where people can look forward to driving to work on a Monday morning. Communicate and help create new business models, best business practices, and adroit peace practices.

What happens if you don't take action today? *Nothing*. Nothing will change. As Henry Ford said: "If you always do what you've always done, then you'll always get what you've always gotten". So, take action now at this time in history!

It is not a secret that some companies are continuing to struggle. They keep insisting on preserving old models. Others are desperately trying to seek new roads, but they do not know which ones to choose, and whether they realize it or not, whether forced or not, whether wanted or not, it is no longer the top floor with the gorgeous view that controls the company. Employees are the ones that are directing traffic in and out of the building nowadays. Why? Because people did not realize the impact of global crises. But we always knew that change is constant. It is the fundamental law of physics.

Leaders that are investing vast amounts of time trying to restore the past are falling behind. For them, it is not about creating something new, but rather restoring the old that can safeguard their spheres of influence. Even today, some leaders argue that crisis or transition planning is not a priority.

Post long crisis leaders must work through their discomfort. The evidence is all around, screaming for leaders to take a different perspective. Context and timing have provided a window of opportunity. If leaders fail to act aptly, then consequences will surely follow.

The creation of something brand new can provide a new mindset, for individuals, teams, and organizations, that can activate leadership to a much higher level of excellence. An inclusive mindset of that can provide everyone with the correct strategies to build capacity.

We encourage you to move forward through our three pillars model, and workbook. We give you the roadmap for storytelling, so you can create your own action plan that can support your well-being at work and in personal life. Both lives have a profound effect on each other.

As you implement our professional tips, clinical tools, and experiential insights, the ego will slowly begin to slip away thereby revealing an authentic and skillful you. You will complain, resist, and blame less. A new, improved, nimble mindset will emerge and activate success.

Each chapter will provide a unique perspective on leadership style that can help you to adapt and transition. We want you to bring forth your full potential this year, so that you can become more impactful and influential on the rapidly evolving global stage. But *you* have to be willing to *learn* and unlearn!

We have designed the chapters so you can utilize various leadership styles in your workplace. You will probably have a propensity towards a certain leading style, but do not get too comfortable with only one style. It will be to your benefit to understand how you can use the various leadership styles for contexts, cultures, and people.

As authors, we acknowledge our own propensity towards a certain leadership style, however we have cultivated the habit of turning our motivators and Activators on. This allows us to become flexible so that we can create inclusive workplaces that can provide us with qualitative and quantitative data that is measurable for positive outcomes and successful sustainability.

In summary, an organization is comprised of employees. An association is made up of members. Work is about people. Never lose sight of your people. Listen to and value them.

Perspectives

We discovered, through the long crises, that one of the greatest atrocities in the workplace was the exclusion of diverse and inclusive perspectives. We are certain that every workplace has words that reverberate in the hallways: "The crisis is well over, now let's go back to how things were". The unhealthy insistence on sustaining competitive models that undeniably resulted in inadequate understandings, does not provide progress for anyone. This scenario is toxic, but toxicity can be changed. The exclusion of diverse and inclusive models will bring about excessive trials and tribulations for three levels: individuals, teams, and systems. An individual brings their bias, a team can bring about groupthink, and a system can bring about bureaucracy. (Irving Janis, 1982). A group can easily make faulty decisions due to group bias and pressure. Therefore, change will need to happen in all three levels, and not just in one.

Systems are made up of unique individuals. They try to succeed amidst a number of barriers that stretch beyond crises, war, destruction, scarce resources, and new technology. Humans innately want to succeed, so they will ask their leaders as to what they need to do and how they can acquire knowledge to keep up with the demands of the workplace. They have the desire to fulfill their job duties, so they can keep their jobs and retirements. Of course, their qualifications got them hired, however, human beings are much more than their resume.

The human being is made up of five constructs that function simultaneously to maintain *homeostasis* (balance/equilibrium): biology, psychology, social, cultural, and spiritual. A team is made up of independent individuals that formulate a collective consciousness to function in synergy, again a balance. A system is made up of teams that yield outcomes, again to maintain balance and equilibrium.

An individual may be carrying a gene for a certain ailment, but that ailment will not emerge unless the external conditions are just right to bring it about. This is called Epigenetics. Flight, stress, and burnout, on individual and team levels, have a drastic cost effect on the company. Absenteeism and retention rates due to ineffective communication and conflict have led to legal and violent implications for many organizations. An unfavorable outcome is the result of the interaction of a person's biology, psychology, social, cultural, and spiritual components against the environment. The human body desperately tries to maintain homeostasis (balance) in environment.

The importance of discussing, identifying, developing, and exploring something new is defined in this book as the "**New Normal Phenomenon**". It is going to take much more than "hurry up and get back in the buildings". Why? Because workers are trying to manage trauma.

From this phenomenon, we have discovered that Millennials, Gen Z, and Alpha generations are courageously showing boldness. The renewed boldness is their authenticity. Unlike their grandparents who endured the workplace without offering their perspectives. Newer generations are in constant communication with each other through social media, and this generational reality of knowledge sharing is a challenge for many organizations. As the philosopher Voltaire (1700's) said: "I may not agree with what you have to say, but I will defend to death your right to say it".

If you believe that crises affect individuals (and we do), then you can reasonably assume that long crises also have an effect on teams and systems. The three levels of individuals, teams, and systems are living, breathing entities that have a profound effect on one another. It is imperative to get to know each other, because we do not want any employee to be left behind.

We are completely aware that the constructs of power and status have their place and time where they have an impact at all three levels, formally and informally. People well understand that leaders have the power to exert power (they get it!) but *how* that power is defined and articulated is crucial. If you use power and glory, you will lose your people. Do not use power to destroy, or people will walk away. The truth is the cost of everything has gone sky high; people need their jobs to meet their basic needs. They desperately need their jobs. We want you to use power to do something spectacular in your niche. Activate your potential to make a positive impact at all three levels.

Doing something spectacular is not an easy feat. No single or solitary solution exists for every level — individual, team, or system. Context and timing will dictate appropriate solutions, understand what you, as an individual, want. Then, understand what you, as a team, want. How can you help others? Use this book as a foundation to begin an honest conversation with yourself and others.

Talk about how you can introduce new mindsets and business models with relevant designs. It is the C-suite that decides what is best for their people, but why not ask your people what they want as well? Leaders can no longer afford to put forth one solution or model in every region of the globe. It is not a one-size-fits-all world. Consider various perspectives, viewpoints, and new environments. Henry David Thoreau (19th century American journalist and philosopher) said: "The price for anything is the amount of life you exchange for it."

Environments

The world crisis single-handedly yanked civilization out of a daze.

Every niche (education, health, business, and other) in this world must seize this opportunity in history to make a positive change. Thoughtful decision-making, artful programming, interdisciplinary communication, and common sense can help all niches and the three levels comprised of individuals, teams, and systems. We can do this through all types of learning environments: in-person, virtual, and hybrid.

No bigger impact has been felt than the small business entrepreneur and students who have been the hardest hit and profoundly obstructed by the world pandemic crisis. With looming debt, lack of funding, lost revenues, and government mandates they are trying to stay afloat as best as they can. Will they be able to survive? It can only be possible through reinvention! Strategic alliances that leverage individual businesses potential can thrive. As John Steinbeck said: "I wonder how many people I have looked at, but never seen". We encourage people to continue to reach out until they are seen.

Professionals have gotten proficient at standing at podiums and proselytizing but fail in implementing systems that yield a humane outcome for all. This is a critical juncture for the education systems to evolve from the Industrial Age to the Technological era; it is an opportune time for healthcare to create open doors; and a great time in history for reflection in how we do things in the business world; this is an opportunity for all of us to change.

As society searches for a 'new normal', our willingness and readiness for growth and development will help all of us in meeting a humanistic collective vision. Decisions made for post-pandemic societies need to be inspired through sustainable partnerships, knowledge-sharing, allocating limited resources, and with a genuine consideration for environmental factors. Without humane consideration, the environments in which we work and live will dwindle and grow stagnant.

Learning to Lead the Self

Effective leaders understand that leadership is not about power and glory, but rather about knowledge and understanding. Leadership is about managing individual learning *and* managing individual learning within a group. What we mean by this is: do you learn through ego or empathy? Back brain or frontal lobe? Be aware of how you learn when you are by yourself and also in the presence of others. By this we mean: do you learn through autonomy or social influence?

Understand that people learn differently when they are by themselves versus when they are surrounded by people. Similar to the Hawthorne principle which states that people will work differently when they are alone versus when they are working with other people watching them. Also, understand that everyone has differing learning styles (auditory, visual, kinesthetic), and multiple intelligences (niche interests) that work in conjunction to what the brain is memorizing and retaining. The conscious brain will learn what you want it to learn, what you focus on, and what you give attention to. Your subconscious (unconscious) will remember everything else. You may be under the assumption that your behavior is under conscious control, but most of your behavior is dictated by the subconscious. Until you make the unconscious conscious, it will direct your life and you will accept things as destiny.

We want to bring to your attention that connects of underlying assumptions in the Single & Double Loop Learning Model of Argyris and Schon (1978). They highlight Single Loop Learning that connects results to goals; and Double Loop Learning that connects results to defensive reasoning and underlying assumptions. Their model helps in understanding how we think and arrive to certain conclusions; for this reason, metacognition or thinking about how and why you think the way that you do is vital as you move into the future.

Being open to learning new models is critical for self-discovery and change. If you are already in a leadership role or if you want to take on a leadership role in the future, you must first learn the art of self-leading.

Our roadmap will help you to cultivate transferable or *durable* skills; we do not call them soft skills, because they are not soft, and we support Forbes magazine in their efforts to remove the word 'soft' when it comes to skills other than job-specific skills. You can gain superb durable skills through specific *actions* (*Activators*) that are vital for work, leadership, and life success. This approach takes a marketable shift in leadership because non-textual and non-historical solutions provoke reactions domination, and punitive measures; not conducive for empathy and teaching.

For example: If someone wants to learn how to ride a bike, we teach. If someone wants to learn how to swim, we teach. But when someone fails at work, we complain, get frustrated, and seek to penalize. Why not teach, re-train, and offer assistance instead? This reorientation will take practice, because you are conditioned to work hard for the performance review and not for altruism.

We encourage you to cultivate empathy in the workplace. It was not long ago that you were a neophyte, so try hard not to make it a 'me' against 'them' mindset. Shift your mindset for cooperation instead. It is natural that you are 'for you'; that's what the back survival brain automatically does, but when you work in a team, whether a project team or a C-suite team, you must bring awareness and intention into the mind to support others as well. Upskilling not only refers to your job-specific skills, but especially for your durable skills and mindset.

Contents

Introduction

This *Activate Success: Tips, Tools, and Insights to Be a Leader in Your Niche* book encapsulates three core pillars that are seamlessly threaded throughout its pages:

Pillar #1: Self-Discovery – Navigating internal fundamental inquiries

Pillar #2: Change Readiness – Building capacity for adaptation

Pillar #3: Sustainable Impact – Equipping yourself with an activator mindset

Each chapter in this book contains information related to its respective title, enabling you to easily navigate through the content. We have placed icons throughout the chapters to bring your attention to items that can help you to activate success at work and life. We have written chapter content as the 'drivers' for you.

The fingerprint serves as a guide to practical, professional, and brain (neuro) tips that can simplify your work and life.

The microscope gives you details.

The telescope gives you a bigger picture.

The eye provides insights.

At the end of each chapter, we have placed a section for *Change Management Insight* and *Effective Communication and Conflict Resolution*.

<u>This book provides you with the following items:</u>

1. **Twenty-seven Activators**
2. **The Ives-Horton Leadership Model**
3. **Foundational Constructs:**
   - *Feelings, Values, Stressors Formula*
   - *Empathy-Ethic Principle*
   - *New Normal Phenomenon Concept*
4. **Change Management Insight**
5. **Effective Communication & Conflict Resolution**

The *Activate Success* book is complemented by a hands-on companion called '*Activate Success Workbook*' that will help you to actively immerse yourself in self-discovery to find purpose and meaning in work and life. The very word "Act" is in our title because you cannot activate success without action.

Now that you've familiarized yourself with the preface, and introduction, it's time to start *your* journey by delving into Chapter 1 for some 'Getting Started' information. Once you've received the foundation in Chapter 1, proceed to Chapter 2, where you'll truly embrace the journey with interactive exercises and insightful content. And Chapter 3 and onwards contains leadership education, application, and practice.

We have intentionally brought our life to you as case studies from which you can learn through *Four Essential Questions*:

1. **Who am I?**
2. **Where am I going?**
3. **How do I get there?**
4. **How do I stay there?**

As you write about yourself, you will begin to understand that who you currently are is based on past *learning*. You might decide to *unlearn* what you have believed for so long. After all, wounded people raise wounded people. Make a commitment to discover your true self, because that's all you have that is real and tangible in life.

As you think about *where* you want to go, think about how your unique interests, skills, and passions intersect. As you think about *how* you want to get there to achieve your goals, make a list of priorities. As you think about *how* you will stay true to yourself, make value commitments to yourself. As you ponder change, be open to support the life that you are trying to create through new learnings.

Chapter 1

Getting Started

Welcome to the ***Getting Started*** section of this book, where we embark on an elevated exploration of leadership through our three pillars. In this section, we lay the foundation for understanding leadership as a profound calling, and not merely a position or role. We delve into the conviction that learning, unlearning, and helping others is not just a choice but a deep and altruistic social responsibility that defines the essence of leadership.

Engagement is a core element of this journey. It takes center stage as we explore how meaningful connections drive the leadership experience. As we navigate forward, you will find that expert-level knowledge is the compass that can guide you through the ever-evolving landscape of self-leading and leading others. Finally, we underline that leadership is not a destination, but an enduring journey filled with continuous self-discovery, change, and impact. Let us embark on this enlightening leadership journey to gain powerful momentum.

Leadership is a multifaceted and dynamic concept that encompasses a wide range of skills, traits, and philosophies.

I.   Self-discovery

Free Will: You have power and control over your choices and are making implicit and explicit choices each day. Awareness and intention will help you for sensible decision-making and problem-solving. Your life today is the creation through the choices you have made. If you want different results, then you will have to make different choices.

Learning: The brain was made to learn. Learn how you manage your learning as an individual, so you can understand how you learn as an individual within a team. Attend professional development workshops and seminars at every turn. You may have to unlearn some things from your past. Understand that cognitive dissonance is a barrier to learning.

Emotional Intelligence: You must learn how to manage your emotions so you can best be able to communicate effectively and resolve conflicts peaceably. Empathize with others and build strong interpersonal relationships. Effective leadership is a continuous journey of growth and development. Use metacognition as a guide to improve emotional intelligence.

Strength & Courage: Build strength and courage to take risks to step outside your comfort zone. Face challenges through curiosity and resilience that can yield hope.

Trustworthiness: Your openness and transparency will allow you to easily navigate through integrity and consistency. Transparency and honesty can save everyone's time.

Responsibility: Be responsible with work and life duties. The leadership tasks, local and global levels, come with a huge responsibility to self and others. Responsibility is the main reason why you should accept leadership positions, and not for power and glory.

Adaptability: Be open to change your habits and reset your behaviors under new situations. Adapting takes practice, because the back brain wants to keep you in your comfort zone. In this day and age, adapting or pivoting is an upskill.

Communication: Articulate your expectations, mission, and vision often! Utilize all modes of effective communication to ensure that you are heard and that the message resonates for others.

Don't forget common sense – be extra clear in your emails; there are no nonverbals there.

Cultural Humility: Acknowledge that you don't have all the answers. Be open to learn about cultures, nations, and practices. We invite you to upskill your leadership habits and patterns to include cultural humility, because there is a tendency to view the Western mindset as the best one for all regions of the world (Ives, 2024, NCDA white paper).

Inspiration: Learn how to inspire and motivate yourself, so you are not reliant on others to do this for you.

Conflict Resolution: Address conflicts promptly and diplomatically. Turn conflicts into opportunities for growth and collaboration. We will teach you the magical formula for effective communication and conflict resolution in this book.

II. Change Readiness

Mindset: Be open to change through an open mindset that can allow you to navigate through change. Your back brain ego will insist on holding you back; resist and fight those survival urges.

Role-modeling: Demonstrate positive behaviors that lead to modeling, coaching, mentoring, and scaffolding.

Empower through Empathy: Encourage autonomy through the **Empathy-Ethic Principle** that supports people's interests, skills, and abilities. Do not compare people but meet them where they are in their lifespan development stages that require distinct needs to be met. Therefore, our definition of our *Empathy-Ethic Principle* encompasses empowering people through an understanding and consideration for their unique skill sets, interests, and goals.

Motivate through Momentum: Get to know each individual, their needs, wants, and dreams. Provide the internal or external motivation items that are necessary for each to grow and change.

Conflict Resolution: Seek consensus through open dialogues that do not have repercussions, understanding through restating and reframing, open-mindedness through free will, and inclusivity through humility.

III. Sustainable Impact

Purpose and Meaning: Individuals need a higher purpose in the daily tasks that they are performing through their interests and skills that can be supported through recognition and celebration.

Lead by Example: Your team depends on you to be an example towards high performance, results, and sustainability.

High-Performance: Understand the strengths of the individual team members to create high-performing teams. Whether you are a team member or leader, you can encourage, empower, and inspire. Provide opportunities and take advantage of learning opportunities.

Strategic Planning: Consider a mission and vision through sustainable development goals that take into consideration natural resources and economics for future generations. Create strategic plans, succession plan, transition plan, and crisis plan.

Habits: Create habits that can cause people to embrace change and sustainability, through evaluation, reflection, adaptability, innovation, and celebration. It is conditioning that can create lasting habits.

Effective Communication & Conflict Resolution: Having a communication process in place that allows for open dialogue, understanding, and acceptance, where conflicts are viewed as opportunities for growth and cooperation. Ask people how they wish to resolve disagreements; set ground rules; and explain how they can move from storming to forming in a peaceful manner.

Co-Elevation: Develop an attitude of curiosity, Empathy-Ethic, interconnectedness to achieve collaborative results.

Positive Organizational Culture: Bring people together through common values, cultural humility, collaboration, inclusion, and innovation. The workplace is home away from home, where you spend at least forty hours, so pay special attention to creating a positive company culture.

Leadership Defined

What is the first thing that comes to mind when you hear the word *leader*? The topic of leadership invokes many thoughts, feelings, and images from the past. Leadership, as we define it in our book, refers to a **role identity** that is both implicit and explicit, in which that distinct **role** impacts yourself and others. *Role* impact will be evident through your perspective in how you make decisions and problem-solve, and your focus on human relationships.

Various sectors use the word *'leader'* interchangeably with *'manager'*. For clarity, generally leaders accomplish their *role* through a *telescopic* lens, and a manager implements tasks via rules, regulations, procedures, operations, and logistics through a *microscopic* lens. Leaders use managers to carry out their mission and vision on a daily basis.

Whether you accept a leader or manager *role*, you must begin, first and foremost, with self-discovery. If you do not know *who you are*, then you will not be able to consciously and appropriately lead others, and you will not know the difference between how you lead through your *role* versus how you lead through who you authentically are.

Through our innumerable work and life experiences, we have activated success through personal assessment, an openness to change, and understanding that our decisions will have a sustainable impact on others.

This book is for *everyone* who wants to activate success at work and in life!

Leadership is a Calling

Don't do it because your boss, partner, or parent wants you to do it. It is crucial to understand that leading others is a calling. But how can you lead others if you do not know how you lead yourself? Getting to know your strengths and challenges will help you to activate success in leading others. Leading others requires an understanding of and an openness to diverse perspectives, awareness, reflection, dialogues, and more. If your feelings get hurt when people express their perspectives, then leading others can wait until you have cultivated growth and awareness. Without leadership people skills, there will be colossal miscommunication that leads to calamitous consequences.

Unfortunately, too many workplaces are filled with miscommunication, hostility, and toxicity. Workplace toxicity is sneaky, invisible, and insidious, and it can jump out when you least expect it as a cruel blindside. The leader of the future will need to learn how pertinent and durable skills can help to prevent toxicity.

Today's conflicts are emerging from older models that no longer work today: working 9-5 by using company equipment; predefined work; no voice; corporate focus. The new employee wants to work anytime, anywhere; use all devices; wants to create their own ladder to leadership; wants to be creative and do customized work to accomplish tasks; wants to collaborate through a myriad of technologies; and through values, democratic learning, training, and knowledge-sharing.

Employees want to be taken seriously in the workplace, and most of them have come to terms that their boss is their job.

One way to help communication is to collect the team and remind them of the mission and vision of the company. It should not be posted and forgotten, because those tenets are the glue that holds everyone together. Those sentences become especially useful, when people feel like they have nothing in common. In addition to mission and vision, we encourage the creation of a set of values that can be posted where everyone can see them as they enter the workplace. Does your organization have a set of *values*? Many do not. Values such as having a strong work ethic can bring about effective communication in the workplace.

We encourage you to embrace the value of an open mindset that balances your results-oriented approach in the clinical workplace. Yes, you read that correctly: clinical. We view the workplace as highly experimental and qualitative and refer to it as "***Work Science***" because it is a setting where people judge and behave through strongly held beliefs. For this reason, we encourage you to adopt the scientific method where you can logically observe without judgment or bias. This all begins with you first.

To get you thinking about self-leadership, let's start with a question:

How would you describe your relationship with yourself? Answering this question may take a moment, so please take a breather here and think about the relationship you have with yourself.

Your needs motivate how you pursue specific skills, and those skills lead you to a particular employment niche. This is fine on the basic level and everyone operates this way, but you must dive deeper if you want to work well with others. You must make the time to dive deep and learn how and why you lead yourself the way you do. You may not have achieved certain desires because your thoughts and feelings may have unconsciously hindered you. Only through introspection can you learn how to evolve yourself to conscious self-leadership.

Some people get stuck in basic emotions such as anger and jealousy. These negative emotions can eventually exacerbate their stress-induced biological somatology, which then has an effect on attendance and retention. They wallow in ill feelings where anger, as a secondary emotion, emerges to be in a chronic relationship with the self. If they are in an angry relationship with themselves, then they will be in an angry relationship with others.

Part of learning how to build a healthy relationship with yourself is to listen to negative self-talk, limiting beliefs, and metacognition (think about how and why you think the way you do). There is great value in assessing and building a great relationship with yourself through positive self-talk and thinking. The relationship you have on the inside will determine a similar outcome on the outside. Do you like yourself? If not, then you alone have the power to change that.

Stay the course and keep committed to self-improvement, so you can work with others.

Helping Others is a Leadership Responsibility

Helping others does not impede your own success; in fact, it significantly enhances it.

Life's purpose isn't about taking from others or putting others down to gain for yourself. A scarcity mindset will lead to a limited existence for you. Embrace the idea of an abundant world with ample resources for everyone. Focus on bringing value and integrity into the workplace, so you can help others to cultivate it for themselves in turn. Some may have more education than you, while others may have more experience than you. Embrace them and help them activate success towards their goals and dreams.

Actively listen to others so you can make a strong connection with others. Even with people you think you do not like. Understand the myriad of cultures that are represented in the workplace and accept that backgrounds affect their thinking and behavior. There is great value in this. Do not be afraid to learn from diversity – color, race, or perspectives.

What happens when someone you have helped gets a promotion before you do? Has this happened to you, and how did it make you feel? This is one of those valuable lessons in the workplace. Sometimes people get "Leapfrogged". This term refers to someone behind you that gets the promotion instead of you. The reasons may encompass many variables: from politics to broken systems. And "leapfrogging" will certainly cause a reaction in the biology and psychology of you.

As a leader, you are also a human being with feelings. This lesson is a good example for self-discovery. The biological sensation in your gut are sensory neurons (sometimes called 'butterflies'), and they will tell you if you are feeling jealous or resentful. If you feel ill feelings, you will attract hurt. And hurting people hurt others. So, the best thing to do when this happens is to feel those ill feelings, then intentionally and consciously let them go. Feelings are visitors. You do not have to hang on to them or invite them into your body to stay. Leaders and managers are not exempt from experiencing ill feelings. We are all human beings that have a primitive back brain where negative feelings reside.

The grass will always seem greener on the other side, but remember they are watering it with positivity and that's why it's so green. It was Carl Jung (1875-1961) that warned about a "shadow side" that is dark and negative and needs vigilance. Be aware that this side of you does not take over your rational, sunny side.

The sooner you reorient and let go of ill feelings, the sooner your turn will arrive. Be patient and kind, so that the right time and place will arrive sooner than later. Everyone has a star above their head. Just because you did not get something today does not mean that you will not get it at all. NO stands for "Next Opportunity". Trust that something better is coming for you.

When you intentionally and consciously let go of hurt, you will be better equipped to activate success through your conscious brain. Cultivate a cathartic desire to discover your true self, because that will *cause all of your other worldly desires to cease.*

Remember this saying: *When things go my way, the world has my back. When things do not go my way, the world still has my back.*

Engagement For Change

Change can either be viewed as difficult or easy. It can be either avoided or embraced. A leader's experience with change can determine their ability to change. The key is self-awareness. Leaders need to put their bias and schema aside to fully support the people they lead. When it comes to change readiness, we encourage leaders to adopt an engagement-focused approach that is void of bewilderment and confusion. Effective communication is the pinnacle of engagement and connection, where engagement and connection are antecedents to relationship-building and conflict-resolution. Therefore, effective communication means that you must connect with people; and connection takes commitment, time, and effort.

Learn how to communicate effectively and do not assume anything. Be as specific as possible in team interactions and during conversations with individuals. People cannot read your mind. It will not be their fault if the results they produce do not match your instructions. You must provide explicit directions and repeat them often through multiple modes of communication.

People need reminders. The brain needs repetition to bring information from short-term (STM) to long-term memory (LTM) storage. Generally speaking, the human species have terrible memories, so we must use strategies to help memory. Strategies such as repetition, writing, and mnemonic devices to remember things, as well as lists, email reminders, alarms, timers, and visuals can help people conduct their business without the forgetting curve (Ebbinghaus, 1913) hampering their success.

Explore these questions: Was there a time where you discovered that your memory was unreliable? When do you feel you deserve success more than someone else?

Effective communication is one of the best 21st century skills that you can cultivate. The quality and candor of your values in your speaking and writing will determine the results you achieve from yourself and others. And while change is constant, you can still intentionally remain consistent through how you speak, write, and act.

Dependent and independent variables are relevant for individuals, teams, and contexts, because change is constant. This is a law in physics. Due to changing variables, it is important for you to remain aware each day. It is mission, vision, and values that can greatly assist you in staying consistent in your communication. And it is the *meaning* that you assign to people, places, and words, that will lead you astray.

Observe people's behavior, and do not *absorb* it.

Effective communication requires a rational response. Remember this:

My reaction to an event determines the outcome! My reaction to an event determines the outcome! My reaction to an event determines the outcome!

We bring you an example from a Hollywood actor who had a professor that took him out to a bar, treated him to a beer, and told him to find another career choice. He could tell the story in a negative way, but the consistency of his values shines through when he tells the story in a positive way: "This is the only professor who took me out and treated me to a free beer!".

A great leader will be someone who helps others overcome and manage external *and* internal challenges. What distinguishes one leader from another is their attitude, skills, knowledge, and values.

Negotiating for change requires the ability to create a positive mindset. The good news is that the brain has neuroplasticity, whereby the brain can make new connections to evolve and grow.

Clearly Define the Change You Want

Change requires negotiation skills. Before entering into negotiations, it's crucial to have a clear and well-defined understanding of the change you are advocating for. This includes identifying the reasons for the change, the expected benefits, and how it fits with organizational goals. These are the strategies that worked for us.

Effective Communication:
Clearly communicate the rationale for the change, its potential benefits, and how it aligns with the values and goals of the organization or community. Tailor your message to resonate with the concerns and interests of your audience.

Create a Win-Win Scenario:
Seek solutions that benefit all parties involved. Emphasize the positive outcomes and advantages that the proposed change can bring to different stakeholders. This approach increases the likelihood of gaining support.

Be Open to Compromise:
Negotiation often involves give-and-take. Be open to compromising on certain aspects of the change while still maintaining the core objectives. Flexibility can help overcome resistance and foster collaboration.

Highlight Success Stories:
Provide examples of similar changes that have been successful elsewhere. Real-life success stories can serve as powerful evidence of the positive outcomes that can result from embracing change.

Anticipate and Address Resistance:
Proactively identify potential sources of resistance and develop strategies to address them. Whether it's concerns about job security, fear of the unknown, or other issues, addressing resistance, instead of ignoring it, is crucial for successful negotiation.

Use Data and Evidence:
Support your case with relevant data, research, and evidence. Demonstrating the facts and potential benefits of the proposed change can strengthen your position and build credibility.

Be Patient and Persistent:
Negotiating for change is often a gradual process. Be patient, persistent, and prepared for setbacks. Consistent communication and a positive attitude can help overcome obstacles.

Seek Feedback:
Encourage feedback and input from stakeholders throughout the negotiation process. This not only shows respect for diverse

perspectives but also allows for adjustments based on valuable insights.

Understand Stakeholder Perspectives:
Recognize that different stakeholders may have diverse perspectives and concerns. Understand their interests, needs, and potential objections to the proposed change. This information is valuable for developing a negotiation strategy.

Build a Coalition:
Form strategic alliances with individuals or groups who share a common interest in the proposed change. A united front can strengthen your negotiating position and provide additional support during discussions.

Expert Level Knowledge is Necessary

Malcolm Gladwell's book "How David Beats Goliath" states that being an expert means having 10,000 hours of doing something repeatedly. All workplaces have policies, procedures, and regulations that require job-specific skills, so be sure you have the necessary years of experience to call yourself an ***expert***. Your expertise will enhance your credibility, and your credibility will improve your reputation where you can use your reputation to help individuals, teams, and systems.

Ensure that your reputation is not tainted via ego that self-inflates your ability to do something as an expert. There may be people you dislike and some will not like you either, for this is the fundamental reality in work and life. People will accept that you have a certain level of expertise in a certain niche, but it is your ego that can cause people to dislike you. Self-leadership requires you to keep your ego in check so you can help others without instilling fear and anxiety in them.

The last thing you want to hear someone say is, "I can lead far better than they can."

You may have years of experience, but you must be able to articulate *why* you want to be a leader. Understand that leadership is a professional responsibility to others, and the goal of leadership is to bring respectful clarity (not confusion), upskilling (not down-hilling), and expertise (not contempt) to the table.

Being a leader means that you will have to shift from doing to leading. This means that you will have to know your people very well. Know which people can solve which problems. You will have to delegate, communicate, coach, and not dictate or abdicate solutions.

Everyone's brain is different. We all think and process information differently. What is fascinating is that the primary function of the human brain is to learn. The human brain has the ability to learn and unlearn. Specialized structures allow the brain to *sense* (through six senses), *think* (through perception), *feel* (through emotions), **perceive** (through focus), and *judge* (through bias).

Everyone has the same anatomical structures, yet everyone's brain takes them through these functions uniquely. This uniqueness is unavoidable because people all have learned *beliefs, assumptions, habits, and experiences.* The brain never sleeps. It constantly engages in: thinking, judging, solving, reflecting, and imagining.

Each person has a different past history that contributes to their beliefs. No wonder there is so much miscommunication and conflict in the workplace. Everyone has different expectations and expositions, just as you have noticed through our Essential Questions.

With our expert knowledge, you can use the information in this book to unify people.

Perhaps your experience, education, certifications, and training landed you on the leadership track. However, it takes much more than a résumé to be a great leader. You must pay attention to the existential threat against everyone as a whole.

The **The New Normal Phenomenon** will require much more from you as a leader. Return-to-office and flexibility battles will ensue, and workers will demand stability in company culture. The C-suite needs to take note that empathy will gain much more importance than it ever has in the past. Presenting yourself as an expert in a niche speaks volumes, but everyone is on the same level now because not many leaders have expert knowledge of how to activate success from a global crisis.

Leadership is A Journey

Leadership is akin to taking a mountain expedition, ocean voyage, or a long scenic drive.

Each person that you encounter is on their own special journey in life. Hence, it is no big surprise that leading people is about meeting people where they are on their roadmap of life, and not projecting your bias or expectations onto them at work. You must learn a wide variety of techniques and methodologies different from those you use when there is no crisis, war, or trauma.

Getting to know the journey that your team members are on will save millions of dollars for your company, because taking the time to know where their mindset is can help retention efforts. Make the time to get to know who they are, where they are going, and how they intend to get there. Are you connecting the dots?

You will find that some people need a *hands-on* approach while others require a *hands-off* approach. They will have different learning styles, multiple intelligences (Howard Gardner), and different personalities, and various preferences. Given these independent variables, you must communicate with your team in a myriad of leadership styles, not just in one way or one time.

Today, leadership exists in a tech heavy decade, so use that to your advantage. The term 'diversity' is widely used through multiple definitions, and for us it encompasses culture, but also modes of delivery, thinking, and doing. Through virtual communication, you may notice neurodiversities on the team, but do not be put off by this fact, because creativity is an asset. Just look at Elon Musk, who has a neurodiversity. Almost one-third of your team will have undiagnosed or diagnosed mental health needs. We urge you to understand and accept the plethora of diversity and traumatic brain conditions that exist on the biological, psychological, social, cultural, and spiritual levels. This is knowledge that was nonexistent in the last decade but is a part of work and life today.

Biologically speaking, the brain is the master organ. It judges all day, and this judgment can quickly take you down a negative road. Through awareness you can intentionally safeguard confidentiality and common sense. Judging others reveals aspects of you and may prevent you from promoting someone due to a neurodiversity. Elon Musk publicly announced his neurodiversity to the entire world on the show 'Saturday Night Live', and through his public disclosure, he made a plea for companies to accept everyone at work without judgment, and shared that neurodiversity is accompanied by creativity and innovative thinking. Whether you like him or not is not relevant, our point here is that Musk opened the door for neurodiversity to become untabooed.

Our research proves how beneficial a supportive leader who provides a supportive environment can be. And although people do not refer to a workplace as a *clinical* setting... it absolutely is!

The leadership journey is an exhilarating road to travel. It is filled with promise and purpose and brings exciting leadership challenges. Do not allow the fear of change to prevent you from getting started on the right path towards workplace fulfillment. Your willingness to change will be proportional to the activation you need for success.

Roles

Roles include daughter, son, father, mother, cousin, worker, friend, neighbor, doctor, lawyer, engineer, statistician, chemist, baker, fireman, comedian, soldier, etc.

In your *roles*, you bring the sum total of your biology, psychology, social, cultural, and spiritual self. All of these constructs affect who you become and how you behave in your *roles*.

The biology of you is made up of eleven systems working together through genes, environment, hormones, and neurotransmitters to maintain homeostasis (balance). For example, dopamine (a neurotransmitter) is released upon task completion; oxytocin (a hormone) spills into the bloodstream when you shake hands or hug; serotonin (a neurotransmitter) enters when you actively engage with others; and endorphins (a hormone) when you receive positive feedback, recognition, or celebration. The eleven body systems will react based on food and drink, too. Healthful eating, personal hygiene, and sleep radically affect your eleven systems. The good news is that all of your cells are on your side: they have a to-do list and healing miraculously occurs overnight. Think of a paper cut that heals by the next morning or an alert that your stomach is not up to par, or an increase in body temperature. This is evidence on a physical dimension that your body knows to give you signals to help it to heal and regain homeostasis. Can the mind do this as well?

Your psychology of you is comprised of metacognition, which is *how* you think. There are ~74 thousand thoughts that pass through your brain each day. Your brain judges, perceives, thinks, and your mind feels, opinionates, and reacts due to past experiences you remember through memory storage. Learning new things, reading, math, music, and delayed gratification positively activate your cognition, memory, and behavior. Reading great books is the single best thing you can do to create new pathways in the brain.

The Social of You focuses on parents, siblings, extended family, school and teachers, music and books, and social media that have influenced your values, beliefs, assumptions, morals, and interests. Your choice of peer groups, books, and music will affect your values. The social of you also includes your involvement, engagement, burnout, relationship navigation, decision-making, and problem-solving.

The Culture of You has an impact on cementing your values, beliefs, assumptions, and biases through traditions, customs, and birth language. Finding habits you enjoy, having meaningful dialogues with people, and traveling are essential for growth.

The Spiritual of You is the inside voice that speaks to you as "Me, myself, and I." The spirit of you believes in something greater than yourself and brings your head-brain and heart-brain together. Spending time alone, meditating, praying, and contributing to a just cause are all things that can satiate the spirit that resides inside of you.

You don't have to be from another country to be in a culture. Every family is a culture because each has traditions, celebrations, and norms that they habitually repeat. For example, two American people can have much conflict in their family even though they both come from the same race. Conflict concerning culture is not relegated to cross-cultural circumstances alone but has much more to do with what people believe, assume, and value.

You bring the biology, psychology, social, cultural, and spiritual of you to each role that you undertake. These five constructs show up each and every time you engage with another person.

Schema

The way you were raised and what you have espoused inside of you is called your *Schema.* Your beliefs, assumptions, experiences, and biases walk into work each morning. If you are unaware of your Schema, it can create havoc for you at work and in life. **Connect The Dots** here: you are a human being with a set of behaviors that you bring to work each day, which are due to the formation of your distinct schema. Your schema gives you your perception, where you are one hundred percent correct from that perception because it is your worldview.

You bring your Biology, Psychology, Social, Cultural, and Spiritual sides to work each day. Look at your hands and think about what they have written, cooked, cleaned. Look at your eyes and think about what makes them stare. Look at your feet and think about where they have taken you. Look at your lips and think about what they have said. Understand the five constructs and how they affect your every move.

This makes *ten* properties implicitly or explicitly influencing a given interaction between two people. This is what makes every relationship highly complex. People rarely consider these items when interacting, but now that you have this pertinent information, you can use it to your advantage in your interactions at work and in life. This knowledge alone will save you time, heartache, and thousands of dollars in therapy.

You are the common denominator in situations that you find challenging, so please heed our advice to self-discover and improve yourself before questioning why others behave the way they do. Be open to receiving and implementing the words you are reading.

Whisper to yourself: "I am open to receive."

Now say it out loud: "I am open to receive, I am open to receive, I am open to receive."

Habits

Your behaviors have turned into patterns that have turned into habits. *Is what you are currently doing working for you?* (Pause and really think about this for a minute). Your subconscious mind is built on habits. It is not logical, but emotional and literal; it records everything, and is always awake.

Changing habits takes lots of practice, so get to know yourself as best as you can before you tackle the second step of making changes in your life. Taking the time to think about and writing down *who* you are, *where* you are, and *why* you think the way you do will genuinely help the true self emerge on paper. And what you were truly meant to do at work and in personal life will certainly be a liberating moment for your life.

A good psychologist may say that you are **stuck** (a clinical term), and you may be. Most people get stuck because they are subconsciously committed to a pattern of behavior. At some point, those behaviors become more harmful than helpful. Experiment and flip the script in your head, and you will surely get a different result. If your self-talk is negative, flip the script and see what happens.

Most of your thinking comes from the Limbic System, which is the emotion center of your brain. That's why you react quickly, instead of taking the time to sensibly respond. One of the first things you must do is to discern your feelings precisely. Be mindful of what feelings upset you easily. Try and get your "I'm offended" list to a minimum. Any little thing you say or do has the potential to activate another person's primitive back brain—the tone of voice, a look, a whisper, how they chew their lunch, etc. If you are feeling offended, ask yourself why, and take a long hard look at yourself. What is causing these feelings to resonate within you?

Feeling offended can be narcissistic. Why do situations offend you? Situations cannot create feelings; only your thoughts about the situation can create your feelings for you. It is your perception about a certain situation that causes certain feelings to arise.

The key is to get your "I'm offended" list down to zero. Remember, just because you are offended does not mean that you are in the right. Any relationship that can be ruined from a candid conversation regarding your feelings is not stable. What offends you, and why? When you feel offended, stop what you're doing and ponder this: Something is resonating inside of me (in my subconscious) that is causing these feelings to come into my consciousness.

Anything that offends you teaches you something. Perhaps you need to learn patience? Anything that angers you is teaching you empathy. Something you detest is teaching you about acceptance. Something you fear is teaching you about courage. Please understand this.

People carry their poor habits into the workplace, and this results in conflicts and toxic environments. People do not leave jobs. They leave people. For this excellent reason, we are bringing you a golden formula for effective communication and conflict resolution that will help you to understand human behavior and eradicate toxic workplace environments.

Power

Every leadership program must provide a course about how to use power. When we talk about power we refer to the control and influence that a person has on individuals, teams, and organization.

We want to make certain that leaders understand the full ramifications of the power that they are entrusted with and to use that power in organizational, social, and interpersonal structures in a humanistic manner. Leadership means responsibility. And responsibility means power.

There is a great deal of responsibility that comes with power. Leaders quickly understand that they hold much power, but great leaders will also understand and use it to motivate and empower through fairness, and without malice.

Consider a time in your life where you had a bold leader that led with impartiality and fairness? Now, think of a time where you had a bold leader that led through power and glory?

Be aware of the ego. Having power feels good to the ego. Do not allow the ego to take over. This is why the first pillar of self-discovery is of utmost importance. We want you to be aware of how your unconscious can easily misuse power. The potential for greatness is vast when the power you hold is used in an egoless manner without politics and self-glorification.

A power-hungry leader cannot possibly make a positive change, because change requires patience and humility. The image of their arms behind their heads and their feet upon their desk is a powerful ego stance and a is popular way that the ego shows the world who holds power.

When power and ego find each other, there is no trust or goodwill for humanity.

How to ACTIVATE Success

Believing that you have a superpower is a prevailing strategy that many people use to activate success, but you may be subconsciously impeding your success through a static mindset, unhealthy ambition, or self-doubt.

Take control of your learning, because change can come effortlessly when you think and do the right thing. If per chance, you do not do the right thing, then do the next right thing. As long as you are moving in a positive direction, you will never fail to activate and accelerate your success. The Japanese believe in "Ikigai," meaning "a reason for being." Learn who you are when you are alone. Learn who you are with others. A reason for being who you are gives you passion and purpose to do the work you do.

Be aware that change is a critical process that takes time. It may take a few months to transform casualty into conscious understanding. You may not be able to change yourself overnight. Keep at it, and do not lose focus.

Much internal strife manifests due to secret hidden wishes. Have the courage to ask for what you want at work and in life. If you don't get what you want today, ask another day. Write down exactly what you want on paper so you can look at it and where it is stares back at you. Do not wait for your boss to come to you, because you may be waiting for a long, long time, and that waiting time will make you resentful.

Learn to treat everyone with respect. You don't have to like someone to show respect; you just need a professional standard for yourself. That's what a best professional practice looks like.

Use this book to create positive ripples and conduct deep dives by exploring your sunny and shadow sides. You can create change through your narrative. We invite you to use the **Ives-Horton Leadership Model**, which is our three-pillar model that activates success. Make a change through *Self-Discovery, Change Readiness, and Sustainable Impact*. We want you to keep remembering these three pillars throughout the book. Use the

Activators that we provide for you to spur your success onwards. In the body, enzymes are needed to create chemical reactions; *activators* work as enzymes in your mind to help psychological activity towards success.

Answering our **Four Essential Questions** will help you to become an effective professional human being. How? Through an awareness of how you *manage your learning* (self-leading) and how you *manage your learning with others* (change).

Ives-Horton Leadership Readiness Model™

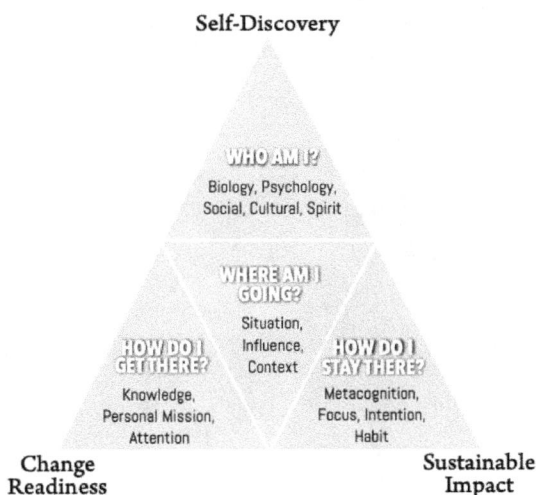

Self-Discovery

WHO AM I?
Biology, Psychology,
Social, Cultural, Spirit

WHERE AM I
GOING?
Situation,
Influence,
Context

HOW DO I
GET THERE?
Knowledge,
Personal Mission,
Attention

HOW DO I
STAY THERE?
Metacognition,
Focus, Intention,
Habit

Change
Readiness

Sustainable
Impact

Don't rush. Your brain will disagree with you if you rush the process. Act as a third person and try to notice your thoughts. What are you gaining from your current thinking? Why do you feel the need to think this way? What would happen if you didn't think this way?

What people do and what they need to do are two entirely different things. Take time to challenge your thinking so you can make a change.

Chapter 2

Embarking on Your Journey
Activators: Essential Questions

As we move into Chapter 2, ***Embarking on Your Journey and Essential Questions*** we invite you to explore the very core of your existence. This chapter is a pivotal point in your search to find purpose, meaning, growth, and success.

You have been working in shallow and murky waters for years, but the time has come for you to take a deep dive inside yourself to make sense of who you have become through nature and nurture. It is introspection that will help you to understand who and what you are and delineate where you want to go the rest of your life.

There are fundamental questions that lay the strongest of foundations for your work and life. It is through self-discovery that you will consciously become aware of your schema, and through self-leading how your schema has affected the decisions you made in the past. Through this section you will gain valuable insights about yourself that will allow you to make a powerful and sustainable impact on those around you.

There are ***Four Essential Questions*** that are the foundational steps to your inward journey that you must answer!

1. **Who am I?**
2. **Where am I going?**
3. **How do I get there?**
4. **How do I stay there?**

We authentically share our own personal stories, as case studies, with you to set you on a journey towards attaining tips, tools, and inspirational insights. Like you, we had to learn through trial and error, learn-as-you-go times, repeated losses, missed opportunities, emotional and irrational decision-making, and interpersonal conflicts.

After you read our stories, please take the opportunity to embark on your own journey of self-discovery by reflecting on and writing down your responses to the *Four Essential Questions*.

Four Essential Questions

Sujata's 'Who Am I?'

Aside from life, my Southeast Asian parents, Ravi and Ratna Kolhatkar, modeled unwavering courage, a love for knowledge, and an adherence to diligence and hard work. Through an authoritative parenting style, they expected nothing less than my best in return.

My childhood, in India, was filled with delightful curries, sweets, spices, colorful Saris, fabrics, Bollywood music, dancing, and Indian holiday traditions ascribed to numerous auspicious events and unfavorable storms during my lifespan development stages.

When I was six months old, my father left India to go to America to get his Master's Degree; he returned when I was four years old. I called him 'uncle', because I didn't know him, aside from his picture. My mother was, principally, a single mother for that time. She would talk about her dream to go to America every day.

At age eight, I found myself on a huge 747 headed for America. As the plane was landing, my eyes were unprepared for what I saw: the grand lady Statue of Liberty was a sight to behold from the airplane window. After we deplaned, the sights and sounds of New York city overwhelmed me with excitement from the top of my head to the tip of my toes. This was a brand-new world, and I knew I would need to be a brave little girl.

My parents' perseverance was well worth the wait. It took them seven long years to get a US Visa; they never gave up. My father was wise in getting his education, earlier, in America, because this made the transition much easier for him. Their determination was fruitful, and their eyes shone with glee because they knew that the American Dream had begun.

We lived in a small rural town in upstate New York, where traditions, values, and patriotism caused neighbors to watch out for each other. We were the first Southeast Asian family to move into that town. As the movers were unloading the truck, an elderly next-door neighbor came up to my dad and said, "I see that you are not black. I see that you are not white. *What* are you?" To which my father replied, "We're beige." Everyone laughed and all was well. For an accountant, he had a good sense of humor and knew how to diffuse situations. The neighbor got to know us better and even attended my school plays, piano recitals, and swim team meets. This show of support and acceptance from the townspeople was most welcomed. We were fortunate that the town was curious and interested in learning about India. We welcomed their engagement at that time because this was not the case for some minorities.

Lives are shaped by consequential and inconsequential events that can lead people a long way from what they intended for themselves. For me, a consequential event came through my parents' dreams and a brand-new culture that would have to be carefully juxtaposed with the Indian one. It didn't take long for me to realize how different the two cultures were, and how carefully I would have to make decisions. It was hard for me to navigate two languages and the customs of two cultures. There were words in Marathi (my birth language) that could not be found in the English language, and vice versa. Certain values overlapped, while others did not.

My teacher told me to go home and watch a lot of TV to learn English; so, I watched a lot of "I Love Lucy" and thank goodness I learned English from Lucy and not from Ricky! They say, English is the most difficult language to learn, but it can be understood though through thorough thought (now say that three times!).

Coming to America was my parents' greatest dream. My father emphasized how lucky I was to be in America and made me promise that I would "give back" to America for all the freedoms, opportunities, and doors offered to us. Education and spirituality were his top two values.

They met through an arranged marriage. My parents, that is. They only saw each other once before the wedding day, when she was to serve High Tea. This practice of High Tea before the wedding day was to ensure that the bride-to-be could walk and did not have any deformities.

Their parents arranged the union through the standard dowry of jewels to settle an agreement between two families. She was a beautiful, light-skinned (the coveted skin) girl; and he was a handsome, skinny fellow. Both families had been converted to Christianity by Scottish missionaries that resided in the state of Maharashtra.

No one asked my mother if she wanted to get married and have children. No one asked my father if he wanted to have the responsibility of a family. In my large photo album sits the picture of my parents on their wedding day, and it is akin to people at a funeral. Her parents felt they needed to get her married off because her mother was dying. My mother was not ready for marriage, because she loved school and wanted to pursue a career. She was only fifteen, an adolescent, and the epitome of angst and confusion.

And my dad? He was ten years older than she was, as is customary in arranged marriages. He was happy with numbers and accounting, and had found his place in a very large Brahmin family headed by Dr. Krisha L. Kolhatkar, MD.

My father relied on the values and tenets that his father had instilled in him. And they were the lighthouse light that guided the family through acclimation and challenging times. His greatest value was peacekeeping.

"We do not accept Indian credentials," blurted the New York University admissions officer. My mother was brilliant and the valedictorian of her high school and college, where, as a little child, I had a front-row seat during her valedictory speeches. Even at my young age, I beamed when she stood confidently and spoke eloquently at podiums. She was a born leader, but a woman born in the wrong culture. When the admissions officer rejected her credentials, she was devastated. But her tenacity and determination did not allow her to stay down. She quickly enrolled at NYU and became the valedictorian in her class once again and began to shine as a leader in the dietetics and nutrition niche. Academically speaking, she was a great model for me, but not beyond that.

One night, I heard her whisper to my father to teach her how to use the checkbook. As she began earning her own money, she opened her own bank account, and she bloomed even more through financial freedom. My father supported her every step. He was the kindest man I'd ever met and did his very best to keep her adolescent hormones and behaviors at bay. Her young personality was difficult. She would think you were arguing when you expressed your thoughts; she was committed to misunderstanding you; she would shame you if you were being truthful with your feelings; she was dismissive, hurtful, and even withdrawn at times.

Despite her tantrums, my dad always kept calm. I learned, well, the meaning of "commitment" from him. She didn't care, because divorce, in the Indian culture, was unheard of at that time and she knew that he would never leave her. She had our love (my father's and mine), and she knew that, but refused to reciprocate, because that would mean that she had accepted the decisions that others had forced upon her life. I spent my college years thinking about how different life could have been for her and us, if she had forgiven her past.

There are things that you learn about yourself when you are unfree from someone's behavior.

Those early days in America were tough and frugal. My mother had two jobs. My father had two jobs. And eventually I had three jobs — daytime, evenings, and weekends. I was an international admissions counselor during the day, a graduate student at night, and a part-time salesclerk during the weekends at a retail store. All three of us worked endless hours like ants; all three of us had great potential. All our money went into one pot. That pot paid for rent, food, clothing, health, and education. It took the first ten years of sacrifice to gain momentum in achieving the American dream.

Millions of internationals try to find funding to come to the US; we were so lucky. Migrating to America gave us access to career paths we could not have had back in India. It was determination and perseverance that activated success for the three of us. You have to be willing to work hard and make sacrifices; you have to be willing to give up certain things. For immigrants, it takes even more: effective integration, acclimatization, and learning a new language. Adopting cultural norms and fitting into the American culture took time, and there were times when I felt alone and misunderstood.

During recession periods, my dad never lost hope. His faith kept him focused on his goals. We saved every penny. It's funny that they never seemed to have the money when I asked them if we could go to the movies, but they always had money for piano lessons, school trips, and books. This taught me the importance of setting priorities. Education and knowledge always came first before anything else.

With each passing year, I witnessed how liberated my mother became as she took advantage of the rights offered to women in the US. She was relishing making choices she would not have had back in India. She felt free from the subservience she was expected to display as a young Indian wife. She savored autonomy from the directives of the Indian culture; however, she just could not help but to use aggressive rebelliousness as to teach this world a lesson.

I took careful note of my mother's interests, skills, strengths, and weaknesses. She was incredibly book smart but was an emotionally underdeveloped teen who was forced to marry a total stranger and ended up with a baby nine months later. Hormones were raging through her young body, and she lashed out just as teens do when they do not understand adult expectations. Most of the time, she left the people around her feeling aggravated, perplexed, and stunned. I found myself raising her to do the right thing, and I took on the parent role. It was parentification in action. Little did I know, then, that children who parentify grow up to have perfection issues.

My father, in his wisdom, was absolutely correct in taking her away from a subservient culture. America was a gift that he gave her. He realized she was born in the wrong culture the day he married her. She never fit in, and he took it upon himself to do something about it as her groom who had professed an oath of commitment in a public church ceremony. Women cannot always live life on their terms, especially when they come from a different region of the world.

We do not ask to be born. I was divinely placed in a particular family on an Easter Sunday morning. People, places, and things only mean something if you choose them to mean something. You have to let go of things that have lost their meanings. This is part of lifespan development.

The hardships and sacrifices were well worth it because the proudest day of our lives was when my parents and I recited the Pledge of Allegiance out loud during our Naturalization Ceremony to become American citizens. I value this country tremendously; I'm giving back to this nation as much as I can!

Gandhi said: "Be the change you want to see in this world". My life experiences in two cultures have momentously impacted who I am today, what I want to do in this world, and with whom.

Nature and nurture have contributed to my unique sounding voice that has become a symbol of hope for thousands of people. I am not a victim; I am a ***product*** of my past. I remember my past, but do not reside there. I am free to be who I want to be, and for this inalienable and indivisible freedom, I am eternally grateful.

YOUR TURN: Circle the words that stood out. Why do those words resonate in your mind?

<u>Sandra's Who Am I?'</u>

The first few breaths of my life were in a hospital incubator as a four-pound baby; struggling to survive by myself and alone in my tiny crib, I thrived against the odds.

Through this challenging and isolated start in life, connection, and attachment would be the central theme that would persist my entire life. But would be balanced by love from my parents and grandparents who saw something in me that was exceptional where at some points in my life I may not have truly felt this to be the case. Unconditional love would prove to be my grounding blocks throughout my life. No matter what came my way, my parents always had my back.

Powerful parental actions can greatly impact a child's perception of the Self and their attitude towards their abilities in life. My parents trusted and encouraged me to be my most authentic self, as they constantly told me, "just be you" throughout my rather lonely childhood and into early adulthood.

But expectations can also prove to be very powerful, especially when they come from your parents! Parents can either assist you, or they can limit you unknowingly. Having well-established and educated parents as leaders meant I was expected to achieve and succeed, which is something I did. I was supported and acknowledged for my abilities. But, when performance and achievement out weights finding personal acceptance and internal success I had not been successful.

My parents modeled great leadership. They were local community leaders who were also community builders. My leadership journey was so not like my parents in that each had found their calling early in life and followed their own paths all of their lives. For me, I would characterize my early self as someone who loved to simply dive, jump, or run head in to things easily. Always taking charge and leading the parade forward. But many times, without a well thought out plan or exit strategy when things would not work out. I was daring and caring, and I lived my life passionately and fully during my youth and early adulthood. I sought out challenging opportunities and thrived in competition. In my early work world, I found it easy to excel in my leadership by facilitating, selling, organizing, and being innovative to bring new things to life. Truly, it was easy for me to lead, just like my parents and grandparents. What was not so easy was for me to know and my own self-worth and leadership because of my untold suppressed childhood trauma story.

I realize now that Who I am is based upon two parts: genetics – the influence that comes from inherited genes and, hence, traits; and the second is my adventuresome life experiences and challenges circumstances that made me who I am today.

My parents had such different life stories that supported them to stand in their leadership. My father, Dr. John Lewis (Jack) McManus, was calm, empathetic, and highly intellectual and led with a quiet voice and big heart. On the other hand, my mom, Gwendolyn (Gwen) McManus, was energetic and action-oriented and led with self-determination. She followed her interests and abilities even in sectors where there weren't many women.

My grandparents, Gladys and Fredrick Kemp on my mom's side were well known within a strong social circle of friends. My grandfather was remarkably charismatic and, upon his return from WWII, naturally fell into city leadership roles.

My Grandfather was ahead of his time and embraced the premise that his daughter (my mother) should be given opportunities that were previously offered solely to men. As you can guess, he was certainly not the norm. He rooted, in my mother, a spirit of adventure and independence. My mom's eyes were opened wide and ready for the possibilities that an independent, self-sufficient woman could aspire to, including leading in the health care sector. She showed me how a woman could be both a professional, wife, active healthy sport person while being there for the family.

My dad, on the other hand, came from major loss and hardship. Sadly, he lost both of his parents to polio when he was only eight years old and was raised by his siblings. After returning from WWII, he followed his passion into veterinary medicine.

My parents met and married later in life. They say, 'opposites attract,' and my parents were opposites in many situations. Regardless of their upbringing, each parent still held similar values and worldviews. They shared their passion for each other and their mutual love of family, animals, education, lifelong learner, and to be a successful contributor to society.

At the same time in my mother's life, there was a sad reality that she had to be the primary caregiver and resource to manage her father's (my grandfather) addiction, and the negative impacts on family.

I took notice that relatives on my mom's side wanted to continue the success that was enjoyed through generations, while on my dad's side, having only his sister as family, they wanted to achieve to overcome poverty and loss. Nature and nurture were working together to create me. My genes (nature) and their leadership influence (nurture) influenced me.

It wasn't till about ten years ago that I began to unlock my personal leadership story earnestly and deeply. During this year, I learned to understand myself from the inside out, and a story that I had kept unconsciously hidden for years. A profound shift occurred where a life-changing perspective allowed me to unravel early chaos and trauma. During a simple graduate exercise, I unearthed my thirty-four-year suppressed story of being sexually assaulted as a child. Those traumatic memories were overshadowed and suppressed by schoolwork, extracurricular activities, sports, and friends, and was consistent across my adult life. On top of this I was also a victim of repeated childhood bullying that continued from Kindergarten to High School. It took the right time and place to feel safe to reveal these unfortunate events from my childhood.

In awakening to my life's purpose and my trauma story, I realized that there were patterns of codependency, victimization, and personal loss that had impacted me and guided my path in how I reacted, not responded, and lead my life. For forty years, I was only focused on external motivations that allowed me to focus on financial success which in reality I now understand kept the pain away. It was through awareness that the layers came off and I understood the impact of my past on present as an adult.

What stands out as a lesson to me is the importance of learning to observe the Self in how you think and act. If I had slowed down and learned to listen, I could have become more self-aware, and many of my life lessons may not have been repeated. I was always on the go, and as a leader, I perpetually tended to react to life instead of responding to life.

A few years ago, I made a significant leap by learning to live through gratitude. By having a clear understanding of the universal law of attraction, I was able to connect my mind and body to my purpose, and this gave me a whole new perspective and meaning in my life.

This new way of thinking transformed my life completely and for the better. I learned that I could program my subconscious mind to keep the positive at the forefront, and to remove the negative self-talk and limiting beliefs that had found a house in my mind and body.

I understood (for the first time) how my childhood experiences and parental influences had shaped me! Knowing and accepting this, I was ready and able right there and then to stand on my own two feet and choose how I wanted to live pain free from certain expectations.

YOUR TURN: Circle the words that stood out. Why do those words resonate in your mind?

Sujata's 'Where Am I Going'

Where I am going in life has much to do with my Bicultural identity. My Biculturalism effects the biology, psychology, social, and spiritual of me. I am a brown-skinned girl with a jiggly voice, and that's the first thing that people notice about me. I am much more, but only the people who take the time to get to know me, know that.

Managing two cultural selves is not for the faint of heart. More often than not I faced internal conflict while I was trying to balance my identity through the influence of two cultures. Going back and forth took identity integration, awareness, and intention to mitigate emotions that came along with identity plurality.

Visualize your front door and imagine that door to be the gateway between two distinctly different worlds. When I opened the door to my home, it was India, and when I opened the door to go out, it was America. I couldn't choose between the two, because I look Indian and that would always stand out first. I felt that I had to become the best for both worlds.

No achievement earned was good enough for my parents; they didn't let me have time to enjoy my achievements because when I accomplished one goal, they would ask, "What's next?!". So, I was always doing something and going somewhere; not busy, per se, but actively making good use of my time to 'give back'. Little did I know that it would take more time for me to know where I was going, because they were always telling me where to go. My locus of control was quite small, because they controlled where I was going.

I stayed true to my bicultural identity by observing cultural values and customs. I decided to take values from each culture. I took the best of both cultures to become the best person I could be – for myself and the people around me. I didn't want to turn into my mother or my father; I wanted to be Sujata!

Like Legos, I tried to assemble the pieces that fit me. I stepped out of that front door to go into an independent, accessible, and resourceful world where I could live my bright values and leave subservience behind me. Through awareness and intention, I conditioned myself to be on the American side of the front door, most of the time.

College taught me and supported me in sharing my own perspectives that arose from a distinct part of my inimitable brain. This was a critical juncture and an 'Aha' moment, because I understood that if I could self-lead accurately, then I could lead others effectively.

My parents' tense relationship influenced my decision to not have an Indian-style arranged marriage. I wanted to marry for love. If that was a mistake, then it would be *my* mistake and no one else', because there is a price for free will.

My parents chose my college major. They said that I had to major in biology, so I did. My college courses helped me to better understand human nature, and as I became more educated, I felt my mind expanding and that gave me confidence to find my own true voice.

After I graduated college, I came home one day to tell my parents that I was not going to agree to have my marriage arranged; that I was going to find my own true love. The muck hit the fan! There was yelling and screaming, because "I had taken away their privilege to choose my mate" (they said). I held my ground and stood firm that I was going to marry for love and prayed that someone wonderful would find me.

True love found me through friends who arranged a blind date between a handsome naval officer and me. So, I tell this part of my story as an ironic occurrence: it was not my parents who arranged my marriage, but rather close friends who arranged a union.

I felt myself going in a direction towards what I believed was for my greater good in the only life that was divinely given to me. It was love at first sight with the American-born military officer of (ironically) British descent. We fell madly in love, married, and began moving around the globe. We had beautiful children, loving dogs, and dear military friends that have stayed close to us for decades.

I went from my father's house to my husband's house. During my childhood, I was known as Ravi and Ratna's daughter; then after marriage, I was known as "Rob's wife". As a lieutenant commander in the submarine service, he was out to sea half the year – the life of a military wife is not for the faint of heart. My in-laws were the best people I'd ever met. "Salt of the Earth," they were. Accepted me with open arms and filled in the gaps during Rob's absences. Of course, the kids and dogs kept me busy too.

The life of a submariner's wife, particularly, is a lonely one. The divorce rate in the military is 52%, and we both knew that we were not going to be a part of those statistics. Many of our military friends got divorced and we kept committed to each other. Going through the plethora of travels gave me a great appreciation for countries and cultures. I knew that 'my turn' was coming someday, so I made the decision to go back to school to get my PhD in psychology. My kids and I studied at the dining room table at the same time, and this role-modeling gave erudition values to them. My dissertation, *"The Impact of an Online Orientation Program on the Impostor Phenomenon, Self-efficacy, and Anxiety"* By Sujata Kolhatkar Ives, can be found online at ProQuest.com

I was grateful to Maslow, Jung, Dyer, and Tolle, that helped me to better understand how to manage my identities and roles in life. I always strived to stay true to my identity through my purpose and passion. My doctorate studies gave me insight to look beyond my vocal cord limitations. I adopted a humanistic mindset and started inspiring others, and that was a brain changer for me, because it took the focus off of my limits and placed it onto my purpose.

I was going to get there through my left brain's facts and logic, and through my right brain's cultural humility that caused me to stay grounded in examining my biases and *beliefs.* I was going to keep improving myself; in essence, I was a case study, just like the case studies I read about during my doctorate. There were many correlations, but *correlation does not equal causation in psychology.*

It was Erikson's psychosocial theory and Piaget's cognitive theory of human development that caused me to take a close look at my Lifespan Development Stages line that has seven slots:

Early Childhood – learning and lessons from two cultures.
Middle Childhood – learning a new language, customs, and norms.
Late Childhood – A push to fit into the majority culture; academic interests; activities.
Adolescence – angst; lack of control regarding money and decision-making.

Early Adulthood – Independent work; more freedom; marriage; children.
Mid-adulthood – A supportive husband; grown kids; gratifying work; perspicacity.

My nature/nurture or genetics/environment work together in helping me understand where I want to go. Each passing year, people ask me: what are your goals this year? What is your dream job? A better question would be: *What values and responsibilities make you feel fulfilled?*

I implore you to fall in love with learning, just as I have. It has worked wonderfully for me; read all great books by great authors. Write how you feel through journaling each day. It is George Orwell that said: "If you cannot write well, you cannot think well, and if you cannot think well, then others will do the thinking for you".

Ask yourself: what do I *need* in my life? What do I *want* in my life? What do I need to let go of? What do I need to do to step out of my comfort zone?

YOUR TURN: Circle the words that stood out to you. Why do those words resonate in your mind?

Sandra's 'Where Am I Going?'

I have always visualized myself in a meditative state up on a serene mountain, feeling a breeze on my face, looking down at the majesty of the land. This is where I am able to think clearly.

For me the step of activating success and gaining clarity is by setting my own direction and not through others directing me. To lead self is all about setting your own direction. This direction setting allows you to then share with others to follow. But, for my journey and perhaps, for you it may require more time, space, to unlock, open up, bridge past traumas, circumstances to be ready now. Not having clarity led me to negotiate with myself to find faster, quicker, and easier ways to come to end results. I valued speed and quality. Doing so led me to burn out as I was working and living on full throttle most of my life. This realization that I could not push or pull life in ways I wanted was huge for me to learn. Learning to catch myself daily when emotions get going, or I feel the need to reeve up the speed of things or take on too much on to my plate is still a challenge. I dial back down or turn the thermostat to a lower temperature so not to catch ignition or blast off. Stopping to reflect and be still has been my antidote.

Moving through those early adult years (which turned into decades), I realize now that I had lived in a state of numbness. Being unaware of signs and symptoms of repression proved to be my hardest lessons. It is both intriguing and a bit frustrating that I could be so highly functioning but yet so unaware of the impact that my past, my habits, and my patterns had on my life and others around me. The truth was I never accepted myself. I only recently realized this truth in my life. Wow, that was a real realization in my life! I now lead myself with purposeful intention and attention to follow positive habits I have created to keep me on track.

As a leader, I learned how much influence words have on and the labels we attach on our self-identity. I realize that I have challenged and redefined myself through these decades in order to see more clearly. I learned that as a mother, a divorced woman with a child, and then later as a single woman with two kids, I could stand on my own two feet when facing challenges and without the need to rely on someone else. I knew I would be successful because I was committed to family and thought I found a way to balance my career and kids as a single mom. In reality, balancing was a great struggle in relationships in personal life. I was attracting the wrong types of people in my personal life that had numerous challenges but didn't realize why. My subconscious mind was attracting people that had more problems than the ones I had to face, but it was my positive spirit that helped me grow, get clarity, and stay true to self-leadership. Anything is possible! My optimistic outlook and action steps propelled me to provide momentum, even during the dark and stormy times of my life.

To align my direction, I learned to define my values, and this allowed me to become adaptable, flexible, responsible, independent, and open. I was a woman in constant motion, hovering, juggling, and trying to work through stress, and this was the duality of my life at that time.

As a woman that was constantly on the go, I never had the time to or understood the need to assess my feelings. I lacked the awareness of the impact that my thinking was having on my person. Eventually, I was stopped because my body broke down into illness. I don't know how I survived those crazy years! I think I just subconsciously remembered how strong my mother was and emulated her.

Recalling setbacks and obstacles was a critical learning step essential to my continued growth. It may seem simple, but it is a powerful reframe from being a victim to standing in my power. I learned how to view my challenges, setbacks, and trauma, then transformed them into growth and learning lessons. By shifting my understanding, I could reframe past situations (childhood trauma) and circumstances (challenging relationships) to serve my present personal growth as a leader, mother, and wife.

What worked for me was:

1. Build self-confidence so that you are resourceful enough to make the right decisions, without relying on someone else's advice for your life. Speak to yourself through inner confidence, so you can be heard. Your words matter and you deserve to be heard.

2. Check-in with your internal guidance system in your heart and gut brains. Allow yourself to be vulnerable without being gullible.

3. Align with your values and moral compass, through self-trust. Do not push or pull, but allow yourself time, space, and faith so things can fall into place.

4. Learn to negotiate and understand that you are in control, and you have the power within you to stand up and demand accountability.

5. Build new self-awareness tactics to become present in your moment. Through my story, I hope you understand how important it is to self-lead through Connection, Observation, Reflection, and Engagement (C.O.R.E. Change Model).

Ask yourself if you are growing from the inside out and be sure that your head is connected to your heart.

Right now, I am championing you to take a long hike so you can sit up on a mountaintop for a new point of view. When you are up there, think about where you are going.

YOUR TURN: Circle the words that stood out to you. Why do those words resonate in your mind?

Sujata's 'How Do I Get There?'

I am proud that I have a great Bicultural sense of self in my work and personal life. I perform my *roles* through gratefulness and openness, that act as *activators* for success. Every role that I hold gives me transferable skills that help me to evolve into my best self and prepares me for the next role.

Going through the military wife role gave me a wealth of transferable skills that were, and still are, an asset in helping me to 'get there'. The navy submariners taught me their saying: Loose lips, sink ships. I learned military culture as a newlywed, and the Captain's wife expeditiously gave me a book entitled *"Service Etiquette"* to speed up my indoctrination into the military culture. That book got me acclimated quickly, because the chapters delineated appropriate customs, norms, and protocols. Soon, I became the belle of the annual submarine balls; I enjoyed dancing and conversing with captains, admirals, and foreign dignitaries. I was proud to publicly wear the navy wife tee shirt that said, "Navy wife: best job in the navy", when I shopped at the base commissary. I was delighted to support my husband's and children's educational and professional goals. Neighbors and friends got promoted, demoted, or died in wars. For the first time in my life, I became astutely aware that enemies exist at the global level, where nations fight against nations for domination.

If you want to hold a military meeting each week, don't hold it on the same day, same time, and same tent each week. When the widows told me that the enemy blew up that tent, my heart sank. Predictability is what the enemy looks for. I cannot help but ruminate over those tent deaths. Our friends died in that tent. I would give my first-born to be invited to a military meeting towards peaceability. Not that I am better than or smarter than military leaders, but rather, as a military wife, I have vast education and a different lens that I can bring to the table. I know my world geography, cultural history, geopolitics, and can offer perspectives without judgment. The military wife is an untapped resource that is not utilized. I believe that the military wife is the *most* untapped resource on the globe. Military wives are important stakeholders. Our husbands are willing to die for this nation, and we are willing to help keep them alive.

If I were to be invited to a military VIP meeting, the first thing I would do is to have emerging leaders, midshipmen, and cadets play the game of 'Risk'. As weird as that may sound, it is the best place to begin learning about strategy, cat and mouse games, hidden agendas, and blindsides. Another example from history is the attack on Pearl Harbor. The US fully expected an attack via the East Coast; it never occurred to them that an enemy attack could happen via the West Coast. If you are reading this and have the power and authority to include a military wife, please contact me!

The mother role gave me transferable skills in planning, organizing, adapting, communicating, pivoting, resetting, time-managing, decision-making, problem-solving, and self-leading that became indispensable during the nineteen moves. I coped through those moves through my love for learning. Ten years after defending my dissertation, the publishing, presenting, and dialoguing honed my skills even more to make a contribution to the global stage. I am passionate about topics surrounding leadership, interculturalism, bias, mindsets, conflict resolution, and building effective teams/groups/alliances/partnerships. I get there by training as many people as I can, so they, too, can find peace of mind that they have done all that they could in their control.

I get there by being mindful, where mindfulness takes me from my back brain protective mode to the rational frontal lobe. Making time to be silent helps me to be quiet and listen to the answers that quietly flow into my brain. You cannot erase historical hurt, but you can make the choice to accept it and let go. The back brain is always in survival mode because its job is to protect the psyche. And even internal self-talk can trigger defensiveness in the back brain; it doesn't have to be something external. Being aware and comfortable with silence is an upskill. You have the locus of control to *Code Shift* – your brain has been coded through conditioning, but you can uncondition, unlearn, and create a new code in your brain. The brain is plastic, and this means it has Neuroplasticity to create new connections every day.

The pinnacle influence for human beings is **memory!** It is through memory (short-term and long-term) and perception of what we can remember that we make decisions and solve problems. Given this information, how can I be angry with someone who is not conscious of who they are. I absolutely cannot and will not; and I will not compare myself with anyone else's life chapter either. We need to give people some grace, because they are still in the process of self-discovery where the learning curve is not linear.

Have you discovered your memory to be unreliable? When do you hold onto something longer than you should?

My schema was formed through how I was raised, my skin color, and my culture that gives me a certain bias that I must always be mindful of. I reflect on a myriad of perspectives, sit still, intentionally let go of unwanted thoughts, and bring my attention from the back survive brain to my frontal thrive brain. It is through the frontal lobe that I can continue to evolve, transcend, and arrive at discernment. My wisdom and enlightenment come from a *discernment* called **Perspicacity**. That *discernment* replaces all judgment. The suspension of judgment makes room for contentment and wisdom.

I believe that there are special neurons, called **Neurodots** that connect with each other and bring us those 'Aha' moments that only make sense to us, and us alone. And when those neurodots are activated, I feel exceedingly joyful and confident. I feel as though I have freed irrelevance and find the reason why I was born – each time that I find *perspicacity*, where perspicacity marks affluence of mind. This is my theory and I call it the *'Ives Neurodots Theory*™*'*.

Please understand there is a vast difference between pursuing a goal and running away from something. Running away doesn't help anything, but pursuing something does.

Work and life fulfillment are entirely possible. If you think you are *missing something* at work or life, then keep reading to discover your unique *activators* for success.

YOUR TURN: Circle the words that stood out to you. Why do those words resonate in your mind?

Sandra's 'How Do I Get There?'

My pathway has gone up and down, winding around curves, and definitely unclear at certain times. But now I realize that it was all about perspective and having a growth mindset that allowed me to look at what was important to me (my values, beliefs, assumptions) and how I was aligned to them to create action steps for myself.

When I read Dr. Carol S. Dweck's book, Mindset: The New Psychology of Success (2016), I learned that there are two mindsets that she calls Fixed and Growth. Whichever mindset your parents, guardians, teachers, or mentors exposed you to during childhood usually tends to be the outlook you will adopt and carry into adulthood.

My "Aha" moment came when I realized that I wished that I had been taught a Growth mindset. I would have had a head start on viewing situations as lessons and not punishments.

In living with a Fixed mindset, I was upholding high standards, expectations, and focused on financial success. By doing so, I realized that the combination of a Fixed mindset plus the childhood trauma created a void inside. My fierce competitiveness, in the workplace, yielded high work achievements, but I still felt stuck and unfulfilled because that competitiveness was not coming from my loving self but as a defense mechanism. The Fixed mindset exposed me to much criticism, negative self-talk, cynical judgment, and blindsides from my environment, all of which were not good for my soul.

The good news is that over time, and with intention, I was able to change and shift my internal dialogue to move myself into a Growth mindset to create positive habits and goals. I was able to understand what I needed for growth, clarity, and connection. I am proud of myself now!

I learned how to self-lead by evaluating my thinking and actions and how I could lead consciously. The process of learning, living, and leading is fundamental to how you can get to where you want to go. Learning more about myself has allowed me to reveal parts that were uncomfortable, sensitive, awkward, and, at times, may have been perceived as risky in some business circles. Living through my values has helped me find great joy and gratitude in all aspects of my life and work.

Learning is a core value that I live by every day.

So, what happens to those who do not choose life-long learning? Or where learning does not come quickly? Or where there is a learning disability? You may not have guessed, but that was me too!

Some things come easy, while others need support in getting there. Despite my learning impairment, I was able to pivot through shame and guilt, to become resourceful, cultivate a Growth mindset in reaching high success.

Never give up on yourself. Stop, breathe, and choose to see the situation differently. Just know that even if the words don't come out easily, accept yourself wholly and know you are beautifully imperfect. No matter how long acceptance takes to arrive. Resist the temptation for negative self-talk and limiting beliefs. Understand that you can reprogram and repattern beliefs in changing your life at any moment. It's your choice.

Everyone has a choice to see things in a particular way. I chose to see myself as a powerful, positive, impactful person with unique gifts, and so can you! No matter your challenge, you always have a choice—a choice to have a winner's attitude so you can learn and grow.

Never give in to the impairment, disability or challenge, no matter how hard the battle is before you. Trust the process. Everything and all things form a web of interconnections. I seek to ensure that I am conscious in the present moment to stop, breathe, and reflect to align with my purpose and journey where I am meant to go. If I find myself falling backward into my old, fixed ways, then I stop again, breathe once more, and begin to move forward through self-discovery.

Your Turn: Circle the words that stood out. Why do those words resonate for you?

Sujata's 'How Do I Stay There?'

I stay there through a commitment to my values in cultivating peaceful workplaces, and through hope that this world will create something significant for its people. It was Friedrich Nietzsche that said: "Original minds are not distinguished by being the first to see a new thing; but instead, by seeing the old and familiar thing that is over-looked as something new".

It is the Bio-Psycho-Social-Cultural-Spiritual Model that I utilize to help others. I have perfected the art of open-ended questioning, that allows people to express their true desires in life. Sometimes, when random people in a long grocery line ask me what I do, I answer: "I ask good questions". I have a keen gift to lead people to the success they are unable to see. People have power, but they do not know how to use it. They have survival power that can translate into motivation, and psychological power that can translate into hope.

My brain is the center of my life and plays a significant role in how I perceive my internal and external world. In real estate, they say: 'location, location, location,' but in psychology, they say: *'perception, perception, perception.'* No one knows true reality because the story we all tell is always from a point of view where we are always the hero in that narrative. I call this *"Survival Bias"*, because we are always 100% correct from our point of view, and this is something I believe is a survival mechanism that is built into the brain.

Everyone has a story. We talk to ourselves and tell each other stories every day. We listen to our inner dialogue. We should not believe everything we think or feel. We listen to our clients. Make others feel heard. As we listen to others, we also learn something about ourselves.

Do you feel like you deserve success more than others? I stay there by being fair, impartial, and nonjudgmental – to myself and to others.

My evolution as a global leader is an amalgamation of my experiences during my lifespan development stages, happenstance, travels, transitions, and growth. My nineteen global moves gave me a wonderful appreciation for this world and the people in it. There are times when I feel as though I am still transitioning and acclimating out of military life.

The freedom this country gave me allows me to make a difference in this world, thereby creating a legacy for my children to discover the purpose, passion, and contribution in their own lives.

I long for an egoless place that does not exist yet, and that's what keeps me working. A place where we can tell authentic stories and listen to them with empathy and without judgment.

My article, published by the Society for Human Resource Management (SHRM), addresses common sense leadership:

www.shrm.org,resourcesandtools,hr-topics,behavioral-competencies,pages,post-crisis-common-sense-global-leadership.aspx?linktext=post-crisis-common-sense-global-leadership

My talk on the global stage addresses the miracle of the brain and how it helps us activate success through discernment: *"Perspicacity: Consciously Connecting the Neuro-dots for Perspicacious Leadership"*

Professional associations have helped my transition into the real world. There, counselors understand that military transitions, acclimation, and integration effects well-being. NCDA, APCDA, MCDA, MCA, ACA, and ICC are the spaces where I love sharing my findings with global peers. Conferences offer credible opportunities where people can share their passionate work through theory and practice, where we can gather to Connect The Dots together. I believe, together, we can move mountains.

I stay there through recognition from my esteemed peers and colleagues. I was recognized for my work by the National Career Development Association (NCDA) when they awarded me the 2023 Diversity Initiative Award. This organization uses an operative power word: *Convergence*. It is the convergence (union, conjunction, and merging) of perspectives, cultures, and ideas that can propel us forward.

I stay there through my contribution as the current President of the Maryland Career Development Association (MCDA) where I encourage people to unite and help each other. As Co-chair of the Program Committee at the Asia Pacific Career Development Association (APCDA) I feel honored to connect with seven regions of the world. I am delighted to educate people through my role as Community Group Coordinator of the World Council on Global and Intercultural Competency, partner of UNESCO. I feel privileged to be Chair of the International Committee of the American Counseling Association (ACA) this year where I have had a great opportunity to unite counselors from Egypt, Canada, UK, Singapore, Philippines, Korea, China, and India.

I stay there because of camaraderie. This year I had the opportunity to conduct a Needs Analysis in a year-long study in the 2024 NCDA Leadership Academy. This study provided results in the areas of cultural humility, interculturalism, and leadership styles.

My worldwide reach made me the 2023 recipient of the OtroMundo 6th Congress' 'Global Visionary', Colombia, South America, where I educated and inspired audiences that nothing is impossible. If you have an idea or value, then all things are possible.

Be still and know. I stay there through silence, and through empowering audiences that appreciate my unique voice. I stay there through opportunities that come my way. Please listen to my NCDA podcast where I share my personal journey of triumph: https://www.buzzsprout.com/1963679/14242733

If I do not have an accurate portrayal of myself, then I cannot portray you accurately. It is through clinical tools that I am able to stay there, and by customizing work-life designs for each unique client. These tools will help you to assess and measure the constructs necessary to live a balanced and successful work and personal life. It is through your narrative that you will be able to discover the true meaning in the life that you have been divinely given.

1. True Colors – is a personality assessment. Begin with this one so you have a distinct paradigm and language to express yourself and understand others.
2. Values inventory – helps you to figure out what you value most in the workplace.
3. John Holland's Hexagon Code – provides six specific areas of personality and how they join together with certain vocations. I Connect The Dots by bringing Holland and the OCEAN model together, because certain vocations are extroverted, and others are introverted.
4. Interests inventory – helps you decipher what niche you are interested in.
5. O*NET inventories.

6. The Johari Window is great because it brings your attention to your blind spot and hidden self that is awaiting growth and awareness.
7. Myers-Briggs MBTI test – puts brain functions (thinking, sensing, perceiving, judging, intuitive) together so you can understand yourself and others better.
8. Clance & Imes Impostor Phenomenon Inventory - is the original one regarding self-doubt, uncertainty, and attribution of success.

Home is where the Navy sends you. In the military, home is not necessarily a physical place, but one you get to create through the heart-brain and capacity-building.

Inclusive professional association teams are where you can send yourself, and they too can become your home.

Be ready and prepared to say something of value to people. I recommend memorizing a short elevator speech when people ask you what you do. You can start by filling in these blanks.

1. Because I value _____ I'm an _____.
2. I feel _____ when I help _____, so people can _____.

❝

Watch your thoughts, for they become words.
Watch your words, for they become actions.

Watch your actions, for they become habits.
Watch your habits, for they become character.

Watch your character,
for it becomes your destiny.

~Lao Tzu~

❞

YOUR TURN: Circle the words that stood out to you. Why do those words resonate in your mind?

What does it take to become successful at work and in life? And how can you stay successful? That's the story here in this book.

I have never told my story to anyone before, and the way that my story emerges in these pages is far different than the one I was feeling when I was a child. The way that my narrative has unfolded reminds me that we completely rely on our memories, growth, and life stages to tell us what happened to us in the past, and it is precisely those memories that give us feelings, emotions, stressors, values, setbacks, and triumphs.

It takes excellence, failure, creativity, and autonomy to achieve success in the workplace where you are expected to highly perform individual, team, and organizational tasks. Success goes beyond simple metrics like financial gains, power, and glory. For long-term success, you must invest time and effort so you can thrive, flourish, and create an altruistic environment everywhere you go.

Just as your workplace success is marked by strategic vision, effective leadership, and a commitment to ethical practices, I want you to transfer that to your personal live too. Both lives require a genuine collaboration, adaptability, and resilience, where everyone can contribute meaningfully to the goals you have created together.

Success takes effective communication and conflict-resolution skills. Setting clear, achievable goals and encouraging a collaborative environment where people valued and engaged is critical. Promoting continuous learning and professional development can enhance individual and collective capabilities. Strong leadership that emphasizes transparency, accountability, and empathy can create a peaceable foundation for success.

It takes building strong relationships. Don't just think about yourself and your needs and wants. Think about others and what they may need and want. Come together, talk to each other, find common ground, and make it a goal to have a win-win outcome for everybody.

In the post-pandemic long crisis workplace, transferable skills for everyone's wellbeing are paramount. Organizations need to implement robust and flexible work policies and technologies that recognize the importance of work-life balance. Mental health support and initiatives that foster resilience should be prioritized to address the long emotional toll of the pandemic.

Keep clear communication channels, both virtual and in-person, that are crucial for maintaining connection. Embrace diversity of thought and cultures, as is a continued focus on digital literacy and upskilling for evolving technological landscapes. A strong organizational culture that values empathy, creativity, and dexterity is foundational for success in the new normal. Work and family leaders must guide their teams and families through change with transparency and understanding that adapts to the lessons learned. That's how you can activate success for work and family because the result will be resilience, camaraderie, and viable relationships.

The workplace is filled with an array of exciting changes and choices that can cause people to fight, flight, freeze, or fumble. It is a time of numerous transitions. Use your voice to create brave spaces where people who have good intentions and curiosity can come together to encircle people of all cultures, backgrounds, perspectives, and personalities.

Some personalities sit back and wish for success to come to them, while others take initiative and strive to succeed. The problem comes when they go after success according to a set of behaviors. People must learn how to quiet the mind so that they can listen when discernment arrives in the frontal brain. All behaviors are a result of memories; of what we can remember. Our memories provide us with feelings and emotions and those affect our decisions and ultimately make us who we are. As a species, (scientific name: Homo Sapiens) we have terrible memories, and the unhealthy ones may be accentuated much more through the back brain versus the happy ones. Therefore, when people experience setbacks, they disengage before they arrive at the opportune time to make a difference. Interests and skills may not be enough. Timing is critical, so never give up. The set of behaviors and habits you currently have may not be the right match for your future success. Upskill and read what you need for your future self. I encourage you to become an avid reader so you can cultivate behaviors and habits that can work credibly and successfully for you.

Investigate empirical and credible sources that can help your decision-making and problem-solving by giving you different perspectives. Making a change in habits and behaviors requires knowledge of theories and practice.

There are plenty of theories that are relevant to the biology, psychology, social, cultural, and spiritual of you. You do not have to remain in your back primitive brain.

Sandra's 'How Do I Stay There?'

Life has a way of happening to you. Either you direct it, or others and the universal laws of attraction will. So, which is your choice?

I stay there by understanding my life and my leadership story as a daughter, woman, mother, and conscious leader, I have shared my story of overcoming and going through hardships to arrive at a place where I feel balance, alignment, and clarity in my thinking, actions, and sense of being. Life has happened to and for me, shaping who I am today. Reflecting, I see how my lack of clarity and blurred vision has led me to live my life, perhaps not how I may have preferred it to go, but one I was destined to live.

My early leadership was framed, directed, and influenced by others (some with positive or negative intentions) because I had lacked, but now possess, the inner integration and outer manifestation of my conscious leadership framework. I truly mean a deeply held connection between my heart, mind, and a higher purpose. This profound alignment has allowed me to let go, release, and trust myself to become a conscious leader who responds to challenges in humanity.

I stay there by asking better questions as a leader through the growth within helped me to arrive at this place by answering these two questions:

1. Am I courageous enough to go within and consistently explore and check in on how I am defining my self-concept?

2. Am I honestly looking at myself "openly in the "present" moment?

In my journey, I have found that by embracing these questions, you can move through change and stay there. You can choose to modify your self-concept, or you might choose to remain the same. There is a risk, though, of not looking at yourself objectively. *"If you don't like something, change it. If you can't change it, change your attitude."* -Maya Angelou

My self-concept involves my self-image, self-esteem, and ideal self. By continually exploring and answering these questions, you can become better able to be more self-aware. Self-awareness, as I define it, is the ability to tune into your feelings, thoughts, and actions. Self-awareness is central to clarity, sustaining growth, facilitating self-change, and being in the present moment.

I stay there by being present and open to possibilities and opportunities. Effective leadership must entail honesty through awareness and attention to the present moment in which you find yourself. What I mean by 'the present' is giving attention to my emotional self-awareness and to the emotional awareness of others in that distinct moment. Being present does not consider the past or the future but instead intentionally staying in the present.

As you stay in the present moment, words, silence, and time will be present. Do not be afraid of a pause because the silence will add to the richness of that present moment. The pause gives your subconscious and conscious minds a chance to greet each other.

Therefore, to live my life fully, I must take the opportunity daily to take stock and respond from an open, honest, and truthful place. What I mean by this is to challenge our perceptions of ourselves (look within) and decide to apply actions that allow us to make informed decisions in our personal and professional lives.

Unfortunately, my story shows that when too much information is happening in our minds or external situations cause it, we can become overwhelmed and lose our sense of direction and ourselves.

When this happens, seek clarity as soon as possible by reducing and eliminating mindless clutter. Ask informed questions of yourself and commit to the improvement of your self-awareness. Doing so will reduce the uncertainty, allowing you to define and move in a direction of your choosing.

I stay there by doing new things to support my own growth. Activities to help you *shift to a positive mindset.*

Go ahead and begin each day anew. The first step is to begin to have and express gratitude. Gratitude allows you to awaken to all that is around you. Begin to purposefully use all your senses to inform and shift your subconscious mind favorably past old patterns into new ones.

According to my mentor Rex Sikes, "The subconscious mind is a learning machine, ... it is a reliable and faithful servant" (Life on Your Terms, pp.43-44, 2021). Take the control back and direct it, or it will direct your actions based on your habits and biases.

The work by Denis Waitley, the author of "The New Psychology of Winning" taught me to connect my values to my work and life. I was able to create a new me which brought a new perspective. It is possible: whatever age you are, whatever ethnicity, whatever religious belief, whatever gender. You have an opportunity to be your best self and make a contribution from this moment on more than at any other time in history" (2021, p.36).

I stay there by finding balance and peace.

A leader must understand the importance of balance, alignment, and peace. This powerful practice allows one to bring alignment and flow into mind and body for the True Self.

As a leader, I hope you answer the following pivotal questions with a resounding 'yes'!

Questions to keep you in balance and peace:

1.   Are you open to allowing a new way of living and being to emerge?
2.   Are you open to a deeper connection with yourself and others?
3.   Are you interested in exploring how you can develop a heart-mind connection to your purpose?

The wonderful news is that anyone who answers yes to even one of these questions can find their heart lit and their leadership elevated. I must say, though, that it requires and demands us to have faith—a faith in self and purpose that is beyond us in a manner that fits your beliefs.

To achieve balance and peace, ask yourself, "What does your heart need to be and heard?" By "heard," I mean that you become aware of the nuances of how your emotions presently show up and impact your emotional reactions inside your body. These are what I call "heart signals," they alert you when certain thoughts and words trigger you. It is safe and okay to release and let go of the triggers – those thoughts – those words. The act of surrendering is one key step to inner peace and transformation. Gaining clarity and knowledge can give you a realization of habits learned, some say your egoic side of yourself, that you have permitted to control. The job of the ego self has a purpose in keeping me alive but is not sensible in keeping me stuck in old habits of thinking, being, and doing. I choose to respond more consciously.

I stay there by being of service to others through my work with the Tri-Cities Chamber of Commerce membership, volunteer committee service to connect local businesses together. Especially my work with the Chamber, Women in Business Committee. A committing dedicated to supporting women through advocacy, connection activities, while strengthening women's skillsets, talents and leadership potential in the Tri-Cities.

As Vice-chair of New View Society, a not for profit who is committed to support individual's living with chronic and persistent mental health challenges. A commitment that I know makes a difference in the lives of many in our community.

I stay there by offering my professional services in change management and project leadership to improve healthcare and enterprise-wide initiatives. Leadership development through emotional intelligence assessments, team-building exercises, and facilitated strategic planning sessions with various sized businesses and industries across the lower mainland of British Columbia, Canada.

Change Your Perspective: Change your life!

<u>YOUR TURN TO REFLECT</u>

1. Circle the words that popped out at you while you were reading Sujata's story.
2. Circle the words that popped out at you while you were reading Sandra's story.
3. Why did you choose these words? Write down the importance of those words in your work and life.
4. What are your Feelings, Values, and Stressors?
5. What opportunities are you still searching for through your strengths and skills?
6. In thinking about who you are, where you are going, how you will get there, how you will stay there, how have you shown your adaptability for change?
7. What are your short-term goals? What are your long-term goals?
8. Have you noticed your behavior with others? How do you communicate with others?
9. How do you meet your needs, goals, and dreams within a team and a company?
10. What does 'success' mean to you? What does it feel like? What does it look like?

Answering the Four Essential Questions is the first step to self-discovery, self-leading, and self-cueing, so please honestly answer those questions to create the momentum you desire to activate success in your work and life.

Ask yourself: How does my personality affect my work and personal life?

Connect The Dots was a child's game that Sujata loved as a child learning English. Today, she is known as the '***Connects The Dots***' doctor! So, we want you to *Connect The Dots* from theory to practice, brain structures to mind patterns, emotional intelligence to emotional labor, consciousness to aims, and inertia to transformation. Strive to make connections between why you think the way you do and your behavior; this is called Metacognition. Gestalt psychology tells us that we think and see things in our world through patterns and symbols, whereby the brain tries to make sense of the parts that make up the big picture.

People don't fail at learning, but rather in not applying what they have learned.

Ask yourself: How can I incorporate what I am learning into my work and life?

Many people do not understand *where they are going*, because they do not know *how* they learn, and *where* they are going because they do not understand *who* they are. Most of the time, people merely mimic where they are going due to Conditioning (Behaviorism psychology) and external influences. Whether you realize it or not, you are being *Conditioned* each day, where conditioning results in positive and negative behaviors that develop due to reward.

Toxic behaviors continue because a person has been rewarded through a smile, a high-five, money, or praise. For example, social media gives you an excellent example of lust, but not for love. There are highly persuasive commercials that cause you to spend your money. There are mirror neurons in your brain that cause you to mimic behaviors. This is why awareness and intention are important *activators* that can help you assess why you are doing the things you are currently doing.

Many people do not understand *how to get there or how to stay there*.

You must distinguish between *who* you are and *what* you want versus what the world wants you to be for them. Take the guesswork out of the equation. Whether for your parent, spouse, or boss, make the distinction between your true self and the *role* you play during the various stages of lifespan development. Your role is not who you authentically are. For example, when you accept a role as an employee, you carry out the duties of that role through a set of behaviors that have been ingrained in you through past learnings and habits. Sometimes those set of behaviors work and sometimes they don't.

Activating success for personal growth involves adopting intentional strategies and cultivating habits that contribute to your self-improvement and overall well-being. You cannot jump to blame others for what you are feeling. Take responsibility because, most of the time, it is not their fault if you feel unheard, judged, disrespected, controlled, or unworthy. Learn how to express your needs in the workplace and in life. You are the common denominator. Everywhere you go, there you are.

Activating success in the context of change involves adopting a positive and proactive mindset, leveraging effective strategies, and embracing the opportunities that change can bring.

Change is a constant in life, and success often comes from how well you adapt and flourish in changing circumstances. By adapting to a more proactive approach, setting clear goals, and leveraging your strengths, you can activate success in the midst of any change.

Personal growth is a continuous process where success becomes a journey, and not a destination. By integrating the information in this book into your daily life, you can activate success for personal growth and create the fulfilling and meaningful life that you long for.

Application & Practice

Are you ready to learn more?

We invite you to use what you have learned so far to continue your journey and explore the possibilities in the next chapters.

We want you to apply the results of your Four Essential Questions (Who You Are, Where You Are Going, How You Will Get There, and How You Will Stay There) and connect it to the information that's coming in the rest of the book. Chapters 3-14 contains leadership education, workplace applications, and best practices that include:

1. Activators for success
2. Problem statements
3. Relevant research
4. Ideas and possible solutions
5. Change management examples
6. Effective communication and conflict resolution
7. Tips, neuro tips, tools, and insights
8. Inspirational quotes
9. Your turn
10. Contexts for Self-Discovery, Change Readiness, and Sustainable Impact
11. Take the time now to write out your Four Essential Questions. We have also given you a chance to do these four Essential Questions in the Workbook, just as a reminder of how important they truly are!

As you absorb the information, pay attention to how you feel and what you value in work and life.

Take responsibility to change what needs to change. Make a commitment to applying what you are reading and learning so that you can build your capacity to open up more opportunities. That is what "Your Turn" means, and this will reinforce positive habits for your successful future.

Keep your momentum going. We want you to be successful.

Chapter 3

Thrive Through Relationships
Activators: Grow & Flourish

Effective Communication and Conflict Resolution

Feelings, Values, Stressors: The Foundational Golden Formula for Effective Communication and Conflict Resolution!

In this section, we give you a technique to increase effective communication and reduce work and life conflicts.

Let's face it, who has not worked with people that were: arrogant, obnoxious, mouthy, conceited, controlling, cruel, cynical, deceptive, vindictive, disrespectful, egotistical, evil, forgetful, greedy, hostile, immature, impatient, inconsiderate, loud, liars, mean, manipulative, messy, nosy, pushy, rude, selfish, sneaky, spoiled, angry, stubborn, traitors, irresponsible, thoughtless, unstable, or vain.

People walk through the door with minor, major, and tragic personality flaws. These stay because they have become habits. Perhaps people have tried to tell them, but "the lightbulb has to *want* to be changed".

Minor Personality Flaws: sarcasm, cynicism, fear, paranoia, jealousy, selfishness, passive-aggressiveness, inappropriate humor.

Major Personality Flaws: prejudice, pride, grudging, gossiping, bullying; "The rules do not apply to me" mindset!

Tragic Personality Flaws: harassment, greed, need for constant praise/recognition, pathology.

There is a landmark case study in psychology of Phineas Gage who went to work one day, and a steel rod struck his face and went through his eye. It has been documented in the field of psychology, as a case study, that his personality completely changed after this traumatic brain injury and his easy-going demeanor got replaced with a mean one.

There is no magic to getting along with different personalities. Relationships take desire, time, and effort. When you comprehend what you value and accept what the other person values simultaneously, it's called 'symbiosis' in the biological sciences. You will no longer project or displace your feelings onto people by putting your desires above another, called 'parasitism' in the biological sciences. We are making the point that just as it is in the animal kingdom, people must also strive to work symbiotically through awareness of their schema and personality traits.

The underlying effectiveness for the modern workplace is *empathy*: a feeling that prompts an authentic desire to understand another human being, and not just going along to get along. Empathy is the skill that you want to bring into the 21st century workplace.

We encourage you to institute empathy and other *values* into the company mission and vision for the sake of effective communication and conflict resolution. People are committed to staying the same, so the addition of *values* in the workplace can help people to take a look at their behavior. Usually, people will put up with toxic behavior and pretend because that is more comfortable than rocking the boat (change). However, ineffective communication and conflicts will continue to create an imbalance in the environment. It is the small things that become gigantic in the workplace setting. It is the mosquitos that bother people from day to day; not the tigers.

Whether your workplace is a comedy or a tragedy, workplace conflict puts people into uncertainty, doubt, and confusion. In general, people are not taught conflict resolution skills, and they have vastly different ways to resolve conflicts based on their past experiences. Factors, such as cultural differences, will require an understanding of how people resolve conflicts through cultural norms, practices, and a traditions lens.

Effective verbal communication entails the use of

- understandable words instead of jargon;
- restating and reframing instead of assuming;
- responding fairly instead of judging; and
- providing suitable responses instead of emotional reactions.

Effective nonverbal communication necessitates a. low tone of voice; b. appropriate facial expressions; c. relaxed body stance; and d. proper use of hands. Notice that we did not include eye contact here on this list, and that is because different cultures have norms regarding eye contact. Especially with superiors. Understand that they may not be looking straight into your eyes, because it may be disrespectful in their culture to do so.

Workplace toxicity is highly preventable. Do not wait until your emotions have run amuck. As soon as you begin feeling uneasy in the biology of you, take action to introspect those sensations. We have observed far too many people make the wrong choices, where they could not control their emotions and chose violence instead of communication. We want to be sure that you have a detailed understanding of your *needs* and *wants*, so you can effectively communicate and resolve conflicts anywhere. Because, guess what? Everywhere you go; there you are! The common denominator is always you. We cannot change others; we can only change ourselves. There is a saying in psychology that goes like this: "The lightbulb has to *want* to be changed", and this means that a person has to be willing to change.

At a small scale, a conflict may arise from someone not picking up after themselves in the employee lunchroom, to a large full-blown conflict that stems from harassment. However small, we want you to learn prevention and intervention methods that can help you create, build, and sustain workplace and life relationships.

Effective communication comes from the head, heart, and gut. You have three brains that speak to each other via neuronal communication. Your head brain thinks in two parts: back and front. When was the last time you listened to all of them? The process of empathetic communication, of watchful verbal and nonverbal communication, can help forge a better understanding between people. You need ***Internal Active Listening*** skills so you can purposefully listen to what your heart brain is signaling your head brain. Internal Active Listening involves intentionally listening to both the back and front brains and cultivating the skill to now allow your back brain judgment to cloud your rational frontal brain. Internal Active Listening takes practice, because we have a terrible habit of interrupting – ourselves and others.

Through self-awareness, you can become cognizant of how you communicate – internally and externally. As you learn the importance of the **Feelings, Values, Stressors Formula** that is presented in this section, you will be ready for any change that comes your way. And as you practice your active listening skills, you will be able to create positive habits and patterns. The brain needs 21 days to create a habit, so keep practicing the conflict-resolution skills that are written here; especially now that people are heading back into buildings and hybrid work settings.

People rarely quit their jobs because they cannot perform job duties. They leave because of conflicts. Usually, personality conflicts. Not all dogs like each other, and that's okay because it's in the animal kingdom. You don't have to be best friends with the people that you work with; you just need to be respectful, empathetic, and communicate well. People must learn how to work well with others regardless of opinions, emotions, or judgments. The same thing that was on your kindergarten performance evaluation – do you play well with others? is on your current performance evaluation: Do you work well with others?

Companies hire people based upon job-specific skills. But there is much more that walks in through the door. That new hire with the job-specific skills also has a certain set of behaviors. Human beings are comprised of habits that emerge and are cemented from feelings and values; and these may vastly differ from others that you work with. It is here that misunderstandings and conflicts erupt. You may think that you don't have anything in common with the people you work with, but that's not true. Think about the mission and vision of the company that you all work for: that is the glue that ties you all together.

Humans are emotional creatures where emotions such as fear and anxiety are the default setting in the back survival reptilian brain. A brain structure called the 'Amygdala' is solely in charge of fear and anxiety, so everything that is perceived is routed through the emotional brain first. It takes a moment of awareness and intention to leave fear and anxiety back there and bring yourself into the frontal lobe and rational part of the brain.

Emotions have a language of their own, and if not resolved they can spread inside the cells of the twelve systems of the body. The mind and body are deeply connected where symptoms such as headache, stomachache, sleeplessness, brain fog, asthma, back ache, and more can appear due to the mind's perception of emotions.

How Do Emotions Work?

Anger is a *secondary* emotion. You will always get a *feeling* first. Therefore, it is critical that you know precisely what you are *feeling*.

You become angry as a result of a specific feeling, and it is the individuality of a certain feeling that can lead to anger. Anger is destructive and can cause you more work because you have to go back to make things right with another person. Anger can cause you to enter a cycle of steps: event, anger, revenge. Some people hit things, stomp, or throw papers, so there is a physical component here where the body tries to reduce the discomfort. The physical actions are due to the adrenaline (a hormone from the endocrine system) that is spilled into the bloodstream. The only way to get adrenaline out of your bloodstream is through physical movement. Run in place, go for a walk, jog, jump, or dance. These are all physical things that can help dissipate adrenaline from the body.

Adrenaline falls into the category of emotional chemistry, as do noradrenaline, dopamine, oxytocin, GABA, acetylcholine, glutamate, endorphins, and serotonin. All of which are based on perception and threat. Deficiencies in these neurotransmitters and hormones can cause procrastination, demotivation, fatigue, and hopelessness. The brain eats 25% of your daily intake, so choose your food wisely. You must learn how your individual mind and body works, so you can become accustomed to your sensations and symptomology.

If you remain angry long enough it can turn into stress, and if you experience chronic stress, it can lead to burnout.

Dr. Hans Selye was the first researcher to make the connection between work, stress, and disease. It looks like this: ***Feelings → Anger → Stress → Burnout → Disease***

You have the opportunity to take control of yourself at the *feelings* stage. At the stage when you experience ill feelings, stop what you are doing and introspect. Ask yourself: *"What is resonating inside of me that is causing these feelings to erupt?"* Always begin with the self. Do not blame. Every feeling has a different solution, so it's important to memorize a cluster of feeling words that you feel often. For example, offense may be something you feel often, and that feeling is highly subjective. If offense is what you are feeling at that moment in time, then you have to stop and figure out why.

When the neurons in your stomach signal you that something's not quite right, then start asking clarifying questions. Be genuine when asking; not cynical.

1. What do you mean?
2. Can you please explain more?
3. That's interesting. Can you please give me an example?
4. That's thought-provoking, can you please describe that?
5. How do you prefer to be approached during disagreements?

You are rarely upset for the reason you think. Asking such questions will allow you to calm your insides down a bit. It will give you *time* to bring your thinking from your back reactive brain to the frontal rational part. Why? Because that process takes *time*. That's why kids get put into time-out. A time-out for you would be a good thing too; and correspond time-outs with age, so if you are forty, then take forty minutes for a time-out. For a three-year-old, the recommendation is three minutes; for a four-year-old, the recommendation is four minutes; you get the idea.

There is a 5x5 rule: is it going to matter in five days? 5 weeks? 5 years? If not, then let it go. You have to choose your battles at work and in life.

First, make a list of *Feeling words.*
In fact, do that now so you don't forget!

Keep that list handy and write down when and where those feelings come up. This is extremely important. Why? Because, like we said before, *every feeling has a different solution!*

For example, if you are feeling sad, this will require a different solution than if you are feeling left out. Be sure to understand this. Once you comprehend this concept, work and life will become conflict-free and enjoyable for you and others.

We invite you to use this formula at work and in your personal life to effectively communicate in any context. You will find that communicating with people through this formula will result in healthy human relationships.

The implementation of this knowledge will put you, your team, and company decades ahead of others. Connect The Dots to the biology, psychology, social, cultural, and spiritual of you. Human communication, active listening, and conflict resolution are part of **"Work Science"**.

Connecting The Dots Between
Feelings, Values, and Stressors!

You *feel* a certain way because you *value* something, and when there is a breach of something that you *value*, it makes you *stressed! Got it?*

We have given you a feelings, values, and stressors chart at the end of each chapter for each leadership style. This will help you to understand yourself and others.

"A value that is missing = ill feelings = stressors" is genius information for you to understand, because it will eradicate most conflicts. When you create a habit of using this formula at work and life, you will be free of the stress symptomology. We assure you; you will never miss the toxicity.

Feelings (positive and negative) List

Accepting, Open, Calm, Centered, Content, Fulfilled, Patient, Peaceful, Present, Relaxed, Serene, Trusting, Aliveness, Joy, Amazed, Awe, Bliss, Delighted, Eager, Ecstatic, Enchanted, Energized, Engaged, Enthusiastic, Excited, Free, Happy, Inspired, Invigorated, Lively, Passionate, Playful, Radiant, Refreshed, Rejuvenated, Renewed, Satisfied, Thrilled, Vibrant, Angry, Annoyed, Agitated, Aggravated, Bitter, Contempt, Cynical, Disdain, Disgruntled, Disturbed, Edgy, Exasperated, Frustrated, Furious, Grouchy, Hostile, Impatient, Irritated, Irate, Moody, On edge, Outraged, Pissed, Resentful, Upset, Vindictive, Courageous, Powerful, Adventurous, Brave, Capable, Confident, Daring, Determined, Free, Grounded, Proud, Strong, Worthy, Valiant, Connected, Loving, Accepting, Affectionate, Caring, Compassion, Empathy, Fulfilled, Present, Safe, Warm, Worthy, Curious, Engaged, Exploring, Fascinated, Interested, Intrigued Involved Stimulated Despair, Sad, Anguish, Depressed, Despondent, Disappointed, Discouraged, Gloomy, Grief, Heartbroken,

Hopeless, Lonely, Longing, Melancholy, Sorrow, Teary, Unhappy, Upset, Weary, Yearning, Disconnected, Numb.

You can get even more specific into the Feelings that you are experiencing. This can provide you with more specifics in finding a specific solution to how you are feeling and what you wish to do about it.

Aloof – Bored, Confused, Embarrassed, Distant, Empty, Indifferent, Isolated.
Lethargic – Listless, Removed, Resistant, Shut down, Uneasy, Withdrawn.
Shame – Ashamed, Humiliated, Inhibited, Mortified, Self-conscious.
Fear – Afraid, Anxious.
Apprehensive – Frightened, Hesitant, Nervous, Panicked, Paralyzed.
Scared – Terrified, Worried, Fragile, Helpless, Sensitive, Alert.
Grateful – Appreciative, Delighted, Fortunate, Grace, Humbled, Moved, Thankful.
Guilt – Regret, Remorseful, Sorry, Worried.
Hopeful – Encouraged, Expectant, Optimistic, Trusting.
Powerless – Helpless, Stoic, Trapped, Victim, Tender, Useless, Weak, Worthless.
Calm – Caring, Loving, Reflective, Serene, Vulnerable, Warm.
Stressed – Burned Out, Cranky, Depleted, Edgy, Exhausted, Frazzled, Overwhelm.
Rattled – Rejecting, Restless, Shaken, Uneasy, Weary, Worn out.
Unsettled – Doubt, Apprehensive, Concerned, Dissatisfied, Disturbed, Perplexed, Rejecting.
Questioning – Reluctant, Skeptical, Suspicious, Unsure, Hesitant, Cautious, Distrustful.

Create a habit of stating exactly what you are feeling:

I feel controlled   I feel ignored
I feel belittled   I feel attached
I feel left out   I feel pressured

I feel humiliated	I feel dismissed
I feel offended	I feel insulted
I feel betrayed	I feel manipulated
I feel dominated	I feel rejected
I feel neglected	I feel judged
I feel powerless	I feel blocked

Learn to express your feelings and values with extreme accuracy. Feeling *dominated* and feeling *betrayed* have entirely different solutions versus feeling *pressured*. It is imperative that you understand this for self-leading and leading others.

Out of all of these feelings, *appreciation* is the one positive feeling that will activate your success toward positive change, so if you are having a bad day, keep repeating this word.

Values List

Second, make a list of **Value words.**

Everyone has different values, and they are usually very dear to the heart. Print out a Values list and keep it on your computer, if that helps.

You will feel stressed when someone does not value the same thing you do. **Values and stress are directly related.** Remember this. This is gold!

For example, if you value education, and people around you do not, then that can make you feel stressed. If you value freedom, and the people around you do not, then that can make you feel stressed. If you value humbleness, and there are arrogant people around you, then that can make you feel stressed. Understand? Once you comprehend this, work and life will become much more acceptable and not just 'fake nice'.

Honesty, Integrity, Wisdom, Autonomy, Loyalty, Abundance, Kindness, Charity, Respect, Courage, Generosity, Gratitude, Openness, Accountability, Compassion, Success, Self-love, Spirituality, Justice, Forgiveness, Caring, Faith, Beauty, Wealth, Acceptance, Humor, Intuition, Prosperity, Change, Gracefulness, Peacefulness, Harmony, Balance, Joy, Fun, Independence, Efficiency, Promise-keeping, Fairness, Sincerity, Accuracy, Goodness, Hope, Honor, Humility, Insightfulness, Influence, Decisiveness, Knowledge.

You can communicate your values:

Honesty is important to me.	Fun is important to me.
Loyalty is important to me.	Money is important to me.
Kindness is important to me.	Family is important to me.
Knowledge is important to me.	Home is important to me.
Health is important to me.	Work is important to me.

You can even communicate your values this way:

I'm a people person.
I tend to be a perfectionist.
I like to be creative.
I'm always on time.
I love solving problems.

We define a value as a fundamental belief or practice of what is most desirable, worthwhile, meaningful, and nonnegotiable to an individual. Values guide your needs, wants, and goals.

A **need** is something you require for survival, like food, water, clothing, and shelter. For example, to eat, to drink water, to sleep.

You do not require a **want** for survival, and it may be something you desire for status or power—for example, a boat, a fur coat, or a watch.

Connect The Dots between your values, strengths, influences, stress, and burnout. Where do your values come from? Do you think your colleagues value the same things you do? Why do you value the things that you do? Did your values change during the world crisis?

Values are extremely dear to the heart brain. People may compromise on their lunch order but will never compromise on their values. What's important to one person may not be important to another. Each person is different, that's why it is critical that you get to know your people individually. The quicker you learn what others value, the quicker you will activate success for yourself at work and in your personal life.

Human vs. human are not the only types of conflicts in the workplace. There are many others: Human vs. self, human vs. tech, human vs. nature, or human vs. nurture.

You can see that there is much room for conflicts in life. Some people will explain it away through 'Murphy's Law – anything that can go wrong, will go wrong". Remember, there will be certain barriers or drawbacks to what you desire; your decisions will be directly proportional to the conflicts you experience; and when faced with choices, they all will have positive and negative consequences.

The funny thing about human psychology is this: the more you admit your shortcomings, the more people will like you. And, the more choices you have, the less satisfied you are with those choices. If you dislike a trait in someone else, you probably have that trait yourself.

Life Experiences

Conscience

Family

What influences a person's Values?

Norms

Peers

Books, music, social media

Neighbors

School & teachers

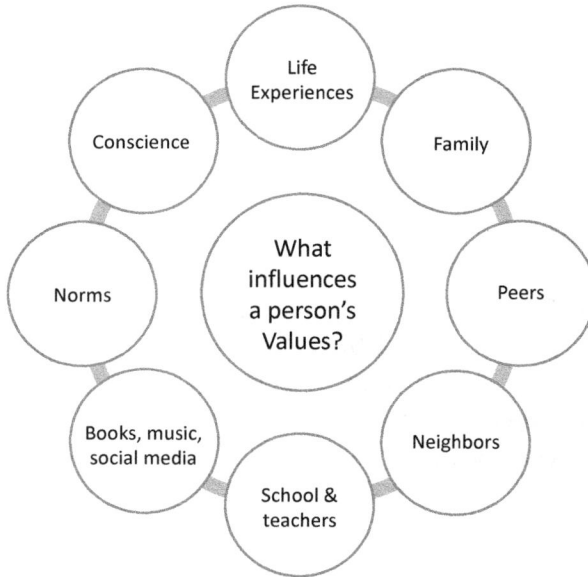

We don't have to give you a Stressors list because stressors are the opposite of your values! For example: peace vs. war; clean vs. unclean; on time vs. late; kind vs. mean.

If you value peace and there is war, then war will be your stressor. If you value fun, and there isn't any fun, then dullness can be your stressor. If you value health and the people around you coughing and sneezing, then sickness can be your stressor. If you value honesty and the people around you lie to you, then dishonesty can be your stressor.

Perhaps you are experiencing or witnessing people putting others down to initiating untruths. These toxic tactics do not work! Unfortunately, some people have sadly mistaken toxicity as a "business professional practice" and have accepted it as a business norm. They fail to realize the ramifications of their actions.

In early childhood, we learn to believe that all people are kind and caring, but as we go through school and contextual experiences, we learn that there is good and evil in this world where both kindness and cruelty exist. At the individual level, we are conditioned from the outside in.

At the systemic level, some organizations have accepted a certain level of malice as socially acceptable and justified it as *assertiveness*. Make no mistake: malice is not assertiveness. We believe that things must change to create empathy in work science and organizational culture.

The workplace is a complex body where contradictory things are psychologically occurring on a daily basis. People sabotage via shunning, which also validates early childhood conditioning and is called 'indirect aggression or microaggression'. Indirect aggression and microaggression is first-order violence. People often give the excuse that they 'lost control,' so pay close attention to your locus of control. Discern what things are in your control and what are not, and learn to accept the things you cannot control, and change the things you can. What the C-suite is missing to take into account is that women prefer virtual and hybrid work, because it allows them to minimize the effects of microaggression, prejudice, and harassment.

Disconnecting from aggressive, non-altruistic behavior takes integrity, intention, and courage. We are not hard-wired to behave in a certain way at work or in life. We are **conditioned**, so pay close attention to what you accept of yourself and others and what you are modeling and displaying in the workplace. This is called *'Impression Management'*.

Fill your head brain, heart brain, and gut brain with decency and civility. All three brains affect each other. Your brain has amazing power. An open mind means there is no room for jealousy, pain, or loss. Race differences are the first thing we see because we are visual learners. Learn to examine what people value, their personalities, and what skills complement yours. The brain judges, so judge people on their character and not for their race or ethnicity.

Make our *"Empathy-Ethic"* your knee-jerk reaction. Believe that your world is abundant where success is infinite. This belief alone will activate and accelerate your success exponentially. Please understand this!

Here is a sample script to understand someone through impartiality and fairness (our values):

- Tell me in your words what happened.
- What were your *feelings* at the time?
- How did this situation affect you?
- Who else did it effect?
- What do you want to do now?
- What can I do to help you?

Intervention is great, but prevention is better. And remember — you can easily get along with anyone if you compliment them behind their back! Leave your back survivor brain and enter your frontal lobe to look for something greater than hurt, envy, and pettiness.

We commend you for bringing your skill-set and passion to the table, but we cannot tell you how many people that are new to an organization do not follow instructions that are directed. Give time to learn the process and follow standard operating procedures during that learning stage. There will come a day when you can go to your boss and suggest another method that may work better for you. Read emails twice, and all the way to the end! And be sure to follow through on those instructions. If there is something you do not understand about those instructions, please ask for clarification. And if you do not know how to proceed, then ask for help! We encourage emerging leaders, especially to practice giving your leader/manager what they want; adopt the mindset that you can make their job easier; then motivate your teammates to help each other.

When you are the newest person on the team please take the time to observe, even if you know something already; get to know every person and connect through common ground; talk to the experts; ask questions; learn that the company product is the problem that you solve; figure out what the low-handing fruits are; and accept feedback as if it were a packaged gift.

If you continue to disregard senior leaders and the existing system, then there will be a crucial conversation at your performance evaluation. You don't want to be blindsided. Gain buy-in from your boss that you are on the right track. You may not be ready or open to receive feedback, and your gut reaction may be to flight and quit, and you may choose that; but the same thing will happen in your new job, because you were not ready to make the change in your last job; so, your choice to not make the change in your behavior will result in the same behavior through habit and pattern, and you will receive the same performance evaluation again. You will sit at the foot of your bed and ask: "Why is this happening to me? Why is this happening to me *again*?" It is you that must change. Be open to questioning your perception, and to what others are perceiving of who you are and how you come across at work.

All behavior in your life comes from your memory.

Your decision-making and problem-solving stem from what you remember. The problem is: as a species, we have terrible memories! That's why we have to engage in strategies like repetition and mnemonic devises that can help us to remember things in the present. The police force also knows this to be true, because they rush to get eyewitness testimonies before too much time passes by where people forget what happened at the scene of the accident.

Human beings have a strong need to belong (Maslow). Therefore, we subconsciously have the desire to be accepted. So, why aren't we all accepted? The systems where we worked were set up for severe competition and not for cooperation, and this derailed the construct of *acceptance*. A highly competitive company culture can result in a great deal of toxicity (back-stabbing, getting even, bullying). It is the psychological equivalent of pinching, scratching, and pulling hair.

The damage done in workplaces has had life-long ramifications for individuals, teams, and organizations. Think back to the places where you worked in the past: segmentation, segregation, separation. These helped no one. The brain's survival mechanism is made to avoid isolation. The brain thinks that there is safety in numbers, therefore human beings are pack animals. Let us all seek to understand each other, shall we?

Belongingness can create healthy relationships within a group, and those can create trust and distrust. Sometimes, the more we care about people the more distrustful we become of them. Caring about others can leave you open for disappointment, but that's a chance everyone takes, because we cannot control others; we can only control our response. Keep consistent in your values and behaviors and give the best of yourself to work and life.

A few people on your team may have undiagnosed or diagnosed mental health challenges. A portion of your team may also have misdemeanors or felonies, for that matter. Whatever the case, you must remember that what people are emotionally experiencing needs understanding. In actuality, people may be suffering from PTSD due to trauma-inducing experiences where they have trusted people and where those people blindsided, bullied, or hurt them.

The triumphs, victories, and challenges for you are quite concrete. Various niches desperately need you. Innovation is critical at this point in history. Step up to the plate and offer your best.

We often ask our clients this question: *"Is what you are currently doing working for you?"* Their answer is always, *"No"*. Then why keep doing the same things expecting different results? Isn't that the definition of insanity?

Be aware of your habits. Get out of your old rut and begin utilizing this chapter to activate success at work and personal life.

The Next Road

Now that you've taken the initial drive and have the book perspective from Chapter 1, get ready to embark on your journey of discovery. In Chapter 2, you will delve deeper into the true self and be able to Connect The Dots.

Let's continue this exciting journey together.

Chapter 4

Theories Matter
Activators: Facts & Research

Have you experienced these barriers to success? Opinions, speculations, assumptions, and biases that have led to less than positive results.

This chapter will help you understand the importance of the *Scientific Method* that all world scientists use for professional peer knowledge sharing and replication of studies. We bring you pertinent theories that have made contributions through scientific methodology, because theories help you to veer away from opinions and assumptions that do not provide credibility in peer reviewed literature.

Just as your house needs a strong foundation for longevity and strength during times of duress, an empirical manner of thinking will ground you in your work and conduct at work and personal life. How you conduct your work translates to your reputation, so it must stand on credible, empirical ground.

It is extremely easy to come to the table with personal opinions, however effective leaders are able to distinguish between opinions and facts. The brain will always provide you with opinions due to the judgment function and steer you in the direction of an emotional rant, however this is not a professional practice, and it will not benefit you in the workplace.

Facts and theories are crucial in every niche. Rather than entertain opinions (yours and another's) it is better for you to create a habit of presenting facts, data, and evidence, even in your daily conversations. Think about what you are hypothesizing, theorizing, conjecturing, and why. Be aware of internal self-talk that mixes opinions in the emotional brain through aggression. The stronger your conviction, the stronger your emotional brain will assert itself and hijack you. A scene in the movie, "A Few Good Men" depicts a foolish leader with an opinion that overrode reality, where he blurts: "You cannot handle the truth".

It is far too easy for the mind to think through the emotional area and not from the rational area of the brain. Your mind wants you to belong to it, but you don't have to believe everything that your mind tells you. Learn how to distinguish between opinions and facts, and more importantly learn when your mind is hijacking you. Just as in speaking, your writing abilities will indicate an empirical mindset and that will showcase evidence that may or may not be supporting you as a leader.

All three levels, individuals, teams, and organizations must work closely with each other and must be motivated to do so if they wish to keep their jobs. The speaking words and writing themes that you choose will impact your actions for all three levels.

- A system will ask you: Do you have potential, and are you using it?
- A team will ask: Do you have skills, and are you interesting?
- You must ask yourself: Do I have the spirit to show my potential through comradeship?

Your qualifications are the position on the playing field, but your reputation is cultivated through empirical credibility in how you present yourself through your own self-discovery as a leader.

In our estimation, the apex of all theories is *Maslow's Hierarchy of Needs*. (1970). Maslow, a humanistic psychologist and author, was a genius whose theory and philosophy applies to every work and life niche. Whether you work in education, health, business, economics, arts, sciences, or technologies, this theory is based on human physiological and psychological needs. It is vital in developing an empathetic understanding for self-leading and leading others, and this master theory that can help you to have a positive impact on humanity.

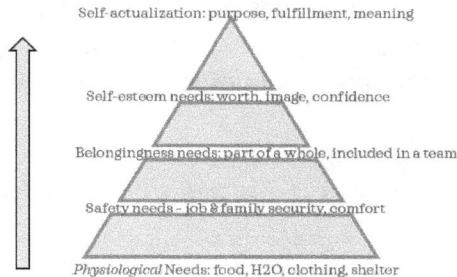

Self-actualization: purpose, fulfillment, meaning

Self-esteem needs: worth, image, confidence

Belongingness needs: part of a whole, included in a team

Safety needs – job & family security, comfort

Physiological Needs: food, H2O, clothing, shelter

Maslow's Motivational Theory is based on psychological health that is structured in fulfilling basic human needs; he prioritizes those needs from the bottom up and culminating with self-actualization on the top. In his writings, Maslow states that a need will not be met unless the previous one is met, and so on. This theory helps you to self-discover so you can lead yourself more effectively to create openness and empathy for other people's needs and motivations.

The attainment of self-actualization is different for everyone, so leaders need to be not to compare individuals. Life chapters will differ from person to person, so please do not compare someone's chapter eight with someone else's chapter one. Everyone is on a unique life journey, as shared in Sujata and Sandra's narratives.

How fast you grow as a leader depends entirely on how soon you accept yourself. Once you decide that you no longer wish to stay stuck *where you are*, things will shift. Taking that first step in knowing who you are and where you are on Maslow's Hierarchy may be scary because you may not like what you discover, but it is the step you need. Once you wholistically accept yourself through the knowledge of your strengths and challenges, you will set yourself on a positive trajectory to activate success.

As we learn and grow, we continue to evolve. Maslow's original five-stage model has also evolved to include 'transcendence'. This newer model encourages us to develop an open mindset and mentality throughout the stages of life. Life experiences move us between the stages of lifespan development (Erikson) — early, middle, and late childhood; adolescence; then, early, middle, and late adulthood.

Erikson's Psychosocial Stages of Development

1. 0–1   Trust vs. Mistrust. Trust (or mistrust) that basic needs, such as nourishment and affection, will be met.
2. 1–3   Autonomy vs. Shame/Doubt. Develop a sense of independence in many tasks.
3. 3–6   Initiative vs. Guilt. Take initiative on some activities— may develop guilt when unsuccessful or boundaries overstepped.
4. 7–11   Industry vs. Inferiority. Develop self-confidence in abilities when competent or sense of inferiority when not.
5. 12–18 Identity vs. Confusion. Experiment with and develop identity and roles.
6. 19–29 Intimacy vs. Isolation. Establish intimacy and relationships with others.
7. 30–64 Generativity vs. Stagnation. Contribute to society and be part of a family.
8. 65–   Integrity vs. Despair. Assess and make sense of life and meaning of contributions.

As you can see, there are only eight stages in a lifetime. Then you pass away. Make full use of the time you have here on Earth to help each other.

If a person has suffered loss or trauma, they may psychologically regress between Maslow's needs and Erikson's life stages. This might be viewed as a setback, but a setback is merely a setup for growth. Self-actualization is currently viewed as a cognitive need where knowledge, understanding, and curiosity are peaked. Self-actualization shows you that as you realize your potential, self-fulfillment, and personal growth, you will experience peak performance. It takes desire not only to *be* but to become the best version of yourself.

Jean Piaget (1960) helps us to understand cognitive progression through the life stages.

Piaget's Stages of Cognitive Development

0–2   **Sensorimotor.** The world is experienced through senses and actions. Object permanence | Stranger anxiety

2–6   **Preoperational.** Use words and images to represent things, but lack logical reasoning | Pretend play | Egocentrism | Language development

7–11   **Concrete Operational.** Understand concrete events and analogies logically; perform arithmetical operations. Conservation | Mathematical transformations

12–Death   **Formal Operational.** Formal operations | Utilize abstract reasoning | Abstract logic | Moral reasoning

At the top of this graphic, you will see Transcendence Needs, where one is motivated by values and spirit. As you grasp that you are part of a larger picture, you can continue on a journey of empathy and understanding. Each experience you encounter will give you a better plan and appreciation for yourself and others.

Which level are you on in Maslow's Hierarchy graph? Your current behavior correlates with the needs of the level that you are currently on. Underneath that behavior is a feeling, and under that feeling is a need. Hence, Maslow's Needs. You will have to focus on the need and the behavior to activate change and success.

Do not compare yourself to anyone. Remember, it is *your* journey.

The one thing we know from physics is that 'change is constant.' The world is constantly changing, and information is continuously updated, so keep up and upskill. Fuel yourself with the knowledge to become an effective cog for your niche. You will need ten thousand hours of experience to call yourself an expert.

Fixed Thinking is in the back brain, and it is negative and exhausting. When a thought rapidly comes into your brain, train yourself to bring it from the back of the brain to the rational Frontal Lobe. When you switch the irrational code in your back brain forward to the rational code, your work and life will be more positive, and you will realize that your only competition is who you were yesterday.

Bear in mind that an environment that is not safe for everyone to voice their perspectives is not psychologically safe. You must Connect The Dots. Basic needs coupled with psychological needs. Fear motivations may include pain, shame, rejection, humiliation, and loss. Evil motivations may include disrespect, hatred, dishonor, pride, greed, revenge, and jealousy. Novel motivations can show up as loyalty, honor, love, and fulfillment.

You automatically think through emotions that cause feelings to emerge.

You must train yourself through awareness of what is happening to your biology and psychology. The mind-body connection is strong and powerful.

The idea is not to suppress your emotions but rather for you to self-lead by controlling them, so they do not control you through an irrational thinking spree. As the Bee Gees lyrics read: If you do not bring awareness into your life, "Emotion is taking me over, tied up in sorrow, lost in your soul".

We are hopeful that you will connect opinions to emotions and facts to credibility and reputation. To transform your emotions and opinions into healthy actions, the work of Salovey and Mayor's Emotional Intelligence (1980), and later Daniel Goleman who popularized this concept in his book, "Emotional Intelligence: Why it can matter more than IQ" (1997), will further help you to self-discover and prepare you for change. You will soon replace automatic thoughts and negative habits.

In addition, the constructs of Emotional Intelligence: Self-awareness, Self-management, Social-awareness, and Relationship-management, will aid you greatly in the fast-growing diverse workforce. To this list, we add Self-cueing, which means how you cue yourself to think, feel, and behave. When you read the narrative that you have written, you will also realize how you cue yourself to behave and manage emotions.

With regard to Relationship-Management, decipher if your story tells you how inclusive you are through your personal influence, and through multicultural dialogues that promote understanding and interculturalism. (www.iccglobal.com). Your past has served its purpose, and you can understand who you have become in the present through your past experiences, but it doesn't do any good to dwell on the past. You are here now, so accept the richness of the present, and focus on making a positive change for the future.

Your values and personality are fluid and will change during the course of lifespan development. The openness in your personality will bring many positive gains. "Openness" is the language in the niche of personality science; while inclusion is the language in the niche of multiculturalism. All niches have certain jargon and language that they use to describe constructs and models.

Costa and McRae's (2005) theory shows that people who consider themselves open-minded are also agreeable and empathetic in their NEO-PIR model of personality. Personality and environment work together for schema formation. Think for a moment if you were exposed to foreign friends, cultural artifacts, foods, music, or diverse symbols. The inclusion of the aforementioned or the lack thereof will influence self-leading and the manner in which you lead others. This work is based on Trait Theory that suggests that certain personality traits are inherent to effective leaders. Traits such as self-confidence, intelligence, determination, and integrity are believed to contribute to leadership effectiveness.

Interculturalism is the avenue for dialogue and interaction that helps people to engage with each other at work and in the community. The reason why we advocate for interculturalism is due to humanism. Recognizing that we are one universal world community will make you a better leader because you will foster an *Empathy-Ethic*. How you do this is through your niche and where (geographically) you are located. Doing something locally that is for the benefit of the globe is called **Glocal** action.

Do what you can, where you are. You can take action given where you are (*Glocal)* with the resources available to you. However small, one step can make a huge difference, globally.

Dr. Urie Bronfenbrenner (1979) offers his Ecological Systems Theory that addresses social influences on an individual. His premise is that your circle of influence widens at each step of the lifespan development stages, where your siblings, aunts, uncles, teachers, church, temple, school, community, music, television, ideas, philosophies, and more have a tremendous impact on who you become, how you think, how you behave, and the life choices you make.

Bronfenbrenner's Ecological Systems Theory has been well received due to the dynamic interactions that environments provide while people are growing, changing, and transforming through lifespan stages.

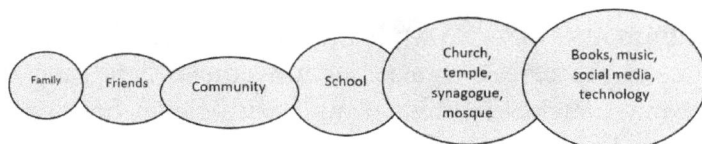

Bronfenbrenner's viewpoint resembles the work of Albert Bandura's Social Learning theory, Lev Vygotsky's Sociocultural theory, and Erikson's Lifespan Stages where the role of the environment is considered to be a vital component in socio-emotional development. Connect The Dots of socio-emotional development to multiple intelligences (Gardner) and needs (Maslow's theory).

Human beings are innately motivated to survive and succeed; you will have to find the strength that resides within you, that will allow your capacity to rise up towards self-actualization and transcendence.

Harvard professor **Martha Nussbaum's (2000) Capability Theory** catches our attention, as we educate and mentor the next generation towards sustainability. Her focus refers to people achieving their skills and abilities while focusing on their capability and autonomy. Nussbaum brought these novel ideas to the forefront because they were excluded from traditional approaches. Similarly, we are emphasizing capacity-building through this book.

Human beings are capable in many ways but need to seek out opportunities to show their capability. The action step is what is needed for change to occur. And action relies on free will. When we talk about choices, it is a humanistic viewpoint that denotes that human beings have free will and willpower that we believe provides motivation required for action, capacity, and potential.

We are grateful for many theorists that have significantly contributed to the world of work, where capacity has been shown to thrive:

Frank Parsons (1854-1908): Is the father of vocational guidance who began the career counseling movement. Trait and Factor Theory that matches individual traits with career options is still used today. People are born with certain temperaments that allow them to do the work they choose.

Donald Super (1910-1994): Focused on career development through life *roles*, self-concept, and through an inspection of how social factors influence career choice. Especially nowadays, where many people are trying to balance the care of aging parents, small children, pets, and single-parenthood at the same time.

John Holland (1919-2008): Is a favorite for his hexagon of vocational personalities knows as the Holland Hexagon R.I.A.S.E.C Model, where he found six categories of personality types that align with distinct work environments that entail: Realistic, Investigative, Artistic, Social, Enterprising, and Conventional. When we discuss Holland with clients, we also link it to Extraversion and Introversion from the O.C.E.A.N personality model. For example: it has been our experience that extraverted people enter the E. for enterprising vocations, while introverted people enter the A for artistic, I for investigative, and C for conventional vocations. Don't be afraid to use more than one model to explain to clients how their personality effects vocational matching.

John Krumboltz (1928-2019): founder of the Social Learning Theory of Career Decision Making, that focuses on social and environmental factors that lead to *learning* experiences in career development. In this book, we emphasize socio-emotional learning, because self-discipline, self-cueing, and self-management is what is necessary to work well with others. How you learn and what you retain contributes to career success.

Nancy Schlossberg (born 1928): founder of the Transition Theory that explains life transitions, management, and career changes. She focused on the psychosocial factors of career development and employment counseling. There are numerous transitions that people go through during their lifespan development. People such as adolescents, military wives, veterans, retirees, immigrants, and returning citizens need an empirical explanation of how they can transition.

Mark Savickas (born 1943): focuses on Career Construction Theory, that focuses on the role of narrative and storytelling through what we term as *career-span* development. You can link his theory with UNESCO's model for Storytelling. Everyone has a story and how they tell it is of critical importance in how we offer help to them.

Empathetic pioneers forged the way for us to be authentic in the way we help people find purpose and meaning in their lives. What counselors and practitioners do is they create a safe space for clients to display their authenticity in what they want to do in life. Done well, it allows the authentic truth to come out into the open, where their ears can hear our loud what they are thinking on the inside. Goal-creation helps people separate authenticity from illusion.

There are several leadership theories that have been developed over the years, each offering a unique perspective on what makes an effective leader. Leadership theories propose that the effectiveness of leadership depends on the strength of the leader. We say that it is about situational awareness.

These are the leadership styles that we chose to focus on in the subsequent chapters. We chose to focus on these leadership styles due to our own work and life experiences and we want to offer you awareness of how you can activate success through building effective relationships with others.

Conscious Leadership: the leader is aware of self and others; able to manage emotions and has situational awareness.

Ego-Centered Leadership: the leader is not aware and does not have control of their emotions.

Transformational Leadership: the leader inspires and motivates people to achieve beyond their expected capabilities; able to bring out their potential.

Pacesetter Leadership: this leader's skills and personality allow them to move a group in the right direction through deadlines and timelines.

Action-Centered Leadership: this leader works closely with managers and expects high team activity and task completion.

Global-Minded Leadership: this leader appreciates diverse perspectives, strategic alliances, and global partnerships.

Sustainable Leadership: this leader is aware of the impact of the globe's limited resources and embeds actions that can help to meet sustainable goals for future generations.

Hands-Off Leadership: this leader trusts their team to complete tasks they delegate.

Co-Elevation Leadership: this leader collaborates and heightens performance through effective communication and team activities.

Evaluative Leadership: this leader's focus on assessment, measurement, and data allows teams to repeat positive outcomes, and reorient to change the ones that do not serve them.

Hope Leadership: this leader focuses on instilling courage and strength for a bright future by encouraging teams to build capacity.

Let's Connect The Dots: Maslow says we all have individual needs and are motivated to meet those needs. Do you know where you are going? Do you know how to get there? Nussbaum says that we all have a certain capacity, where motivation requires opportunity to build individual capacity. Therefore, motivation without opportunity will result in stress, conflict, and unmet needs. Bronfenbrenner explains that the individual is influenced by their social environment and attains their point of view based on what they have learned through their influences. The individual self-leads through their viewpoint; anything that is opposite of what they believe becomes an opportunity for communication and conflict resolution.

Whatever your vocational niche, using the Scientific Method puts you on a professional level with your peers. Viewing life in an orderly and logical way, based on evidence, takes uncertainty and subjectivity out of work and life.

Because you are a professional working in a professional field, it is vital that you stay in the Scientific Method frame of mind. Think about what you observe; write down your observations; ask questions about what you have observed; then find some answers based on research. You can even write down a Hypothesis based on your observation that uses the 'If…. Then' formula that is used worldwide.

Do not be afraid to jump into journals that prove or disprove your hypotheses, assumptions, and suppositions. Decades ago, there was an injustice in the scientific field called the "File Drawer

Phenomenon" where some scientists put gender-related data in the bottom drawer (sciencedirect.com). Do not be afraid if your research disproves your hypothesis. Present your findings in an ethical manner. As a professional, you will be presenting on the stage, so it is a requirement to include valid and reliable sources through credible sources that end in org, edu, or gov. You want as much credibility as possible when you are trying to be the change in this world. As a reminder we have included a section on change management and effective communication so that you can begin to think and do things differently.

Change Management Insight

CEO's carry a great burden through their *role*. Leaders, who are not self-aware and have not taken the time to understand how to manage their emotions, often continue to have high-powered outbursts directed at senior leadership team members, especially in the Board room. What precipitates such outbursts?

Outbursts cause a domino effect in the workplace. People match the energy that is coming towards them, and they do this unknowingly. That is why awareness in self-leading is critical, because it is awareness that can help people to shift from reacting to responding.

A win-lose approach is common in the workplace but is one that no longer works well. It continues because individuals automatically stick to their opinions that are connected to their schema. If they don't know any differently, then they will continue to believe in the win-lose outcome.

The workplace provides an excellent opportunity to create and distribute value for everyone's interests, skills, and goals. You can reorient a win-lose mindset into a win-win one through self-awareness, self-regulation, and relationship-building, and through a focus on facts and evidence. Stop yourself when you have a thought-opinion, collect credible information, and transform that thought-opinion into a thought-fact.

The sooner you realize that the answers are on the inside, the sooner you will begin to enjoy outside the world of work and personal life.

🔏 **Tip #1:** We urge you to read about the master's in psychology —Maslow, Bronfenbrenner, Jung, Rogers, Skinner, Erikson, Bandura, Wundt, Watson, Rogers, Pavlov, Piaget, Erikson, Ainsworth, Bandura, Schacter, Singer, Thorndike, Allport, Cattel, Miller, Chomsky, Seligman, Csikzentmihalyi, Sternberg, and even Freud because he was the one who gave us his genius defense mechanisms list. See the work of Dr. Imants Jaunarajs, Ohio University, Assistant Dean, Career Network, Brain-based career development and leadership coaching. The work of career and change theorists — Frank Parsons, Donald Super, John Holland, John Krumboltz, Nancy Schlossberg, Mark Savickas, Kotter, Lewin, and Imants Jaunaraj makes our jobs easier.

Enhance your credibility to your colleagues and boss:

1. Show the relevance of two grounded theories in the work you currently do.
2. Talk about two sources of theoretical work you have read that you can use in your work.
3. Highlight divergent thinking skills through work and life experiences that you have navigated. What was the outcome, and why? What can you do differently next time?

🔏 **Neuro Tip #1:** There is a biological condition called *Alexithymia*, where people cannot recognize emotions in others. Please give people some grace when trying to understand them. Do not fill in the blanks based on your schema, because, in truth, you do not have all the information about a person. There is also a condition called *Synesthesia*, where some people view numbers in certain colors. They are not color-blind, because they see all colors, however it is the numbers that show up as certain colors.

Tool #1: TED Talk on how scientists learn. https://www.ted.com/playlists/410/how_scientists_learn

YOUR TURN

1. Why are empirical theories important in the workplace?
2. What is your favorite theory and why?
3. Think about a situation where people got opinions and facts mixed up. What was the result, and how was it resolved?
4. Here are some areas that can help you to become a high functioning adult in an axiomatic world. What areas do you need to improve?
   a. How to manage money
   b. How to manage time
   c. How to cope with failure
   d. How to find a job
   e. How to be organized
   f. How to talk to people
   g. How to clean
   h. How to cook
   i. How to accept a 'no' gracefully.
   j. How to manage emotions.

"

Vision without execution is hallucination.

~Thomas A. Edison~

"

Chapter 5

Conscious Leadership
Activators: Clarity & Mindset

Have you experienced these barriers to success? Unawareness, confusion, errors, *learn-as-you-go* attitudes, misunderstandings, broken relationships and severed partnerships.

This chapter will help you to gain clarity and help you to become open and aware of your personality, thinking, decision-making, and problem-solving through our anecdotes and experiences. As you read, keep the results of your four Essential Questions in mind for even more clearness.

Have you read the story of *The Blind Men and the Elephant* by John Godfrey Saxe? It is a story about being conscious of differing perspectives.

We've modified it for modern language and have given a short passage here. For the original and extended versions go to:

https://allpoetry.com/The-Blind-Man-And-The-Elephant

The first approached the elephant
and happening to fall against his broad
and sturdy side, once said:
"The elephant is just like a wall!"

The second felt the tusk and said:
"It's round, smooth, and sharp.
To me it's very clear,
this wonder of an elephant s like a spear!"

The third approached the animal,
and happening to take the squirming trunk in his hands, said:
"The elephant is like a snake!"
The fourth reached out an eager hand,
and felt around the knee. To him it was plain that:
"It's clear enough the elephant is like a tree!"

The fifth, who touched the ear, said:
"Even the blindest of men can clearly tell
that the elephant is like a fan."

The sixth no sooner had begun when he thought
about the swinging tail that was within his reach
and said: "The elephant is like a rope!"

And so, these men of Indostan
Disputed loud and long,
Each in his own opinion
Exceeding stiff and strong,
Though each was partly in the right,
All were in the wrong!

Graphic: From a Jain Temple, India. By Romana Klee from USA –
Sammathi tarka prakarana.

This parable of the blind men and the elephant reminds us of the different perspectives as individual parts. Each brings their perspective based on their knowledge, and when all their parts are put together, they create a complete picture. The moral of this story is that we vehemently hold on to our viewpoint because we feel our perspective is correct. When we accept that our mindset is only one-sided, we can open up to diverse views to gain a bigger picture. We are 100% correct from our perspective every time. Each time we collect around the table, we are like the blind men in the story. Please understand this.

Throughout history, philosophers have given us stories and wisdom about how perception dictates decision-making, problem-solving, and choices.

Philosophical works from the ancient philosopher Plato and his book, *Plato's Republic* (375 B.C.), pondered the question of the qualities an individual must embrace to lead others. His observation recognized the value of great leaders, plus the belief that a person must possess specific characteristics to be a leader. This notion was later researched by 21st-century experts and led to trait theories.

We recognize a significant relationship exists between the construct of leadership and individual traits. Intelligence, adaptation, conscientiousness, openness, and extraversion lend themselves to successful leadership, as do natural ability and intuition. Traits are affected by **Temperaments** (research by Kiersey) and there are three distinct temperaments that a baby is born with: Easy-going. Slow to warm up. Difficult. Personality and traits emerge from the three, so for example, in the workplace you will notice that there will be people who will be easy to get along with, some that are slow to warm up, while some are straight up difficult.

Individual traits and characteristics have been termed the "Big Five" (Costa & McRae, 1978). The Big Five are personality traits that refer to 1. Openness, 2. Conscientiousness, 3. Extraversion, 4. Agreeableness, and 5. Neuroticism. This OCEAN personality model can be considered with cognitive ability, social skills, and values.

Traits and Influence

Five personality traits contribute to personality through the Big Five and OCEAN model (Costa & McRae, 2005). Connect The Dots to the three temperaments discussed earlier. If there are 8 billion people on this earth, are there 8 billion personalities? No. Personality variations stem from this model and personalities repeat in the population. People you meet can sometimes remind you of other people. And sometimes you keep choosing the same type of people to be in your life like in Sujata and Sandra's stories.

Openness: Creativity and authenticity of emotions have been linked to this trait. It is also seen as an important component of a visionary who transforms and inspires. Openness correlates to the 'easy-going' temperament.

Conscientiousness: Although this trait is more linked to transactional leadership, a transformation has detail-oriented skills that display conscientiousness. Conscientiousness can relate to all three.

Extraversion: Although transformational leaders may prefer introversion in their private lives, they emerge as extroverted because they get excited about influencing people to transform their ways. Extraversion relates to 'easy-going' temperament. Some people choose an extraverted profession, even through they are introverts. They could be both: Ambiverts.

Agreeableness: A leader such as this one generally possesses an agreeable nature that stems from natural empathy and consideration. Agreeableness relates to 'easy-going' temperament.

Neuroticism: Neuroticism gives an individual a level of anxiety that is related to productivity. Neuroticism relates to 'slow-to-warm-up and difficult' temperaments.

Dr. Hans Selye called good stress 'Eustress'. It is the good type of stress that motivates a person to get things done. The bad type is called 'Distress'.

Extraversion and Introversion are described as "energy". Extroverted people require more energy from the environment. If you are an introverted person then you require far less energy and may have to recharge in a quiet place.

You cannot control how other people receive the energy that you are putting forth. Everything you say and do is processed through the mind and body of the person receiving it at that moment in time. The same goes for emails; it is not necessarily what you have written that causes an issue; it is the mind and body states of the reader at the time that causes a certain reaction in the two-dimensional environment.

Personality theories state that traits effect preferences, and preferences effect behaviors. And here, we also know that personality, traits, and preferences effect leadership styles.

As the Waves of psychology grew from psychodynamics (the first wave) to behaviorism (the second wave) to humanism (the third wave), so did leadership research and theories, which ran parallel to the waves of psychology throughout the history of psychology.

The Psychodynamic perspective of leadership viewed leaders in a certain way (unmet childhood needs), while the Behaviorists thought of it another way (conditioning and reinforcement), and the Humanists thought of it yet another way (needs). We believe that all three waves and perspectives of psychology contribute to the approach that leaders choose and use.

There is a fourth Wave of psychology, and its focus is on positive psychology that is supported by Dr. Martin Seligman and his friend Dr. Mihalyi Csikszentmihalyi, author of *"Finding Flow."*

These Waves of psychology can be seen in many disciplines and have been used to explain the traits of individual leaders that take on a particular leadership style. Leaders of yesterday were autocratic and made decisions on their own without sharing, and then wondered why people got rebellious and quit their jobs. In exploring how leaders are portrayed through different perspectives, we are aware of the media's stereotypical view of a dynamic, oblivious, stressed, unfamiliar, and blunt leader. Eventually, they got discouraged, depressed, had a heart attack, and dropped to the ground. This Type A (aggressive, yelling, screaming, and throwing) leader has quickly become a dinosaur, and some have even realized that they need to change if they are going to survive in this day and age.

Physicians Meyer Friedman and R.H. Rosenman originated the Type A and B personality concept in the 1950s after connecting heart disease and heightened emotional personality characteristics. Type A patient was the most prone to heart disease due to high-strung characteristics versus the Type B patient, who was more relaxed and able to cope through less stressful means. Perhaps you have known the Type A personality extremes in your own work life.

Some bosses we experienced were forceful, aggressive, and intent on getting their way because winning was the only thing that mattered to them. Type A leaders can be challenging to reach emotionally as they struggle to express or understand emotions. Other leaders that we have had were quite absent and out of touch. Have you experienced such a leader?

Some leaders we've had engaged teams through interactive activities of deduction, where they could be in kinesthetic motion, keeping their brain excited and cognition moving at a rapid pace.

These leaders may find it challenging to commit to something because they are always on the go.

Other leaders we have had displayed a spectrum of emotions. Some were physically and psychologically fragile; some valued their privacy and could be secretive; some were like social butterflies and loved talking to people; some were charming and well-dressed, with an aura of mystery surrounding them. Others were dreamers who were solemn; some were ruthless, dominant and difficult figures who took themselves too seriously; some were unstable, cold, and ignored the needs of others. Some did not know how to create relationships, while others were self and emotionally aware. Some got their feelings hurt quite easily and did not take rejection of their ideas very well. When we look at this paragraph, we feel like we've experienced all types of leaders, managers, and supervisors.

You can see how personality and preferences can intertwine with leadership styles. The importance of self-discovery, then, is the antecedent to change readiness and sustainable impact.

Kurt Lewin (1947) researched leadership styles and performance. He assessed the performance of groups of people in various environments where the leader was asked to use his influence to get tasks accomplished. Each group had a leader who used a different style, and Lewin documented these styles as Authoritarian, Democratic, and Laissez-Faire. For Lewin, leadership is the function of one's environment. Therefore, both the pieces of Nature and Nurture intersect. And you can also say that Lewin was a Behaviorist because he believed that the outside environment (systems) affected the inside.

Systems thinking and how it is applied within organizations has a distinct influence on individuals, teams, and the organization due to individual perspectives. The individual's application of systems thinking to their everyday path can influence their outlook, performance, and outcome.

Systems are structured for profit and performance, and expeditious management of a large numbers of employees from the top down. All levels of leadership structure (front line, middle, and top managers) are motivated to succeed through their perspectives and through job-specific skills towards high performance.

How you perform through your personality traits and achieve high performance through your diverse perspectives and divergent thinking will be unique for you and will uniquely influence the system in which you work.

Employees arrive each day to do an excellent job for their boss, themselves, and for their families. Employees come to work with their skills, but they also come with their needs, wants, motivations, and emotions (Maslow). Your personality and approach will not only affect your colleagues, but it will also have a significant impact on you, your consciousness, and your growth.

Employee and leader are roles. You may have ambition to seek a high-performing role, such as being a leader, that will bring you more responsibility and a venue to help others, thereby activating success for everyone.

Effective leaders are conscious of connecting with their people through suitable leadership style. Whatever the personality and leadership style, modern leadership is about rapport, relationship, and team building, where one-size does not fit all.

When you become aware and conscious of your personality and styles, you can better understand the ramifications of Conditioning (the second wave, Behaviorism) and Schema-development that has occurred throughout your life. The former refers to reinforcement, and the latter refers to the sum total of who you are and what you believe at this juncture. A commitment to self-discovery through the Four Essential Questions is the road to becoming a conscious leader.

What do you want to become conscious of? Make clarity, empathy, openness, observation, responsiveness, and responsibility your goals.

Consider that even though we all come from diverse backgrounds with a myriad of skills and talents, the system assembles us to function as one entity to produce high results. Our own research tells us that you cannot get positive results if you are not consciously accepting diversity of people, cultures, and varying perspectives.

Why wait for a cathartic realization through trial and error? Instead, learn right now to understand people *first*. It's not about winning or losing against each other; it's about doing the right thing at the right time for the right reasons for sustainable impact.

Have you formulated what Conscious Leadership means to you yet?

Conscious leadership means intentionally focusing on people and listening to their values and strengths. After all, you do not want to spend your time managing; you want to build trust and create opportunities so employees can feel heard, cared about, and fulfilled.

Becoming a Conscious leader is a choice that you make. This type of leadership style takes a process to evolve. Leaders are typically judged on character and competence, while employees equate integrity with kindness and empathy. We are designed to think, feel, and act. Take those into your focus to expand as a conscious leader. Work and life are getting more complex by the minute and require homeostatic balance. Pay attention to work-life, work-play, work-family, and work-self.

Between the demands of our jobs and lives, our mental capacities are stretched and stressed to the limits, and our reactions and actions will undoubtedly show whether we are conscious or directed by our subconscious minds. Have you ever found yourself in over your head? Perhaps you have had an experience where you took on too much or were given too much to manage. Seek to gain a healthy balance in your life. The locus of control is in your hands.

In assessing locus of control, you will have to learn how to self-regulate. When you become self-aware, you can better understand when you are overwhelmed or discouraged, and it is at that juncture where you must allow yourself to feel those feelings, but then through free will intentionally bring your focus back to your values and strengths.

Under every behavior is a feeling, and under every feeling there is a need. Become conscious of the behavior; not the person. Never say: "You're a bad person"; this is not effective leadership. Always emphasize the behavior. What did they do that was ineffective? What can they do differently next time?

Tool #2: A great tool that can help you accelerate success in your understanding, that we love, is called "**The Johari Window**."

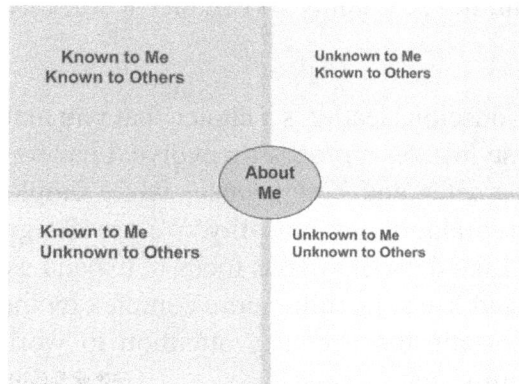

Known to Me **Known to Others**	Unknown to Me Known to Others
Known to Me **Unknown to Others**	Unknown to Me Unknown to Others

About Me

Two wonderful psychologists are Joseph Luft and Harrington Ingham (1955), who created the "Johari Window." The "Johari Window" was named after their first names, Joe and Harry. The Johari Window comprises of four small squares that form one large square. We have used this framework repeatedly throughout the years for coaching, counseling, mentoring, training, and more. The Johari Window sections all our relationships and interactions into four quadrants based upon an individual's awareness about themselves as individuals, in teams, and companies.

The first quadrant is known as the **'Open'** Quadrant. This depicts the information that both you and others know about you. For example, your name, education, interests, and personality are all things that others know about you, and you, yourself, also know about you.

The second is known as the **'Hidden'** Quadrant. This depicts your knowledge about yourself but chooses to hide it from others. For example, you may have a reputation for being a great public speaker, but you could be afraid of public speaking. Or, you may be an avid reader of fantasy books, but others do not know this about you, because you choose to keep it hidden from others.

The third quadrant is the opposite of the **'Hidden'** in that the world knows something about you, where you have no awareness; that's why it is called the **'Blind Spot.'** For example, if you are insecure in public speaking and this causes you to speak in anger, then when you speak in public, others notice some anger in your voice while you are oblivious to it.

The last quadrant is called the **'Unknown'** because this symbolizes knowledge that is unknown to both the person and others. So, there are things we do not know about ourselves, and others do not know. These are things that lay in your memory stores, but you have not retrieved to date.

Most leadership development focuses only on the **Hidden** and **Blind Spot** quadrants because the information in the 'Open' quadrant is known to everyone, and the 'Unknown' is known to no one. Therefore, The Johari Window makes leadership development straightforward because performance evaluations will indicate items that you, yourself, cannot see.

We encourage you to become more approachable and self-forgiving, so you can become more receptive to feedback and overcome that **'Blind Spot'**. The crux of this approach is an assumption that *improvement requires engagement with others*. You can learn about your blind spot through regular feedback and show others your true self by learning what is behind your mask or that which is in the shadow. And yes, we know about "Impression Management". There is an impression that you want to give to the outside world, and you can continue to show the world who you are by the way you dress and carry yourself, but alas, you must also try, through conscious intention, to show your authenticity so you do not have internal strife.

What we're talking about regarding the Johari is not about impression management, per se, but about your blind spot where others see something, and you are clueless about it, and your receptivity to that information when they tell you about what they notice. Do not become defensive. You will always be 100% correct *from your perspective*, therefore it is extremely important that you become open to receive constructive feedback from others.

The **'Unknown'** quadrant is usually ignored in most leadership development initiatives, and this makes total sense because how can a person become educated about an **'Unknown'** factor? The authors, Luft and Ingham, encourage us to look into this quadrant despite logic. They want us to defy logic because we assume that self-improvement comes through a two-way interaction. While this may be true for schooling, the fourth quadrant consists of only one person (you) to open up the "unknown," and this can only be accomplished through reflective questioning of the self: a one-way interaction into one's head, heart, and gut brains, as well as the mind and soul.

Do you talk to yourself when you are by yourself? Everyone has internal dialogue. It's called 'self-talk'; and this can be, both positive and negative depending on mood and context. We engage in explicit conversations with our inner being and our three selves: past self (what we think we were), present self (what we think we are), and future self (what we want to be). Life is about continuous self-improvement.

Our conversation with the Past Self is entirely skewed because we talk to ourselves through our memories. As a species, we have terrible memories, so we tend to add, delete, and alter our narrative. Each time you visit your past, you judge yourself with far more shrewdness than it took to make decisions at that time in your lifespan. Your recollection of the past is far more hurtful than the experience you went through. You are living a life of perception and not actual reality. Your reality is vastly different than your siblings, colleagues, boss, and others around you.

The Present Self is attached to current influences (Dr. Urie Bronfenbrenner's theory), physical pain, and pleasure attainment that occurs through reward and punishment conditioning.

The Future Self. That image is far more idealistic compared to the present self. For example, if a swimmer wants to win in the Olympics, then they train for winning. That swimmer creates a future memory of a winning performance that is visualized with euphoria that triggers dopamine (the feel-good neurotransmitter) in the brain. The harsh realities of training vanquish; arduous training is long forgotten, and the ecstatic ending is emphasized through visualization. Some people achieve this through vision boards and staying committed to the feeling that it is happening in the present.

As you plan to be a leader, you will view your future self as much more idealistic (better) than the Present Self. Some people may call this hope. Regardless, this is why you gorge on food, thinking that the diet will come after the holidays. How many people have had a substantial 'last meal' before starting a diet? In New Year's resolutions, you convince your future self that you will do something, while your present self continues to occupy in current bad habits.

The Johari Window's **'Unknown'** quadrant is that mysterious reflection pool of knowledge from your past. It contains fear-based actions, problems, challenges, and decisions filled with shame or regret. This quadrant is the battlefield between the future idealistic self and the materialistic tactless self. This quadrant has behaviors that hold us back and goals imposed on us by someone else, and we continue to feel conflicted if we should please those people or do what is best for us.

The journey into the **'Unknown'** quadrant will not be easy. It will take maturity, awareness, reflection, introspection, growth, and admission. It will take courage to self-critique, and this will be most difficult because we view ourselves as the hero and victim in our narratives. The Ego self insists on embellishing the past, present, and future self, which always gets in the way of honest, authentic self-reflection. "To thine own self be true," said Shakespeare, and he was right, and it takes determination to ignore the ego.

What we are saying is that if you want to be a good leader, you must understand that leaders spend much time in the *Hidden* or *Blind Spot* quadrants to fix their deficiencies there. The problem is that most leaders believe that leaders are born and not made. We tell you leaders can be made through self-leading, self-understanding, and self-reflection. You must make an effort to understand your strengths plus innermost shortcomings. You know this about others, because you can see the shortcomings in others quite easily, but you must also accept the same for yourself. The most effective way to delve into this is with a great counselor, coach, or mentor who can help you understand your **'Unknown'** self.

In self-leading and leading others, you must listen and observe as you balance your internal self-talk and external talk. There are many assumptions that you will make based on your schema of how things work or how things *should* work. You spend much of your time inferring.

Dr. Rebecca Saxe of MIT University (check out her TED Talk) researched the construct of 'inferencing' and found that this process occurs in your brain's Right Temporal Parietal Lobe. Read about the "Ladder of Inference," (Chris Argyris) where the brain takes you through cognitive steps to come arrive at a certain conclusion. Your brain needs twenty-five percent of your calories as it maneuvers ~74 thousand thoughts per day.

Personal assessment (interests, skills, attitudes) + career exploration (labor market, vocations) = An active road to work and life success.

As the brain goes about inferring and perceiving, it is important to take stock of what you are feeling and valuing. Please note that along with feelings and values, you will also experience body sensations because of the mind-body connection. You can go back to review the feeling and value words earlier in the book. Do you experience some of these bodily sensations? Where and when? Connect The Dots from feelings, values, stressors, inferring, perceiving, and body sensations. When you view the Johari Window through the eyes of activating success, it is an excellent tool that can help you towards Self-Discovery, Change-Readiness, and Sustainable Impact.

Body Sensations that occur through the biology of you that cause the psychology of you that can prevent sound decision-making and problem-solving:

Achy, Airy, Blocked, Breathless, Bruised, Burning, Buzzy, Clammy, Clenched, Cold, Constricted, Dizzy, Drained, Dull, Electric, Empty, Expanded, Flowing, Fluid, Fluttery, Frozen, Full, Gentle, Heavy, Hollow, Hot, Icy, Itchy, Jumpy, Knotted, Light, Nauseous, Numb, Pain, Pounding, Prickly, Queasy, Radiating, Relaxed, Rigid, Sensitive, Settled, Shaky, Shivery, Sore, Spacey, Stiff, Still, Suffocated, Sweaty, Tender, Tense, Throbbing, Tight, Tingling, Trembly, Twitchy, Warm, Wobbly.

<u>You can conduct a weekly self-performance check:</u>

I feel….
I need….
I forgive….
I trust….
I celebrate….

In your evolution as a Conscious leader, you will realize that absolutely no one else has the right answers for your work and life, but you and you alone. You can do your best with what you have been given in your genes and environment.

Change Management Insight

Change is highly complex, and everyone views change differently. Dr. Spencer Johnson, in his book "Who Moved My Cheese", put is plainly and simply: people get defensive when it comes to change. Therefore, implement change through steps that are manageable. When it comes to change, try to gain diverse perspectives you need and even those you do not need. Ensure that projects and tasks have feasible timelines, and use motivation to help people to adapt, implement, and sustain small changes.

Any change, small or large, will bring out a plethora of back brain emotions. When people hear the word "change," they usually cringe, because they are comfortable in their comfort zones, and their perception may be that there is no need to change things. They will go through a series of steps akin to Elisabeth Kubler-Ross's (1981) grief steps before they reach "acceptance." The ego will ask: 'What will happen to me?' So, make the time to reflect on where you want to go with the change; the steps during a change process so you can bridge the discomfort; and support people through their feedback. Here are the emotional steps that people will go through during change:

1. Surprise or shock
2. Denial and refusal
3. Frustration or anger
4. Fight or flight
5. Brainstorming and Decision-making
6. Acceptance

It is the ego that deceives you: "Once everything falls into place, then you will find peace". But it is your true self that will tell you: "Find peace of mind so all can fall into place". Peace of mind can be achieved by controlling the thoughts you give your attention to most of the time. Allow your ~74 thousand thoughts to enter and leave each day. Give attention to only those that serve your sunny side, and not your shadow side. Thoughts are not facts.

We encourage you to use the principles of Kaizen that translate into "a good change" or "improvement." Create numerous opportunities for discussions that allow the many generations in the workplace to express their needs and concerns (without reprisal). Please do not leave them in the dark to their imaginations. Look for alternative explanations and appropriate knowledge sharing.

We invite you to explore the principles of Prosci change management and the ADKAR™ model, which stands for Awareness, Desire, Knowledge, Ability, and Reinforcement.

Inspiration will minimize surprise and denial. Empowerment will reduce frustration and anger. Open discussions will minimize the fight and flight response. Clarity and responsiveness will create a harmonious work environment.

The second wave in psychology, Behaviorism, says that there is no such thing as Free Will, but we are third wave practitioners who are Humanistic and believe that you always have a choice as a leader. You can either force change onto others or you dialogue with and motivate each other through a change process.

Effective Communication & Conflict Resolution

Conscious Leader Values List

Autonomy, competence, curiosity, ethics, focus, growth mindset, ideas, innovation, intelligence, knowledge, rationality, theories, vision, wisdom.

Conscious Leader Stress List

Incompetence, disorganization, ignorance, unfairness, labels, lack of freedom, not knowing something, rigidity, rules that make no sense, lack of clarity, lack of growth

What does this mean?

This means that when there is a breach of something that you value, then that will cause you a great deal of stress. Stress will lead to an imbalance in the biology of you and manifest into negative symptoms in one or two of your twelve biological systems. That, in turn, will affect the psychology, social, and spirit of you as well.

How can you talk to people that breach something that you value? Be honest and accurate with your *feelings*!

Resolution

BE calm. *BE* still and know.

Do not blame, "You do this! You do that!". When you use the word "You", it will completely turn the other person off and they will stop listening to what you have to say. *DO* this instead: a better way is to use "I" statements. Say, "I feel _____ when you _____". For example, "I feel hurt when you refuse to listen to my novel ideas in meetings".

HAVE: a peaceful workplace and personal life filled with communication and understanding!

(Thanks to Stephen Covey for his Be, Do, Have model that we love from his book "7 Habits of Highly Effective People" https://www.simonandschuster.com/authors/Stephen-R-Covey/4).

👁 **Insight #1:** Learn to communicate your needs.

1. Tell them who you consciously are (your values and strengths).
2. Tell them your niche expertise. {*Note: it takes 10,000 hours of experience to call yourself an expert!*}
3. Tell them how they have benefited from hiring you as an employee and conscious leader.

When the time comes for a promotion or a raise, you can say this: "My education, background, and experience reflect how much my performance benefits this company. Is there a salary figure that best reflects my high performance?"

👁 **Tip #2:** To reduce your blind self square, think about how you can move from the blind self to the knowing self. Be open and receptive when others speak the truth of what they see in you. Defensiveness will get you nowhere, so be aware of the ego and its cunning expertise of sabotage.

🔎 **Tool #3:** Go to https://positivepsychology.com/johari-window/ to view an article on "How to Use the Johari Window to Improve Leadership".

YOUR TURN

1. Is becoming a conscious leader important to you? Why?
2. What new learning can you gain by becoming a conscious leader?
3. Are you conscious of your extroversion or introversion?
4. What roles are you in?
5. What do you identify with most of the time?
6. What do you desire that may be residing in your subconscious?
7. What new skills do you need to display a Conscious leadership style?

"

It is the process of choosing
– not just our choices –
that makes us who we are.

~Gina Hayden~

"

Chapter 6

Ego-Centered Leadership
Activators: Power & Awareness

Have you experienced these barriers to success? Conceit, pride, vanity, arrogance, closed-mindedness, hyperactive reactions, arguments, defensiveness, and blow-ups.

This chapter will provide you with the means to attain human flourishing (as potential) through an understanding of personality and leader styles, and through an honest discussion of what the ego can do to workplace well-being.

Employee mental health is one of the biggest issues facing the workplace today. We are not talking only about personality differences, but leadership style that has a profound negative impact on their people's well-being and wellness. The Ego in its ego-centeredness fails to realize the effect it has on others. This, due to an inability to understand how the subconscious ego forces conscious actions. The solution lies in discovering that the authentic self can regain power over the ego through mindfulness and locus of control.

Some people talk about "an intentional positive ego" and others question this because the ego represents all things selfish and self-centered. Through Free Will, awareness, and choice, a balance can be achieved for the back survivor brain and the frontal rational brain. A great leader certainly needs self-confidence, and we are not debating this fact. We want balance so humans can move in a positive direction from survival to thriving, and from thriving to flourishing.

It has been our experience that the egoic leader lacks empathy for the needs of their employees who work diligently to appease. Know that you are not alone. Millions of employees become apathetic, lose interest, get sick, and leave the company altogether (if they can afford it). Those who cannot afford to leave simply *Quit and Stay*, which means they check out mentally, but physically come to work to be at their desks.

The *Great Resignation* is a flight response. People do not leave the work they are passionate about; they leave people who do not appreciate their efforts or don't give them credit for their ideas or are affected by workplace fears.

The Great Resignation brought about *Quiet Walk-out* as well as *Loud Quitting*, where newer generations were not afraid to voice their reasons for walking out. We wonder if it is a lack of experience in working within systems that they made those quick decisions, or whether it was because there were many options for them as their upside. Regardless, the downside to leaving quickly is that emerging leaders can miss out on disciplining themselves and learning how to navigate systems. We're not saying that people should stay in a toxic work environment; we're saying be aware of the decision-making process to weigh pros and cons. Connect The Dots to your readiness for change. Some people end up going into a situation that ends up being far worse than the one they left.

Millennials and Gen Z question authority. Why? Because they have information at their fingertips. They can check the accuracy of the information that leaders and managers are providing them; and they can easily check the feasibility of directives as well. They have a tolerance threshold that can lead them to find other companies with leaders who are better communicators. No one wants to be fearful at work. They do not want managers or supervisors to provoke fear-based motivation. People get it: leaders and managers have the power to hire and fire. Millennials and Gen Z take stock of what their peers say, compare and contrast, and steer clear of egoic company culture. They hold leaders accountable through social media.

The point is that the egoic leadership style no longer works; it is an old and antiquated approach that does not serve the current workplace. If today's leaders wish to stay in their positions, then they must adapt to the needs of newer generations and not the other way around. Current generations desire leaders with open minds and diverse approaches; to consider values, student loans, high childcare, elder care, pet care costs, food, and the overall high cost of living.

In this day and age, systems must care about and for their people. Most importantly, they must communicate with their people.

We live in an age of information overload. Signals can easily get crossed. Misunderstandings can rapidly arise. Conflict can result if an extroverted leader thinks that the introverted employee is disinterested, which may be far from the truth. We have witnessed egoic leaders fail because they misinterpret certain traits (those that they do not have) as weaknesses. There is a saying: "still waters run deep", and this means that the quiet people have much depth of character. Today's leader has to understand the consequences of behavior, learning styles, multiple intelligences, neurodiversities, and personalities.

To further understand ego-centered leadership, we bring your attention back to personality. The O.C.E.A.N model (discussed earlier in the book) of personality is highly relevant in understanding egoic style. The N stands for Neuroticism and the E stands for Extraversion, where egoic behaviors shine. As you know, the brain thinks, senses, intuits, feels, perceives, and judges. Preferences are shown through *degrees* of introversion and extraversion, which have much to do with *energy*.

Comparing to the ego, other leadership styles are better able to sense intuitiveness, feeling patterns, perception, and judging habits. Due to a focus on the ego self, the egoic leader fails to notice what other personality styles exist around them; they also fail to see the value their people bring to the table, because they spend much of their time thinking and judging, not sensing and feeling. We empathize with you if you have an egoic leader or manager. We know how hard you've worked to arrive at the table, only to feel disappointed.

A **Sensing** person is practical, while an **Intuitive** person is creative and innovative. Misunderstanding can stem from miscommunication between the sensing and the intuitive, due to sensitivity in the Intuitive person versus the practicality of the Sensing one. This is a sure set-up for conflict if people do not know how they operate. An open dialogue with ground rules can bring about professional transparency where the Intuitive person can reveal their feelings, and the Sensing person can reveal their logic and pragmatism.

A **Thinking** person is logical, while a **Feeling** person feels emotions. The Thinking person rarely shows emotions (especially in the workplace), while the *Feeling* person responds with emotions. A healthy conversation can openly display feelings, values, facts, and logic.

A **Judging** person is structured, compared to the **Perceiving** person who is more open to options, freedom, and less structure. An open dialogue can display the needs of both preferences and styles, so that people can work cooperatively.

There are many examples of egoic leaders in history that have failed to take into account their vast impact on people. A good example of ego leadership comes from the tyrant Machiavelli. Machiavelli wrote *The Prince* in the early 16th century as a manual for emperors, kings, and rulers on how to gain and exert their powers over people. An elitism existed with a vast chasm and abyss between the elite and the commoners. Machiavelli failed to listen and become self-aware of his behavior. It was not until 1821 that the dictionary even had the term "leadership".

Rulers and emperors inflicted harm on the common masses; people were ostracized and banished if they spoke up. Do elements of these behaviors, of going against the grain and status quo, or challenging leaders directly, exist in your workplace? And are the results the same nowadays in being outcasted from a niche or prevention from access to promotions? You may be viewed as a threat that needs to be diminished.

How do egoic leaders attain leadership positions, and how do they stay there?

They use their charm and influence to get where they are going. Many egoic leaders have created charismatic circles made up of other egoic leaders that turn into an 'egoic support network' that sustains power and influence. Their charm comes from their personality, whereas their influence comes from a conditioned behavior that works for them.

In the 21st century, Board members have exponential power to hire senior executives and C-suite positions, however they exclusively use resume experience and solely focus on company mission and vision. Boards must institute behavioral questions in the interview process for senior leaders and the C-Suite and take into account organizational culture along with the mission and vision. This newer interview model can provide a certain level of quality assurance in detecting ego, personality disorders, and potential misuse of power. The prevention step is clear to us: do not hire ego-centered leaders.

Is egoic behavior difficult to understand, manage, and change?

The ego reacts based on an individual's Schema (beliefs, assumptions, bias) which is formed in childhood and cemented during adulthood. The subconscious remembers everything a person experiences; therefore, it performs behaviors through the mind's Defense Mechanisms to keep ego intact. When the brain senses a threat, the ego comes to the forefront.

When we encounter new situations that we have not experienced before, the survival brain immediately senses a threat. The ego gets activated to protect itself, and the reply is emotional and reactive. People construct mental models to help them through quick reactions. These models come from schema, and most of this process is unconscious and rapid.

Psychodynamic theories explain how the ego justifies behavior through Defense Mechanisms.

Here are some common mechanisms that the ego uses to persuade and influence:

1. Denial, when you refuse to accept something.
2. Rationalization, where you give excuses for yours or someone else's behavior.
3. Displacement, when you take your anger out on someone else that is nonthreatening.
4. Projection, when you project your needs and wants on to someone else.
5. Compensation, where you show that you are good at a skill if you are poor at another skill.
6. Repression, when you do not remember the ill from the past.
7. Regression, when you manage your emotions through acting younger.
8. Sublimation, when you divert the negative into something acceptable to you.

9. Reaction formation, when you act and say the opposite of what you feel.
10. Intellectualization, when you use only logic to explain behavior.
11. Dissociation, when you remove yourself far away from what is currently happening.
12. Faulty Thinking, when you use irrational thinking to explain, persuade, and defend.

These are psychological survival mechanisms that keep the ego protected and intact. There may be more than these that are being used every day, and we want you to keep metacognition to the forefront of your thinking so you do not use defensiveness as a means to activate your success at work and in personal life. Activate success rationally, and not irrationally.

The ego impedes your ability to lead skillfully and effectively. Think about it for a moment. When and where have you experienced the consequences of ego?

Ego leadership style can bring about biological sensations inside of you, and if you continue to live with elevated levels of arousal, your neurotransmitter acetylcholine and the hormone adrenaline will flood your body and create emotional hijacks. Anxiety, high blood pressure, headaches, and more can transpire over time. When this happens, self-care, well-being, and wellness is of utmost importance in getting back to the parasympathetic system that secretes endorphins (feel good), oxytocin (empathy and love), serotonin (good mood), and dopamine (feel good, rewards).

Each one of us harbors powerful emotions inside. It is in understanding how we can best observe and identify what is being triggered that our feelings can be better managed civilly. As you grow in your ability to keep, feel, and redirect your emotions, you will no longer react through negative emotions. It is through emotional self-awareness and Emotional Intelligence (EI) that you can begin to build a new you; one that has consciousness of negative patterns and moods that no longer serve you, and that can provide growth for self-leading and in leading others. We want to remind you that change needs to occur in the five constructs that make up the human being.

Egoic leaders may attempt to manipulate you through narcissism and lack of impulse-control to make you think that workplace toxicity is your fault and not theirs. They will try to turn your perception of what is happening to be false to match their own internal narrative. Here are some cognitive distortions that lead to the faulty internal narrative: All or nothing absolutes, Generalization, Assumptions, Blame, Deletions, and Catastrophizing. These do not provide the insight that egoic leaders desperately need.

The leader's mood will most definitively set the tone for the team; the team's tone can also affect the department, and the company's output will also reflect the same. Teams that have leaders with a positive mood will perform much better compared to a leader who operates with a negative mood. The minute a leader walks into the room, they bring positive or negative energy (personality & mood) into the space. They cannot help but express their mood in words, actions, and nonverbal communication. Signals are transmitted to other bodies in the room that cause an equal and opposite reaction. Is this happening to you? And if so, does the information we have provided help you to understand how to adapt.

This is a law in physics: to every action, there is an equal and opposite reaction, therefore a team can react as positively or negatively charged ions. Leaders have packed schedules of daunting tasks that have to be accomplished, performance evaluations, board meetings, allocation of projects, distribution of tasks, and how they respond in their role in achieving these tasks can be the difference between egoic mood or non-egoic action.

Just as a series of dominoes need to be positioned into kinetic energy to perform their task, people also need their potential energy to be induced into kinetic action so they can perform their tasks effectively and joyfully. The leader is a catalyst and how they lead the team through self-regulation can create healthy teams, otherwise teams shut down or quit.

People want their leader to take the lead, and not behave through mood or emotion. Team performance, behavior, and productivity will directly correlate to the leader's emotional state, mood, behavior, and actions. Empathy is critical because it can save leaders and teams much heartache in the long run.

There is good news and bad news: just as an individual can hold negative and positive bias; a group can hold the same. Humans are pack animals; they want to belong; they search for like-minded people, where shared misery, empathy, or altruism can be common unifying themes. We want you to be aware of a team's collective ego as well. It is not only the individual that needs to be aware of their own specific ego that is inside of them. Groups can also take on a collective egoic persona that forms its own schema. Historically, this has been quite dangerous, because it creates a "we are better, stronger, mightier" mindset. There is a landmark case of Kitty Genovese who was killed while thirty people watched and did nothing to help her, thinking that someone else would help. Psychologists now say that individuals are more likely to help when they are alone versus if there are other people around. This is called the Bystander Effect, coined by Drs. Bibb Latane and John Darley alert people about empathy, altruism, standing up for what is right, and social justice. This is another good reason for self-discovery. Who are you when you are alone? Who are you when you are in a group?

In the field of psychology, we interpret ego-centric behaviors of leaders as *lacking empathy*. Empathy is the construct that measures psychopathy. For the Ego, altruism is replaced by a hunger for power, control, status, money, and prestige. Leaders with large egos truly cannot become what they are meant to be in life because they are unable to develop an identity that genuinely cares about others. Their schema has been formed through certain beliefs and assumptions, so it comfortably thrives without ever discovering what may be dormant beneath the surface of the iceberg. Their Conditioning causes anger and resentment in relationships. Egoic leaders wander the world searching for people who will worship them in order to satiate their ego. But alas, even those who worship them get tired and depart from the worldly things they can offer.

Due to unawareness, the ego orchestrates reactionary behaviors without thoughtful consideration of its impact on self and others. The ego does not care about anything but itself, because the subconscious mind is potent and is formed to support basic survival reactions. What's worse is — the logical mind's "hands" are tied, and it cannot do the rational thing. This is a good example of the two head brains working against each other. If you think about it we all make mistakes where if we fail to do the right thing, then we do the next right thing. For an egoic leader, this is quite impossible because they are stuck in ego mode and unable to shift their thinking.

If you want to be a successful leader, then you must make a choice to journey into self-discovery and self-improvement to examine your existing Schema (beliefs, assumptions, biases) and values. Stop to ask yourself: is there evidence against my current thought patterns? If I viewed my thoughts differently, how would my thinking and feeling change? Are my thoughts helpful or harmful? Thoughts create feelings. It is through awareness that you can replace unhelpful thoughts with constructive ones.

Through our own experiences, we are unequivocally aware of how persistent ego can be and have been subjected to leaders that insist on exerting their power.

We know that it is through Free Will that egoic leaders can change themselves. New thinking can provide the activation they need to eradicate egoic behaviors so they can intentionally replace those with an Empathy-Ethic; and through skillful emotional intelligence that helps to minimize the commotion of the reactive back brain.

From our past lessons, we do not allow the pings and dings of social media to deter or persuade us from our personal mission to search for meaningful activators that can bring success in our lives. We wanted success through leadership because we wanted to accept the responsibility to help others.

We have found that our self-awareness grew considerably through an intentional understanding of theories, models, and books written by Western and Eastern authors. They became the tools that enhanced our understanding of how our leadership styles were formed and how those styles were interconnected with our personalities and needs. Evolved leaders understand the need to take control of their egos so their egos do not keep taking control of their mind and body.

Consequences don't work for the egoic person. Non-egoic people cannot differentiate between 'knowledge' and the *feeling* of 'knowing and having that knowledge' which are distinctly different things. Take a moment to reflect.

Before self-help books began appearing at commercial bookstores, there was a book that could be found in public libraries entitled "Siddhartha." Author, Herman Hesse (1922) stated that the "true self is not flesh and bone, nor thought or consciousness", but "the way to the truth". It was through living a life in a manner that no one else could show another. Hesse posed a question of depth to this world; that there is a limit to teaching. It is the learning that must emerge from within that brings wisdom and enlightenment to a person. A teacher cannot do all the work; the learner must be willing to accept the teachings to find their own, unique, individual truth.

Understand that you are uniquely gifted.... just like the other 8 billion people on Earth. Visualize yourself as a grain of sand on the biggest beach. Are you lost in the sand? Ego-centered leaders are lost grains of sand on a large beach. Do not mimic them. You can make a difference through your unique talents, gifts, interests, and skills. Life without meaning is no life at all. Visualization is a powerful tool.

To be a non-egoic leader means to have integrity, empathy, and conscientious.

You cannot make a difference in this world if you live a life focused on power and insignificant trivialities.

Victor Frankl (1946, 1984) puts it best: "Your search for meaning is a vital journey for your sake and the sake of others that you may lead." Perhaps eighty percent of the people we meet are reluctant to make self-actualization a goal, which is a mystery to non-egoic leaders. Why would we get involved in leading a cause if that cause fails to have depth and sustainable impact? It is our purpose, not our egoic achievements or wealth, that gives us self-esteem, self-efficacy, and meaning.

Do not be disappointed by Egoic leaders who break your personal or team spirit. Genetics and Environment work together, so a built-in genetic propensity coupled with adults who dominated them as a child has resulted in a self-centered leader. Due to unmet needs, they fail to see the error of their ways. Find the courage to stay the course, learn all you can, and stay strong with your teammates.

Mindfulness

We recommend Mindfulness as a strategy for egoic leaders that want to change, as well as to those who work for egoic leaders and wish to cope through stress reduction.

Mindfulness is a strategy that can help quiet the noise and chaos of the egoic brain, if the egoic leader is open and willing to change their ways. Mindfulness is a great strategy to cope with the daily contradictions that egoic leaders display day after day. Being mindful requires the willingness to reorient so clarity can flow into the rational brain. It is in the silence and stillness where the egoic person can find answers. And it is through Free Will that mindfulness can enhance connectedness to the self (Jon Kabat Zinn (2008)). The problem is: the ego rarely wants to change. But we are always hopeful.

Relationships are central for the workplace and in personal life. When you are mindful of and connected to those you lead, you can build trust that can create lasting relationships that can, then, result in rewarding work. Mindfulness can help people create long-lasting partnerships.

The leadership journey will be different for the different temperament types that we discussed earlier in the book. The difficult tempered baby, who requires much attention, sometimes grows up to have an egoic personality that is void of empathy for others. We encourage you to use mindfulness as a tool for *learning* and unlearning behaviors, and in this case where self-centeredness can be unlearned through mindfulness as a best practice for positive change.

Mindfulness can be particularly helpful for people that are working for the egoic leader, because this strategy helps to reduce stress and burnout. The World Health Organization (WHO) estimates that stress costs American businesses $300 billion dollars annually.

Investing in reflective mindfulness can benefit everyone by reducing the high costs of stress.

Do not pre-judge to think that mindfulness is difficult. Ask yourself the following questions during a quiet moment: What am I feeling? Don't judge; observe. Watch your thoughts come and go. Watch your feelings come and go. Be aware and do not allow yourself to get stuck on a persisting thought or feeling. You will pay a price for the time you are willing to stay stuck and may even exchange decades for it.

If, per chance, you find mindfulness is too difficult, then begin with breath work. There are many free breathing apps, so make sure to download one. Deep breathing is the single best thing you can do for your mind and body. Mindfulness takes a bit of discipline. You can be certain that your ego will insist on going back to old defense mechanisms to justify why it cannot change.

It takes self-discipline to master both breathwork and mindfulness. We do not mean discipline as punishment. Self-discipline allows you to wade through trial and error, restraint through impulses, and modification through doubt, shame, and vulnerability.

If you are new to a workplace, you will surely be vulnerable for a few weeks. Please adopt the following behaviors:

- Observe
- Follow instructions.
- Listen
- Your role is to learn first; then, you can talk as much as you want.
- Don't walk in the door as "Fonzie" and say "Hey, I'm here to save the day!"
- Take notes.

- Keep emails brief and to the point. They reflect the quality of your values.
- Have an exceptional work ethic.

We have interviewed numerous leaders who practice reflection and mindfulness because they can feel the benefits in their biology, psychology, and spirit. These results give us hope.

Locus of Control

The Locus of Control is a vital area to examine, because the egoic leader feels the need to have strong control over others. The genesis for this is through their childhood lifespan development. Most probably, they did not have any control over situations in childhood, therefore they crave control as an adult. They fail to realize that they have harbored low self-esteem for decades that has transmuted in an abnormal hunger for power and control over others.

The Locus of Control needs to be assessed each week. What things are in your control? What things are not in your control? Be grateful for the list of things that you can control. Accept the things you cannot control. Be mindful and ask yourself 'What If" questions that can help you to think about things differently and more openly.

Here are things that you can control: your beliefs, attitude, perspective, risks, wants, time, feelings, judgment, mood, empathy, jealousy, and other emotions. There are things that you have no control over: the weather and others.

This world urgently needs you to turn the workplace into a place of understanding and reconciliation. Let go of your need to control.

People are motivated by conscious desires that curb subconscious discomfort. The vast experiences that people endure during childhood and adolescence trauma cause them to turn to subconscious defense mechanisms to survive. Mindfulness and Locus of Control can help people so they can reorient themselves and enjoy their achievements through heart-centered values, and where ego can be replaced by purpose, meaning, and empathy.

Do Not Misconstrue Military Leadership as Ego-Leadership

Military leadership is based on a distinct warrior culture that demands structure, discipline, accountability, teamwork, and precision. Where war is concerned, the risk is life itself. There is no room for errors because it is a matter of life and death for people that make up a nation.

In all military branches, personnel in all ranks are expected to adhere to a code of ethical conduct. Military leaders set clear goals and execute strict completion deadlines. For rapid response, they often use the Pacesetter Leadership style.

If officers find that their people do not adhere to strict timelines to achieve specific goals, they will impart severe consequences, because the leaders is subject to the same consequences. There is a strict chain of command where directives flow from top to front-line recruits. Leading by example where people must follow suit; role-modeling where people must follow suit; and coaching/retraining through consequences (this is Behaviorism in action) are all part of a combination of military-pacesetter leadership style. People are motivated to do their job as a team that serves the whole.

Academies such as the United States Naval Academy, West Point, and the Canadian Defence Academy (Sandra's country) are rigorous in educating and training emerging military leaders. Midshipman and cadets must follow stringent rules and regulations that provide demerits if not followed. Through parades, recognition, and promotion, military leadership takes care of their armed forces and their families to the end. The military community is cohesive and strong, because they have to institutively engage with each other at war time. The military takes good care of soldiers, where the price to pay is adherence to precise direction, global moves, and time away from family.

The general population appreciates the military and the sacrifice they make for their nation. Delve into military history and read about George Washington, Ulysses S. Grant, Napoleon Bonaparte, Golda Meier, Indira Gandhi, who tried to make a cohesive country, Idi Amin, who kicked out all the East Indians who had migrated into his country for safety, Genghis Khan who burned down cities, Joseph Stalin, Adolph Hitler who wanted a pure country void of Jews, Mahatma Gandhi who fought for freedom against British rule, Mao Zedong the communist, Pol Pot, Saddam Hussein, Josef Mengele who helped Hitler's crusade to eradicate human beings is depicted in the movie "Boys from Brazil".

What lessons can be learned from military history?

Tyrants are obsessive; leaders are creators. Tyrants have overbearing personalities that lack empathy; they do not take care of their people and nation. They make promises through loud voices, and their charming ability to appeal to our outrage makes us feel falsely heard. Egoic and tyrant leaders are masters of disguise, and they are masters in creating illusions that make us feel lead. Do not mistake these things for military leadership. Military leaders defend nations and people. They build bridges and support freedom and democratic efforts. They invite partnerships to help solve the world's problems and sustainable development goals. Military leaders unite people so this world can live in harmony. Leaders use a certain language that is firm yet positive. Military leaders are focused on a brighter future, whereas the egoic leader highlights a grim past. Military leaders act as mentors for emerging leaders and support the academies in supporting the best of the best.

Consider what is happening in the world today. Tyrannical leaders can activate stress in our minds, where our bodies end up feeling fearful. The conundrum here is that strangely, it is exactly the fear and anxiety that they create that propels militaries to redirect the tyranny towards peaceability. To achieve this, the military leader may have to adopt the Pacesetter leadership style in rapid response. The military is a means for prevention, intervention, and deterrence. We thank those who are serving and have served in the armed forces.

"

> *Leadership is a matter of intelligence,*
> *trustworthiness, humaneness, courage, and discipline*
> *Reliance on intelligence alone results in rebelliousness.*
> *Exercise of humaneness alone results in weakness.*
> *Fixation on trust results in folly.*
> *Dependence on the strength of courage results in violence.*
> *Excessive discipline and sternness in*
> *command result in cruelty.*
> *When one has all five virtues together,*
> *each appropriate to its function, then one can be a leader.*

~Jia Lin, in commentary on Sun Tzu, Art of War~

"

Change Management Insight

To us, domination is a workplace mental well-being issue. When domination exists, there is no room for compromising. Compromising is a learned skill. For example, notice how people behave in a meeting or in a project huddle when a leader walks in and dominates the group. The leader's mood and extraversion can squelch the mood that the group has created for themselves. That group is happy to share their work with senior leaders, so they need to understand the role that they can play in different contexts: stage, meetings, teams, culturally mixed groupings.

We are at an inflection point in history. We cannot neglect the well-being of employees. As you *reorient* into a new normal, we know that there will be roadblocks — one-way, two-way, and unyielding. Roadblocks will require inspection to decipher pertinent activators that motivate and inspire.

People need *stability*, so stability will be a new word that you can bring into your workplace. Social stability and networking, instead of fractionating at this juncture is central. Collective communication, coaching, mentoring, and creating an atmosphere of mutual respect through the acceptance of diverse personalities is relevant. Self-expression can help to create more stability, where you can express yourselves through values and transparency.

As you work in a variety of situations you may witness greatness or struggle that can emerge from remote or in-person teams, therefore we encourage effective communication, innovation, and work-life balance to activate success. Beware of the survival brain that wants to take over and create a fight and flight (quitting/resignation) response.

Effective Communication & Conflict Resolution

Ego Leader Values

Spotlight, fame, adoration, status, power, money, action, to talk about themselves, looking good, taking credit, worship

Ego Leader Stressors

Empathy, lack of money, lack of fame, lack of status, lack of power, lack of worship

What does this mean?

This means that when there is a breach of something that you value, then that will cause you a great deal of stress. Stress will lead to an imbalance in the biology of you and manifest into negative symptoms in one or two of your twelve biological systems. That, in turn, will affect the psychology, social, and spirit of you as well.

How can you talk to people that breach something that you value? Be honest with your *feelings*!

Resolution

BE mindful. Do not say, "You're not making sense! You never make sense!". When you use the word "You", it puts the other person into an emotional spiral where they will become physically unable to listen to you. *DO* use "I" statements. Say, "I feel _____ when you _____". For example, "I feel uneasy when the sole emphasis is on revenues and not on customer service".

HAVE: effective communication through emphasis of values. Ask "What If" questions.

👁 **Insight #2:** Ask "What If" questions to an Egoic boss:

1. What if we do it this way?
2. What if this doesn't work?
3. What if we find a less challenging way to do this?
4. Have you done this a different way in the past?

🖐 **Tip #3:** Ego loves appearance. Compliments you can give that have nothing to do with physical appearance:

1. I find you inspiring.
2. I like your ideas.
3. I think you're strong.
4. I like to listen to what you are saying about _____.
5. Your empathy is valued.
6. Our conversations make me more confident.
7. Your passion is infectious.
8. You are talented.
9. You restore respect.
10. I wish there were more people like you in this world.

YOUR TURN

1. What does your Ego *need*, and why?
2. Why is it important to be aware of your Ego?
3. Why is it important to be aware of Ego in self-leading and in leading others?
4. How can you manage the Ego at work and personal life?
5. How can you make yourself aware of Ego as it tries to confuse you and others?
6. How can you take responsibility for your *needs*?
7. What can you do to relinquish control over other people?
8. Do you feel vulnerable when you face your Ego? Why? And what can you do about it?

"

Be the change that you wish to see in this world.

~Mahatma Gandhi~

"

Chapter 7

Transformational Leadership
Activators: Inspiration & Performance

Have you experienced these barriers to success? Not taking time to reflect, evaluate, reset, reconstruct to transform individuals and teams into high performance.

For many extroverted leaders, an ultimate pursuit is to be seen as a transformational leader. Why is the word transformation so important in leadership? Why is it coveted in many niches? There are certain leaders with certain personalities that prefer to motivate and influence people through inspiration and empowerment. These are the activators that motivate them; it makes them feel good and that means that dopamine is released when they inspire and empower audiences. This style works for both the leader and the people they lead, because both benefit mutually through the heart-brain.

Take a moment to reflect on leaders, managers, or supervisors that you have had in the past. What characteristics did they have? Did they make you feel respected? Do you want to incorporate some of their characteristics into your self-leading and leadership style?

In this chapter we explore introductory aspects of transformational leadership and provide you with information that can connect mind, body, and values through the heart brain. The transformational leader stimulates their audience through enthusiastic inspiration to gain motivation in individuals and to build team spirit in groups. They empower and influence skills and talents to achieve high-performance systemic goals, and they do it well because this style comes naturally for them.

How do you know you are a Transformational leader?

Transformational leadership requires the cohesion of thinking and feeling. These leaders work closely with their teams, departments, and companies to transform individuals and teams to inspire their potential. This style means that leaders impart a vision through inspiration, empowerment, and erudition. Through these characteristics, they lead through pathos and emotional influence to exact change, thereby elevating growth and achievement beyond capabilities. We hear people saying, "I didn't know that I could do that, but I did it, and it feels great!".

These leaders are able to maintain stability through consistency, attentiveness of people's feelings and emotions, and genuine concern for autonomy and efficacy. The nature of the transformational leader as a positive entity is infectious for any team and organization. Their influence ultimately leads to high motivation, morale, and performance in individuals and group spirit. In short, their *activators* for success are: inspiration, empowerment, and influence. Ultimately, they are able to accomplish self-fulfilling prophecy for the people they lead as well as for themselves.

Psychological safety needs are essential for transformational leaders, and they meet those by connecting, role-modeling, and mentoring, because they want to produce evidence for measurable growth and commitment. Their ability to keenly focus on each person allows them to adapt to diverse needs in situations. We encourage transformational leaders to encourage people to tell their stories. Stories can teach us about what people have been through and what they value.

Inspirational motivation increases as the team commits to the transformational leader through company mission and vision. This leader has self-awareness and sets forth a collective shared vision through reasonable goals that can be met through the skills of team members. Leaders who utilize inspirational motivation can motivate their followers through an intrinsic motivation and attribution of success. They are aware that external motivators work for some people, but not for all people. The Return of Investment (ROI), in turn, leads to increased internal self-esteem that positively influences teammates and the company as a whole.

This leader encourages individuals to inspect their interests, skills, and talents so they can easily see how they fit into the team. They encourage people to look beyond self-interest for group goals. This key piece is the difference between transformation and other leadership styles because the transformational leader has a heart-centered approach that comes from the heart brain, where the head and heart are both connected for decision-making and problem-solving.

By utilizing transformational theories and best practices, we have found that teams become more impactful in their work. It is through actions, and not necessarily words, that people come to know their leaders.

Peter Senge was a systems scientist and senior MIT Sloan School of Management lecturer. He is best known for his pivotal book "The Fifth Discipline (1996), where he shares that a leader must acquire a certain set of skills to become a transformational leader. He states that a leader must have personal mastery, understand their mental models, foster a shared vision, develop team learning, and apply a system thinking lens to become a transformational leader. By applying these practices, a leader will create what is known as a 'learning organization.' A learning organization is the positive result of transformational leadership in practice.

Leaders must master themselves before they can aptly lead others. They must build self-awareness and clearly define who, what, where, and how they will lead themselves and others. The most widely accepted definition of personal mastery is "the process of living and working purposefully towards a vision, in orientation with one's values and in a state of constant learning about oneself and the reality in which one exists." Personal mastery and self-leadership are two important elements for successful transformational leadership.

The attainment of mastery occurs slowly, through the work-life process, and through a voyage that is not binary. When we open ourselves to awareness and intention, personal mastery takes on an authentic commitment to self-leading. A person has choice and opportunity through Free Will in reorienting change as they continue to discover their purpose in life. Once the flame of purpose has been kindled, growth toward actualization and transcendence gains momentum.

Sometimes the momentum ceases through barriers and roadblocks. Especially for women, like us. The two of us had to overcome gender discrimination that limited our opportunities to self-master certain skills, and this kept us from activating our career success paths. Because those circumstances were limiting us, we found ourselves in positions where we could not say No. We ended up catering to bosses who held enormous power over us. Hence, the section on *Refusal Skills* at the end of the chapter.

Those days were especially difficult because they made the achievement of personal mastery distant and out of reach. That external environment made us hypercompetitive against others, causing dissonance because this went against our authentic selves.

As we gained more work experience, we realized that people are not all givers. There were far too many takers. Their feelings of inadequacy caused them to project and displace their anger on us. The story of "Who kicked the cat" is applicable here. That story describes a situation where the boss yells at the man, the man then goes home and yells at the wife, the wife gets angry and yells at the kid, and the kid gets angry and kicks the cat. So, who kicked the cat?

Leaders who have not taken the time to self-discover will always react and make decisions through their emotions. People can make you feel disappointed, if you let them get to you. Do not mistrust your heart brain. Learn from those bosses, but don't dwell on the past. You, and only you, know exactly what you need to construct yourself. To become transformed, we needed our leaders to be givers of information, share their wisdom and insight, and encourage, empower, and inspire us.

Where are you in your transformation for self-leading? Take a moment to reflect.

Becoming a transformative leader requires introspection. Make a choice today to break open your true self and become the best version of yourself that you have the potential to be.

We have noticed that transformational leaders tend to perform exceptionally well in today's workplaces.

Who is Responsible for Transformation?

Besides yourself, both the leader and manager roles can be instrumental in transforming the workplace. Remember that a title given to a person does not guarantee success. A title signifies more responsibilities. The 'how' comes through experiences, personality, vision, and context.

You may be familiar with the phrase "leading by example." Have you ever heard the phrase "managing by example?" Those who lead by example are called role models. They emulate the desired behavior for their direct reports to follow.

Managers can lead by example too: Being creative and motivating the team, inspiring them to want to do better, enabling them to contribute to the organization's success, and empowering them to make decisions without micromanaging. You may have experienced micromanagement from a manager that doesn't know how to transform because they lack introspection and insight.

What do you think of when you hear the word transformation?

To us, it means change. But what kind of change and for whom? There are four things to consider: Individuals, intellectual engagement, inspirational motivation, and ideal influence.

The underlying thread of the four items is woven through mindset. You must believe in yourself, the vision you value, and the path you create to activate success. By doing so, you will motivate and inspire others to accelerate success towards high performance.

We hope that you are learning that transformational leadership is an approach that causes a change within you, as you cultivate the skills to transmute others around you. This style makes a positive difference in teams and develops high efficacy in teams.

A transformational leader will have an open and receptive personality; they may be quite charismatic due to the spirit component in their leadership style. They succeed through a confident belief in engaging their audiences, and this kind of passion, values, and heart-centeredness during wartime, health crises, and financial crashes is imperative.

Transformational leadership theory entails specific rules of engagement and makes the following assumptions: visionary, innovation, creativity, imagination, and deep dives, which are needed during crises. Transformational leaders and followers engage together through a value-centered focus, creating a robust environment to renovate (Burns, 2004).

As relationships transform, so does the transformational leader.

When one person teaches, two people learn.

Relationships can turn into partnerships of exchange, growth, and learning because all sides rise above tasks. People get things done, but also transcend to more meaningful outcomes that are higher order (Bloom's Taxonomy and Maslow's Theory).

The focus is not only on the task at hand or short-term goals but on what is desired for tomorrow and the future. Creating particular Ethos, Pathos, and Logos for tomorrow's world fosters high-performance objectives that can easily lead to connected motivations, such as service and servant orientation.

Transformative leaders accept people for who they are and *where they* are in their psychological journey. They respect people's interests, skills, needs, and desires. They ensure that the words they chose to use are in arrangement with their audience. Their attention to language can result in providing self-esteem, commitment, and cooperation from their teams.

The gains are many when one has committed themselves to transformational leadership style.

Change Management Insight

Whether its individuals, teams, or organizations, transformation is about changing habits and patterns. One of the most important skills to have at work and in life are Refusal Skills! Why? Because people have trouble saying "No". Activate assertiveness and reduce workplace fears. We're not just talking about the amygdala brain fear, but the fear that enters a workplace through stress, mistrust, and change.

Have you ever had trouble saying "No" at work? We have. And we would also add a 'sorry' after we said 'no'! We had to relearn and train ourselves to say "No". We were conditioned not to say 'no' to people, because it wasn't polite, and if we said 'yes' then they would like us.

Wherever the learning happened, you must learn to say "No" without saying 'sorry' or feeling guilty. You may have to avoid situations that could lead to trouble, such as fraternizing or starting personal relationships with clients. Audiences have asked us these questions: what if I get in a situation and have to talk my way out? What if I have a forceful colleague, client, or boss? What do I say?

1. Practice saying No to people.

2. Do not offer reasons, excuses, or apologies. We often think that giving an explanation or justification is required for good manners, but it's not. Don't waste your time coming up with reasons, excuses, or apologies. Just say 'No'.

3. If there is pressure, then ask the other person why they keep pressuring you when you have already given them a 'No' answer.

4. After you say "No', cut eye contact with them so they do not engage with you further! Walk away (if context allows) and refuse to discuss the matter further.

5. Know how to counter the pressure statements people pitch at you. Here are some examples:

Refusal Examples:

Situation #1
Pressure statement: I thought we were friends.
Response: I think you care about me, so please respect my feelings and do not force me to do something I don't want.

Situation #2
Pressure statement: If you don't do what I want, I don't want to be friends.

Response: If that's how you feel, we cannot be friends.

Situation #3
Pressure statement: I know you can do this.
Response: I know what I can and cannot do. Let's not argue about it.

Situation #4
Pressure statement: Touching is the way I show you I care. You have let me touch you before. Why not now?
Response: I let you massage my neck once for a few seconds, but I've changed my mind and have decided to say 'No' to touching.

Situation #5
Pressure Statement: You're acting immature.
Response: No. I am a mature adult who knows what I want and do not want.

Situation #6
Pressure statement: OK, if you can't do it, I'll find someone else who can, and they'll probably get the promotion instead of you.
Response: That's fine.

You can transform your behavior through assertiveness (not aggressiveness). The more practice you have saying 'no', the better you will feel. This, too, is self-care.

Effective Communication & Conflict Management

Transformational Leader Values

Communication, empathy, creativity, friendship, harmony, serving, morality, intuition, relationships, bonding, genuineness, teams, unity

Transformational Leader Stressors

Arguments, judgment, lack of communication, injustice, aggression, battles, lack of support, lack of understanding, selfishness

What does this mean?

This means that when there is a breach of something that you value, then that will cause you a great deal of stress. Stress will lead to an imbalance in the biology of you and manifest into negative symptoms in one or two of your twelve biological systems. That, in turn, will affect the psychology, social, and spirit of you as well.

How can you talk to people that breach something that you value? Be honest with your *feelings*!

Resolution

BE silent, especially when you want to yell. Do not say, "It's your fault! You did this!". When you use the word "you", it will completely turn the Transformative leader off and they will stop listening to what you have to say. *DO* this instead: a better way is to use "I" statements. Say, "I feel _____ when you _____". For example, "I feel uncomfortable when you want me to build a friendship with X".

HAVE agreement and understanding; compromise to build justice, and union.

Insight #3: The term "undiscussables" was coined by Harvard professor Dr. Chris Argyris, where he stated that "an undiscussable is a problem or issue that someone hesitates to talk about with those who are essential to its resolution" (in Kathleen D. Ryan & Daniel K. Oestreich's 'Driving Fear Out Of The Workplace, 1998).

Tip #4: What people are <u>not</u> talking about is equally as important as what they are talking about. Make the time to discuss company culture *often*. Sudden departures signal distrust. People will act to reduce psychological discomfort. Make undiscussables discussable, and not taboo.

Tool #5: Use discussion and dialogue to build trust so you can help people transform into their potential. Create a trust-building discussion that is specific to your workplace challenges and conflicts. To get you started, you can use these points for a whole group discussion: Communication, attitudes, affirmations. Then, ask them to Think-Pair-Share in twos or threes to come up with three positive strategies for each discussion point listed.

YOUR TURN

1. Why is the Transformative Leadership style important?
2. How can you incorporate a transformational approach in the workplace?
3. How can you use it as a leader, at work and in life?
4. How can you become open to receiving change?

"

Before you become a leader,
success is all about growing yourself.
When you become a leader,
success is all about growing others.

~Jack Welch~

"

Chapter 8

Pacesetter Leadership
Activators: Motivation & Results

Have you experienced these barriers to success? Procrastination, standstills, abstract goals, absence of vision, constant shifting of benchmarks, unclear timelines, poor time management, high pressure, and too many changes all at once.

This chapter discusses Pacesetting Leadership style, activators, and theories. Pacesetters are energetic leaders who like to set a fast pace for teams, where members of a team are expected to match their high energy. They lead by example and through role modeling for the purpose of high performance and high expectations they set for themselves and others. They are not going to ask a team to work overtime, without working overtime themselves to achieve the fast results they desire.

Pacesetting style includes a strong drive to get things done immediately. Pacesetters include school administrators, staff, sports coaches, and managers, because this style is results driven. The focus is on winning, and a good leader, who knows their team members well, will know what tasks to disseminate to which team member to get the job done expeditiously. It will be the parts of the sum, collectively, that will provide results for the larger organization.

The Pacesetter utilizes certain *Activators*: drive, speediness, quality, conscientiousness, potential, opportunities, cooperation, and positive energy to activate success.

A Pacesetter knows exactly how to prioritize goals, created through speediness, that are not out of reach and are achievable for the talent hired. Team members may be expecting a slower pace, but in reality the pacesetter leader will ask to keep up with their pace. The pacesetter creates a realistic outlook, a scrutinizing task focus. They know that value of the seasoned team that they are working with and execute quickly on the deliverables.

Pacesetting leaders have the C for Conscientiousness that warrants quality (from the OCEAN Model), and E for their Extraversion towards positive energy. It is important to note that team members to not take their rapid thinking and pivoting personally. Consider how this style can help your team to synergize their knowledge and expertise through their unique personalities and strengths.

The Pacesetter utilizes goal theories and these strategies to significantly increase team performance through engagement, motivation (Humanism), and enthusiasm (Positive Psychology). They are driven to increase team potential and offer numerous opportunities to leverage team skills and talents by:

- Increasing employee engagement within the workplace.
- Improving employee performance by increasing efforts and motivation.
- Providing constructive feedback that gives people a chance to improve.
- Investing in people by creating a positive culture and sense that they have activated success which in turn increases morale, work satisfaction, and retention.
- Listening actively to ensure quality and goal-achievement. Active listening requires the pacesetting leader to listen, not only for the message, but to the team's feelings, values, and stressors.

How can you implement these strategies for pacesetting in your workplace?

The creation of a high-pressured environment is a limitation of the Pacesetter leader. This is a great reason to slow down the pace at strategic junctures and to cultivate awareness in how team members are feeling. As the Pacesetter leader slows down to listen to others, this also provides time for them to expand their metacognition.

If you are trying to activate success as a Pacesetter and you don't feel like listening to someone, then intentionally code shift and cultivate curiosity instead. Having curiosity will cause you to ask questions, and the more powerful your questions, the more powerful the responses will receive. Team members will feel heard. Showing genuine interest in people, by slowing down a bit, will improve engagement, cooperation, and quality. Take a proactive approach to create confidence, determination, and self-efficacy. Your approach will offer team members an opportunity to expand their schemas; dopamine will be released; positive energies will flow.

As you set the pace for self and others, keep awareness and intention at the forefront. Knowing **where you are going** will help you to *get there* and *stay there* through consideration and adaptable structures.

As you lead through a fast pace, your priority will be task completion and how you motivate your teams. You will be the one to answer to the Board and executive stakeholders on how the mission and vision are connected to what you are doing daily, reached with an approved budget, and meeting timelines and deadlines. All by creating healthy workplace relationships through evidentiary and empirical approaches.

Empirical theories help the Pacesetter to take an evidence-based approach, coupled with energetic personality, that helps support others in a more productive manner. The Pacesetter leadership style depends on goal-setting theory. Edwin Locke's Goal-Setting Theory is based on motivation, and based on the premise that setting specific and measurable goals together *with the team* is much more effective than allowing teams to set their own unclear goals. Locke's Goal-Setting Theory of motivation has been tested and supported by a myriad of studies comprised of thousands of participants, and yielded results that indicated positive global changes in the individuals on teams (Locke and Latham, 2019).

To get your team in action, you can apply theories that can provide constructive feedback that connects to the final product. Teams work well when they are given challenging goals that correlate with their knowledge, expertise, abilities, and interests. Undertaking slightly more difficult goals motivates people to work harder to challenge themselves and prepares them for change. While consistent and constructive feedback can provide a sense of accomplishment, the following strategies can increase team self-efficacy through these strategies:

Clarity: In speaking of goals, you must give clear and specific tasks so can be fewer misunderstandings when employees understand project objectives and deadlines. Do not say, "Do you have any questions?" because they will not ask due to schema. This question simply does not work, anytime, anywhere, in our estimation. Instead, you can ask, "What questions do you predict coming up at your desks?" Or, "What's the first thing you will do when you return to your desks?".

Challenge: Goals should be sufficiently challenging to keep employees engaged and focused while performing the tasks needed to reach each goal. Too difficult or easy goals will demotivate and result in less achievement and satisfaction. You can ask, "If you think this goal is difficult, how can you break it into manageable tasks?". Or you can ask, "If you think this goal is easy, how can you challenge yourself to create something better?".

Commitment: Employees need to understand and support the goal they are being assigned from the beginning. Employees who don't feel committed to the goal are less likely to enjoy the process and ultimately achieve the goal. Take the time to check in on your people so you can provide appropriate pacesetting leadership to each individual. We live in a fast-food mentality and want things quickly, but taking the time to apply training and coaching sessions can scaffold your team with effective communication in meeting their needs to perform through timelines. You can even say empathetic statements such as: "Things take time and we don't have extra time, so what resources do you need to meet deadlines?"

Feedback: Feedback is an essential component of the goal-setting theory. Regular feedback should be provided throughout the goal-achieving process to ensure tasks stay on track to reach the goal. Know your individual team members well so you can assess who needs additional support. You can ask, "I will check in with you at the end of this week to see if you have any questions or concerns. I will meet with you alone and the whole group".

Task Delegation: Goals need to be broken down into smaller parts, so they are not daunting. Once each smaller part is accomplished, conduct a review to update team members on the overall progress toward the larger goal. The workplace is about both collaboration and cooperation. Invite team members to communicate cooperatively, like this: "If someone has expertise in a task that someone else is working on, please ask if they mind if you assist!"

1. *Identify the purpose of the goal*
    There are several reasons why a goal should be set. Ensure that the goal is clear to team members who will be working towards the goal.

2. *Meet individually with team members*
    If a goal is being set for a single team member, schedule a meeting to review goals for task completion. Collect opinions

and feelings regarding needs for their goals and confirm that they understand their responsibilities and interdependencies in completing their goals. Especially if their goal completion rests on someone else's beginning. Ask all team members (personalities and roles), what their preferred methods of communication are.

3. *Make sure the team member has what they need to accomplish their goal(s).*
    Before a team member begins, ensure they have the resources to complete the goal. Meet with the person(s) and ask if they have access to what they require, and if not, provide appropriate resources to them before they begin working on that goal.

4. *Provide regular feedback through constructive critique*
    Meet with people regularly so you can review their plans and progress. Be positive and supportive of what they have done and continue to do. Look for the positive and recognize the work done, and then provide quick guidance in what they can accomplish quickly.

5. *Develop a plan using the SMART model*
    The SMART model is an effective way to set and accomplish goals. SMART is an acronym for Specific, Measurable, Achievable, Realistic, and Timely.

We took the S.M.A.R.T model (George T. Doran, 1981) and have added to it by making it ***S.M.A.R.T.E.R.***

a. *Specific for Incremental Implementation*: Specific means that the goal should be as clear and concrete as possible. Rather than saying you want an employee to increase their customer satisfaction ratings, communicate you want the employee to improve their customer satisfaction ratings by 10% over the next month.

b.   *Measurable for Growth and Improvement***:** The goal should be measurable for data collection. So, instead of saying the goal is to increase sales, you would set a measurable sales goal, such as to increase sales by 25% over the next six months.

c.   *Achievable through Reward:* Goals should be challenging to keep employees engaged and provide a reward upon accomplishing them. Ensure the goal is slightly higher than an employee's skill set to keep the employee engaged but still within reach of the employee's capabilities. This is where interests, skills, aptitudes, abilities, and capabilities meet self-esteem, efficacy, and belongingness.

d.   *Realistic and not a Dream:* Setting a goal that seems impossible or out of reach will not offer employees motivational value, resulting in loss of interest and engagement for those working to reach the goal. Set a goal that can realistically be met. You don't want them to give up or quit.

e.   *Timelines & Deadlines:* Goals should have a clear timeframe in which they need to be reached. For example, we want a goal to increase membership by 10%, *over the next three months.*

f.   *Our addition is Engagement:* Goals need to match the mission and vision of the organization, and also meet the interests and abilities of the person working on those tasks. Create Eustress (urgency through motivation), not Distress (fear, anxiety, panic).

g.   *Our addition is Relevance:* Goals should be current and trend setting. Take a risk and try innovative goals that meet the needs of contemporary generations and present-day hot topics.

There are significant gains from utilizing Pacesetter leadership style through the creation of clear goals that are established early in rapid cycles where competent teams work peaceably through continuous improvement to attain company measures.

Change Management Insight

Know that, many times, goal interactions may not be linear or black and white but are part of a more extensive process that moves interests and desires forward through step-by-step vertical and horizontal action.

As you take the responsibility for task completion, ensure that you delegate based on individual strengths. As a Pacesetter leader, be mindful that you do not slip into ancient tactics that revive the ego. It is much more legitimate to inform, reframe, provide and ask for feedback, and give constructive critique. Ask each person how they prefer to receive constructive feedback, so their own imaginative ego does not misinterpret your pacesetting style of leadership. Team interests, abilities, and personalities make up the diverse individuals on a team that you are trying to motivate through your own strengths for extraversion and conscientiousness. Awareness will help you to realize that not everyone on your team will be extroverted or conscientious. Curiosity will be your strength when you are working with introversion or neuroticism on a team.

Here are a bevy of questions you can use to motivate and gain awareness:

1. What was your team's biggest gain this week?
2. What made you happy this week?
3. What made your team happy?
4. Is there something you will change next week?
5. What would you like your team to change next week?

Effective Communication & Conflict Resolution

<u>Pacesetter Leader Values</u>

Goals, aims, objectives, intent, planning, structuring, high pace, conscientiousness

<u>Pacesetter Leader Stressors</u>

Lack of goals, aims, and objectives. Not planning for the near and far future, working haphazardly, untidiness, no calendars, no reminders, timers, or scheduled appointments

What does this mean?

This means that when there is a breach of something that you value, then that will cause you a great deal of stress. Stress will lead to an imbalance in the biology of you and manifest into negative symptoms in one or two of your twelve biological systems. That, in turn, will affect the psychology, social, and spirit of you as well.

How can you talk to people that breach something that you value? Be honest with your *feelings*!

<u>Resolution</u>

BE focused and keep your voice and tone low. Do not say, "Why can't you be more X?!". When you use the word "You", it puts the person into their sympathetic nervous system where their adrenaline increases getting them ready for the fight or flight reaction. *DO* use "I" statements. Say, "I feel _____ when you _____". For example, "I feel nervous and anxious because you expect us to keep too many calendars".

HAVE consideration; communication, thoughtfulness, and understanding.

👁 **Insight #4:** A few points to reflect upon:

1. I am aware of my five-year goals and why I want to become a leader in this company because _____.
2. I connect with others through meaningful conversations by_____.
3. I have learned to self-lead by _____.
4. I feel confident to lead others because _____.
5. We can win on the competitive global stage by _____.
6. I know how to recognize a high-pressure environment and will help to create workplace wellness by _____.

🔖 **Tip #5:** Use intrinsic and extrinsic motivators. The benefits of using intrinsic motivation include curiosity, challenge, recognition, and creativity. Engagement must include ethos, pathos, and logos, where trust and respect begin with you.

🔖 **Neuro Tip #2:** The brain wants you to pay attention to food, exercise, hydration, rest, challenges, habits, learning, and mental wellness. You can stimulate the frontal lobe through opposites: use your opposite hand for brushing your teeth, writing, holding keys, eating, or doing other easy tasks. Do not give in to poor habits, such as: smoking, too much salt or sugar, or rarely talking. Sitting still and also moving around will both help your brain to develop new connections. The brain morphs each day based on your habits, challenges, thinking, and feelings. What type of brain are you creating for yourself?

🔭 **Tool #6:** Perfect planners can be found at: www.erincondren.com

YOUR TURN:

1. Why is the Pacesetting or Goal-Centered style important?
2. How can you incorporate it in the workplace?
3. How can you use it as a leader?
4. When would you use the SMARTER goal method?
5. We talked about goal-readiness. How can you get others ready to set goals for themselves as individuals and as a team member?

"

A goal is a dream with a deadline.

~Napoleon Hill~

"

Chapter 9

Action-Centered Leadership
Activators: Roles & Actions

Have you experienced these barriers to success? Lack of duties, lack of role clarity, procrastination, lack of resources, short timelines, weak skill sets.

The chapter discusses the difference between leaders and managers, differentiation of duties, and leadership and management function.

Leaders and managers have distinctly different duties and roles, whereby the leader shares a broad vision, and the manager supports the leader in implementing and bringing that vision to fruition through daily activities.

There are many leaders that depend on managers to accomplish their goals through day-to-day affairs. If you do not have a manager by your side to help you to achieve mission, vision, and goals, then you will have to be the one to perform managerial actions.

A short list of managerial tasks includes being able to balance process with actions to get tasks accomplished in a timely fashion. This process involves effective communication in a chain of command that flows from organization to department head to team lead, who then allocates strength-based responsibilities to the individuals to accomplish the task (Adair, 1973).

Action-Centered Leadership is a leadership model developed by John Adair. This model focuses on balancing three key elements, the three circles model, to achieve effective leadership within a team or organization: the task, the team, and the individual.

According to Adair, a leader must address these three areas simultaneously for successful and balanced leadership. Here are the core components of the Action-Centered Leadership model:

Task: Achieving the task involves setting clear objectives and goals for the team. The leader must ensure that the team is working toward achieving these tasks efficiently and effectively.

Planning: Leaders need to develop plans and strategies to accomplish tasks. This includes resource allocation, timeline setting, and risk management.

Coaching the Team: A leader must focus on building a cohesive and motivated team. This involves creating a positive team culture, fostering good communication, and addressing conflicts. Be attentive to teams and committees that submit "No Report". Every committee is accountable for their charge, so if you receive such a response, please go into coaching mode and help that team to articulate what they are doing and how they are doing it. Perhaps there are language barriers or a misinterpretation that no report means that all is good, when in reality it shows a stagnant group.

Coaching Individuals: We vehemently believe that leaders must help the growth and development of team members. This includes providing training opportunities, coaching, retraining, mentoring, recognizing individual contributions, and giving credit where credit is due.

Meeting Individual Needs: Recognizing and addressing the personal needs and concerns of team members is crucial. This includes understanding their strengths, weaknesses, aspirations, and concerns. Some committees/teams have a lead or a chair. They may view it as a weakness to ask you for a co-chair or co-lead, so be sure to ask them if they need one.

Ensuring Well-being: Leaders are responsible for the well-being of individual team members, ensuring a healthy work environment and addressing any personal challenges that may affect performance. We go back to the no reporting example to restate that there may be something in their personal life that is impeding their progress.

The key idea behind Action-Centered Leadership is that leaders need to find the right balance among these three elements. Neglecting one in favor of the others can lead to imbalances and potential issues within the team or organization. Effective leaders, according to Adair, are those who can address the needs of the task, team, and individual simultaneously.

This model is often represented as a three-circle Venn diagram, where the intersection of the three circles represents the optimal balance where all three elements are addressed effectively.

In summary, Action-Centered Leadership emphasizes the importance of managing tasks, teams, and individuals concurrently to achieve successful and balanced leadership. This approach is particularly relevant in dynamic and complex work environments where leaders need to navigate various challenges to achieve both task success and team cohesion.

Balancing his "Three Circles" model: The central idea is that effective leaders find the right balance among the task, team, and individual dimensions. Neglecting one at the expense of the others can lead to imbalances and challenges within the team.

The most important trait that an action-centered leader must have, according to Adair, is adaptability. Action-centered leaders and managers are adaptable and can shift their focus based on the needs of the situation. They understand that different circumstances may require different emphases on the task, team, or individual dimension.

The Adair model is practical and flexible, making it applicable to various leadership situations. It provides a framework for leaders to assess and address the multifaceted nature of their roles. Action-Centered Leadership encourages leaders to be mindful of the interdependence of tasks, teams, and individuals in achieving overall success.

We view an effective flow of communication to look like this:

Task: Work that is undertaken and is performed by individual, team, and organization.

Team: A group of individuals within a department or committee who work together to achieve goals and meet deadlines.

Individual: A person that has certain skills that are conducive in helping to support the team in accomplishing their goal.

When using this process in your organization, think about the aspects of performance necessary to activate success in your niche. Effective implementation of tasks involves careful planning, clear communication, efficient execution, and continuous monitoring.

Managerial Tasks: Supervisory

- Get tasks done.
- Identify aims.
- Identify vision.
- Communicate purpose and direction.
- Identify resources (person, place, thing)
- Create a plan to achieve the task
- Establish responsibilities and accountabilities
- Set standards and quality
- Control and maintain activities
- Monitor and maintain overall performance
- Report on progress

- Review, re-assess, and adjust plan

Managerial Tasks: The Group

- Establish, agree, and communicate standards of performance and behavior
- Establish a style, culture, and approach
- Monitor and maintain discipline, ethics, integrity, and focus
- Anticipate and resolve conflicts
- Assess and change the balance and composition of a team
- Develop teamwork, cooperation, morale, and team spirit
- Develop maturity and capability of the group through autonomy and independence
- Encourage the team towards objectives and aims through motivation
- Identify, develop, and agree on the team- and project-leadership roles within the group
- Enable, facilitate, and ensure effective internal and external group communications
- Identify and meet group training needs
- Give feedback to the group on overall progress; consult and seek feedback and input.

Managerial Tasks: The Individuals

- Understand the team members as individuals - personality, skills, strengths, needs, and aims.
- Assist and support individuals - plans, problems, challenges
- Identify and agree on appropriate individual responsibilities and objectives
- Give recognition and praise to individuals - acknowledge efforts
- Reward individuals with extra responsibility, advancement, and status

- Identify, develop, and utilize each individual's capabilities and strengths
- Train and develop individual team members
- Develop individual freedom and authority

Through this information, researchers shifted the perception of managers to encompass their act of leading as associated with communication, decision-making, and problem-solving. This shift made it possible for organizations to separate management from leadership because managers are not necessarily leaders, and leaders are not necessarily managers.

Leading is about having direction. Both manager and leader roles are needed, but for achieving and completing different tasks. Leaders know how to inspire others, while managers focus on managing operations that enable people to do the job. The Action-Centered leadership style helps managers and leaders in three critical areas: achieve the task, develop a team, and develop individuals.

Here are some quality skills and personality traits that can help you to implement an Action-Centered style:

- Planning - seeking information, defining tasks, setting aims.
- Initiating - briefing, task allocation, setting standards.
- Monitoring - maintaining standards, ensuring progress, ongoing decision-making.
- Supporting - individuals' contributions, encouraging, team spirit, reconciling, morale.
- Informing - clarifying tasks and plans, updating, receiving feedback, and interpreting.
- Evaluating - feasibility of ideas, performance, enabling self-assessment.

Make note that we have called the above skills and traits. Some personalities are natural planners, initiators, monitors, supporters, informers, or evaluators, while others need to intentionally cultivate these skills that are required for an action focus. Genetics and Environment, both, play a role in creating a personality and skills.

We would be remiss if we did not mention the importance of how to empower a team. A major portion of an action-oriented leader manager will be to push the team along to meet a feasible timeline for completion of a project.

Effective implementation of a project involves careful planning, clear communication, efficient execution, and continuous monitoring. Here are some key steps and principles to ensure successful project implementation:

Goals and Objectives: Clearly define the project objectives and goals. Ensure that these are allied with the overall business or organizational strategy; adhere to financial goals as well.

Plans and Details: Develop a comprehensive project plan that includes tasks, timelines, resources, and dependencies. Use project management tools to help with scheduling through time zones, and resource allocation from various geographic locations.

Competence: Assemble a skilled and motivated project team. Clearly define roles and responsibilities to avoid confusion. Provide a list of competencies that people can work on.

Effective Communication: Establish a robust communication plan to keep teams and all stakeholders informed. Regularly update everyone on project progress, challenges, and changes.

Risk Management: Identify potential risks and develop a risk management plan. Be proactive in addressing and mitigating risks throughout the project lifecycle.

Quality Assurance: Implement a robust quality assurance process to ensure that project deliverables meet specified standards. Conduct regular quality checks and audits.

Resource Management: Efficiently manage resources, including personnel, equipment, and finances. Ensure that resources are allocated appropriately based on project requirements.

Adaptability: Be flexible and prepared to adapt the project plan based on changing circumstances or unforeseen issues.

Monitoring: Establish monitoring mechanisms to track progress against the project plan. Implement control measures to address any deviations from the plan promptly.

Engagement: Engage with stakeholders regularly to gather feedback and address concerns. Ensure that stakeholders are supportive of project goals. Engagement and connection are key.

Training and Development: Provide necessary training and coaching to team members if new skills are required for the project. Foster a learning environment that encourages continuous improvement.

Documentation: Maintain thorough documentation for project lifecycles. Document decisions, changes, and lessons learned for future reference can be excellent trusted sources.

Evaluation: Close the project systematically by completing all required deliverables. Conduct a post-implementation review to assess the project's success and identify areas for improvement.

Continuous Improvement: Gather feedback from the team and stakeholders. Apply lessons learned to improve processes for future projects. Do not wait for months and months to go by.

Recognition and Success: Acknowledge and celebrate people and their milestones for successful completion of projects. Recognize the efforts of the team members; give credit to others.

Remember that each venture is unique, so adapt these principles to suit the specific needs and characteristics of your workplace. Regularly reexamine and adjust your approach based on progress and changing circumstances.

Action-Centered leadership style works positively for people who have a tendency to procrastinate or those who just do not know how and where to begin. They know how to keep individuals and teams on the right track, focused, and towards task completion.

We want to make sure they include recognition and celebrations too, because all work without rewards don't make for effective conditioning.

Change Management Insight

Meeting individual needs is just as important as recognizing and addressing the needs and concerns of a team or department. This includes an understanding of their strengths, weaknesses, aspirations, concerns, and fears.

Action-focused leaders can especially ensure well-being and stay responsible for the wellness of individual team members. This can ensure a healthy work environment and address personal challenges that may affect work performance.

Personal conduct could lead to fears. Skilled incompetence could lead to even more fear. Create avenues for high performance and values for respect, trust-building, integrity, unity, and continuous improvement. Assess what is under your control and also under their locus of control in order to begin incremental changes.

Effective Communication & Conflict Resolution

Action-Centered Leader Values

Activity, adventure, imagination, rivalry, change, emersion, theater, performing, enthusiasm, high energy, high pace, autonomy, fun, friskiness, novelty, extemporaneity, variety, zest.

Action-Centered Leader Stressors

Tedium, monotony, being on time, procedures, deadlines, lack of humor, paperwork, form-filling, criticism, calendars, waiting, predictability.

What does this mean?

This means that when there is a breach of something that you value, then that will cause you a great deal of stress. Stress will lead to an imbalance in the biology of you and manifest into negative symptoms in one or two of your twelve biological systems. That, in turn, will affect the psychology, social, and spirit of you as well.

How can you talk to people that breach something that you value?

Resolution

BE calm as you show your seriousness. *DO* not say, "You never take things seriously!". When you use the word "you" to a hands-on leader, they will blame you for being too serious, no fun, and boring. Instead, a better way is to use "I" statements. Say, "I feel _____ when you _____". For example, "I feel pressured when you demand me to be present at too many meetings".

HAVE engagement, adaptability, collaboration, cooperation, teamwork.

👁 **Insight #5:** Be sure to observe yourself in self-leading. Look through the microscope as well as the telescopic lens. Here are a few things to say to people.

1. I show up on time, and if I'm running late, I will always call you.
2. I have good manners and am considerate of others.
3. I hold myself accountable.
4. I allow people to be themselves and am adept at asking questions for clarification to increase understanding and reduce conflicts.
5. I am willing to compromise.

🔎 **Neuro Tip #3:** The hands-on approach is not a stand-alone one because it entails action. And 'action' means activity, and that activity can activate success. The brain responds to small success just as much as it does to large success. Highlight small successes too so that the reward chemical, dopamine, is released in everyone's body.

There is a common 50/50 rule between nature (genetics) and nurture (environment), but numerous studies have proven that the environment plays more of a critical role in the creation of an individual (Bandura, Bronfenbrenner, Vygotsky, B.F. Skinner).

Individual motivation, personality, and skill webs with the environmental context. Every leader and manager need to know their motives, so they can seek the appropriate opportunities that match their needs.

🔭 **Tool #7:** Conduct a gap analysis to see where you are and where you want to be. Begin by making a chart that lists your mission and vision. Then, create a survey that asks teams how mission and vision coordinate with tasks and products.

The best AI tools that we have found are: Chat GPT, Copy.AI, Midjourney, Tome, Kaiber, Fireflies, and Soundraw.io

YOUR TURN

1. How will you use the Action-Centered approach?
2. What does it mean to be an Action-Centered manager?
3. What does it mean to be an Action-Centered leader?
4. What is the difference between a manager and a leader?
5. How would you do things differently if you were a leader versus a manager?
6. Are you creating a company culture where it is safe to disagree?

❝

Stand up for what you believe.
Just having that strong determination
can make other people join you in your struggle.

~Silvia Carrera~

❞

Chapter 10

Global-Minded Leadership
Activators: Perspectives & Dialogue

Have you experienced these barriers to success? Disregarding cultures, customs, taboos, diverse perspectives, world geography, history, impact of world events, and foreign leaders.

This chapter will discuss the Global-Minded Leader that understands and values Interculturalism; contributions that have a global impact; diverse perspectives for the purpose of dialogue and peacekeeping; and how to shape a Global-Minded Leadership style.

Interculturalism is an approach that encourages the interaction and understanding of, and mutual respect for individuals from diverse cultural backgrounds. It promotes the idea that different cultures can coexist and contribute to a richer, more dynamic society through dialogues and narratives. The Global-Minded leader values *Interculturalism* as a 21st- century upskill. Successful leaders for this century will be those who are culturally sensitive through cultural humility in their engagement with different cultures and nations.

Interculturalism aims to build social cohesion by creating a sense of unity and shared identity among people from diverse cultural backgrounds. This is achieved through common values, respect, and collaboration. People must learn to live peaceably through a sense of community. Interculturalism acknowledges that societies are dynamic and constantly evolving. Being adaptable to change, embracing diversity, and adjusting to new cultural influences are essential components. These are all great reasons for self-discovery and the change that is necessary for the 21st century to activate success with global partnerships.

A helpful suggestion is for you to create a glossary of terms on hand so you can understand and explain the meanings of those terms to your team. Terms such as: ethnocentrism, multiculturalism, transculturalism, diversity, glocal, global citizen, and interculturalism are used interchangeably. ***Multiculturalism*** is the awareness that other cultures exist, while ***Interculturalism*** is *dialoguing across cultures.* ***Transculturalism*** is adopting customs from another culture, while ***Diversity*** can have a slew of different meanings. ***Glocal*** means that you are doing your part in your local area that can have a global affect, while Global Citizen means that you have the desire to embrace other cultures.

To shape your Global-Minded leadership style, recognize that each culture brings unique perspectives, traditions, and contributions to the broader and majority community that they reside in. You can build capacity by encouraging open and respectful dialogues, fostering environments where individuals can share their experiences, beliefs, and values without judgment, and through empathy.

All individuals, regardless of their cultural background, must be given equal opportunities to participate in society, regardless of who they are and where they came from. Interculturalism promotes inclusivity and actively works against discrimination and exclusion. This is the basis for cultural exchange, therefore encouraging cultural exchange is central to Interculturalism. It is the sharing of traditions, customs, and experiences that enhances mutual understanding and appreciation.

Promoting education and awareness regarding different cultures is also central to the construct of Interculturalism that seeks to raise awareness, challenge stereotypes, and build knowledge to reduce prejudice and foster cross-cultural understanding.

The principles of social justice also correspond with Interculturalism. The Global-Minded leadership style advocates for fair treatment, equal opportunities, and the elimination of systemic barriers that may disproportionately affect individuals from certain cultural backgrounds. Through knowledge, awareness, and peace, a community can build trust. Trust is foundational in intercultural interactions. Fostering trust requires honesty, integrity, and a commitment to understanding and respecting different cultural norms and expectations.

Interculturalism addresses apathy or conflicts arising from cultural differences through dialogue, mediation, and conflict resolution strategies. It seeks to find common ground while respecting diverse perspectives. Through this, we can encourage a sense of global citizenship, where individuals are seen not only as members of their immediate cultural communities but also as part of a larger, interconnected world.

How will you create opportunities to celebrate cultural food and music? Rather than viewing differences as sources of division, interculturalism celebrates cultures as strengths. The uniqueness of each culture is seen as a valuable contribution to the broader cultural tapestry.

Now that you know how to integrate Interculturalism in your leadership style, we want to see every niche gain global and intercultural competency. Why? So that you, as a leader, can help companies acquire the expertise to interact, negotiate, trade, barter, and merge with different nations without misunderstandings and conflicts.

Misunderstandings and conflicts can be mitigated through understanding the concepts of *Reciprocity* and *Transculturalism* which are subsets of Interculturalism. The aforementioned both consider the exchanging of diverse ideas, knowledge, and experiences among individuals from different cultures. It is dialogue, empathy, and acceptance that lends to the transcultural consequences of adopting diverse cultural practices that parallel with the values of the majority.

Dr. Darla Deardorff is a world-renowned expert on intercultural competence and one of the most prolific global contributors to the field of Interculturalism. She has created an extensive forum to activate the success of intercultural and global competencies. She is the United Nations Educational, Scientific, and Cultural Organization (UNESCO) Chair in Intercultural Competencies for Stellenbosch University. She states that intercultural research focuses on socio-emotional learning, emotional intelligence, empathy, compassion, with an overlap to justice, equity, diversity, belonging, and inclusion. She works with UNESCO partners internationally to move from research to concrete practice and to the end point for shared humanity. https://www.sun.ac.za/english/Lists/news/DispForm.aspx?ID=9960

Researcher, Richard D. Lewis (1996), is another author who stands out; his book, "When Cultures Collide," provides a candid framework for navigating people and organizations across cultures. He closely examines cultural norms for meetings and professional interactions, and also provides clear instructions for facilitating matriarchal-patriarchal postures.

We admire Lewis's open perspective for a thorough understanding that this globe and its cultures and languages, and how they cause people to interact with each other. Lewis lists certain behaviors that people from different cultures display during exchanges and negotiations. Therefore, we encourage the global-centered leader to inspect their bias, schema, and cognitive dissonance so they can build successful relationships.

By embracing these principles, individuals, communities, and societies can create peaceable environments through knowledge of and understanding of cultures. The understanding of culture can help to foster inclusivity and cooperation, ultimately contributing to a more harmonious and interconnected world of work.

A Global-Centered leader takes a strong interest in workplace culture and how behavior and actions can embrace diverse cultural practices and nuances that have a great impact on the workplace, much greater than words alone. Cultural nuances can make or break negotiations and relationships if you fail to consider respectful cultural practices. For example, you would not go into an interview without researching a company, and the same applies regarding world cultures.

Let's take respect for example: some cultures do not mind 'rocking the boat', while others would take offence; some will show respect by not having eye contact, while others will interpret this as disinterest; the thumbs-up emoji provides a positive emotion in the western hemisphere but means the exact opposite in the MENA region of the world.

Global leadership and global citizenship go hand in hand, and this means that you must be aware of your beliefs and schema so you can expand organizational culture. Variations in contrary cultural self-expressions can result in miscommunication and misunderstanding. Western and Eastern leaders have different worldviews due to their lived national history in their geographic regions and personal experiences. This can have a profound effect on decision-making and problem-solving.

When you think of yourself as a global citizen leader, you take on a richer perspective that causes a shift in thinking, feeling, and perceiving. Interacting with different cultures will push you to question your bias, so that you can create an open mindset leading to discernment. This attainment can, exponentially, expand your worldview.

When we are exposed to different cultures, it reminds us to take a close look at our own. Through self-discovery and where we are on the lifespan development line, we can become aware of our conditioned beliefs, assumptions, and norms. Worldviews are formed through a multitude of cultural norms: patience, quietness, privacy, socialness, gregariousness, respect, silence, punctuality, structure, losing face, presents, dominance, humility, just to name a few.

Depending on where in the world a person is raised can profoundly affect a person's metacognition, identity, and worldview. Leaders and teams bring this to the company and to the table. Observe and be cognizant of what cultures are sitting at the table. Your actions and behaviors during meetings can strengthen or break relationships. To explain more of how this works, take the example of "**Losing Face**". "Losing Face" is especially prevalent in the Eastern Hemisphere, where it is customary to protect the integrity of another in the workplace and life.

At the table, you may also notice the nuance of words that integrate church and state. Certain nations do not separate government and religion, while others keep the two totally separate. Consider these the following suggestions when you are planning a meeting with international leaders:

1. State the purpose of the meeting and stick to the agenda.
2. Make the list of invitees known and where they come from.
3. State the length of the meeting, and do not go overtime.
4. State the format for questions and answers, so everyone is allotted time to ask.
5. State the format for debate or disagreement, so there are ground rules for fairness.
6. State the steps in the decision-making and problem-solving process.

7. Consider the language gaps between nationalities that are attending and hire an interpreter.
8. Consider conflicts that may be occurring between two nations.
9. Ask the priorities of each nationality before the meeting, so you can conduct a fair meeting.
10. State the timeline for decision-making and completion of topics discussed.

The Global-Minded leadership style grows to understand others through empathy, self-awareness, and situational awareness. This leader becomes focused through their attentive to understanding all people and cultures. Famous author Stephen Covey says: "Seek first to understand, then to be understood." It is thoughtful understanding and empathy that can help to evolve partnerships.

Here are a few ways that you can speak with respect:

1. I understand what you are saying, and I respectfully disagree.
2. You bring up an interesting point that I will consider.
3. Maybe we can find a way to make this work.
4. I see no other choice, do you?
5. I will do all I can in my power to make that work for both of us.
6. Speedy action is necessary in this case, that's why my voice and tone sound urgent.

As a Global-Minded leader who is intercultural, you will become adept in communicating effectively and respectfully across cultures. Adapting an open communication style can bridge cultural gaps that embraces diversity and inclusion, adapts to different cultural, economic, and political contexts, and is a hallmark of global-minded leadership. They foster an inclusive organizational culture because they value diversity, diverse perspectives, creativity, and innovation. Leaders with a global mindset have a broad understanding of global trends, economies, and geopolitical dynamics. They can anticipate and respond to changes in the global landscape, positioning their organizations for success.

You will find that your work comes easier due to the collaborations and strategic alliances across borders in building and nurturing international networks, partnerships to leverage expertise and resources. Their global mindset will help you to take responsibility for contributing to the well-being of the global community by considering social, economic, and environmental impact of decision-making.

The Global-Minded leader is high on the O that stands for 'Open-Mindedness' from the O.C.E.A.N. model as the personality trait that makes them receptive to new ideas, points of view and a willingness to challenge their own assumptions. They have a regard for how language effects thinking and processing in brain structures. They have high regard for how emotions land on the table.

Connect The Dots from previous chapters because connecting the *why* will help you to be aware of respect. Observe yourself in the third person, so you can get rid of any barriers that prevent you from building relationships with other cultures. The sooner you accept that you have to make changes in how you currently do things, the sooner you will be on your way to activating success.

Most of all, please listen to stories and tell stories!

Change Management Insight

Conducting a meeting that has a myriad of countries represented at the table is like steering an orchestra. The more you prepare in advance, the better your performance will be. Of course, there will also be moments where you will have to improvise, so be sure to have expert knowledge on the day's topic.

Part of improvisation is to listen to what and *how* others are 'playing', and what they are expressing through their word choices and nonverbal communication. Pay close attention and learn how people motivate themselves through their esoteric traditions, customs, and norms. Be sure to portray that your goal is to achieve a win-win outcome through compromise.

Effective Communication & Conflict Resolution

Global Leader Values

Inclusiveness, cultures, outreach, missions, internationalism, policies, world issues, travel, compromise, listening, understanding, empathy.

Global Leader Stressors

Exclusiveness, lack of multiplicity, miscommunication, unfairness, injustice

What does this mean?

This means that when there is a breach of something that you value, then that will cause you a great deal of stress. Stress will lead to an imbalance in the biology of you and manifest into negative symptoms in one or two of your twelve biological systems. That, in turn, will affect the psychology, social, and spirit of you as well.

How can you talk to people that breach something that you value? Be honest with your *feelings*!

Resolution

BE still and listen. DO not say, "You never! You always!". When you use the word "You", it turns on the emotional center of the brain the Limbic system where the Amygdala hijacks you in to reacting and not responding rationally. *DO* use "I" statements and say, "I feel _____ when you _____". For example, "I feel dismayed when you ignore my contributions at the table".

HAVE fairness, communication, equalness, impartiality, acceptance.

👁 **Insight #6:** Here are some suggestions to begin an effective dialogue with a diverse group of people.

1. A current article you read and why it was important to you.
2. Your global concern and why it is important to you.
3. Your cultural experiences and why they are important to you.
4. Your global and travel exposure to cultures.
5. Discuss a metaphor related to culture and perspectives.
6. Instead of "Where are you from? You look different", ask: What is it about your culture that you would like me to know?

Tip #6: Create a glossary of terms that compare and contrast DEI and Interculturalism. The DEI movement is connected to the civil rights movement in America, while Interculturalism refers to dialogue between cultures for the purpose of peacebuilding. There are distinct differences when it comes to culture-speak.

We encourage you to invest time in reading books that are written by great and international authors because their divergent perspectives that can help to provide a distinct competitive advantage you need for the global landscape.

Neuro Tip #4: When you challenge a thought, think of 3 positive thoughts, and this will train your brain to go from back brain to frontal lobe. It is *you* that must do the "good work" that Carl Jung talked about. Your shadow side and sunny side are both in your locus of control. Your shadow side contains thoughts of: self-doubt, fear of failure, fear of success, helplessness, hopelessness, powerlessness, and negativity. Challenge your thinking: how do I know this is true? What evidence supports my thinking? Is the thought helping or hurting me? What is in my locus of control? Am I assuming the worst? Am I making this personal?

Tool #8: Use UNESCO's storytelling model to improve communication and understanding. Interculturalism tools can be found at: www.unesco.org, www.un.org, www.icc.org, and global-in-circle.org

YOUR TURN

1. Why is the Global Leadership style important?
2. How can you incorporate it in the workplace?
3. How can you integrate Interculturalism into the workplace?
4. Do other cultures frighten you? Why or why not?
5. What disability do you fear the most?
6. How can you encourage strength through weaknesses?
7. How does your location on Earth impact your mindset?

"

When you know better,
you do better, so be open to receive.

~The Authors~

"

Chapter 11

Sustainable Leadership
Activators: Legacy & Impact

Have you experienced these barriers to success? Imbalance, inability to build relationships and partnerships, disconnectedness, lack of influence, resilience, and wellness.

Social, environmental, and economic issues in this world are drastically imbalanced and have become of great concern to leaders around the world. With a plethora of tasks on a leader's to-do list, these additional points can pose a challenge in how to build partnerships that consider social responsibility, nature, and resources. Time is running out; therefore, there is a need for a sustainable leader who can balance challenges, navigate with increased risk and liability, for the protection of the Earth and future generations.

Indigenous peoples across North America share stories of the frivolous human consumption of the Earth's resources, environment, and economics and have had a long-standing practice of decision-making with consideration to seven future generations. The notion of sustainability was brought to the attention of leaders and managers by the Brundtland Committee and brought into academic circles by pioneers of this construct, Pearce and Turner (1990).

Hargreaves and Fink (2004) developed a model of sustainable leadership based on the educational organization to maintain and promote in-depth and extensive learning, future planning and dialogue, improve justice and diversity, and promote appropriate policies and procedures to enhance learning and standardization for nations.

Through academic research and publication, the business sector realized that a new leadership style was warranted for sustainable impact. Avery and Bergsteiner (2011) provided best practices that could help the sustainable leader to meet sustainable goals. These included: basic practices that could be instituted at the individual level; high-level practices that could be instituted through teams; and key performance drivers that could be inaugurated at the systems level. It is the responsibility of individuals, teams, and systems to address sustainability.

Utilizing this information along with the current state of the Earth, the United Nations Secretary-General brought about a strong focus on the relationships between people, environment, and resources through his 2030 Sustainable Development Goals (www.un.org). For the first time in human history, attention was brought to the protection and intersection of man, nature, and economics. Decision-making and problem-solving now must involve decisions that value something existentially greater than all of us.

Sustainable leaders take into consideration the global impact that their decisions have amongst nations, where poverty, hunger, land, oceans, equity, housing, clean water, gender equality, and human wellness can be brought into the forefront through wise decision-making and problem-solving.

We bring your attention to our three pillars of Self-Discovery, Change Readiness, and Sustainable Impact, where the third one is imperative to achieve and activate long-term success.

Sustainable leadership refers to a leadership approach that prioritizes long-term social, environmental, and economic sustainability, instead of making these areas just areas for fiduciary donation. This type of leadership is characterized by a commitment to responsible and ethical practices that consider the impact of decisions on not only the current generation but also future generations. Sustainable leaders strive to create positive outcomes for the planet, society, and the economy, recognizing the interconnectedness of these elements. We support sustainable leaders that actively search to embed solutions, advancement, and global partnerships in their already existing company framework.

Tool #9: https://www.frontiersin.org/articles/10.3389/fpsyg.2022.1045570/full

Here are some key principles and characteristics associated with sustainable leadership that can be integrated in what you currently have in place:

Sustainable leaders consider the **triple bottom line**, which includes social responsibility, environmental challenges, and economic factors. The sole focus need not be on financial profit, but on through consciousness and inclusive of the goals that have formulated for "The New Normal Phenomenon".

They have an enduring vision where they must focus on long-term goals rather than short-term gains that can aid sustainable practices. They do this through partnership engagement; a focus on diverse perspectives, cultural humility, interconnectedness to work together and share resources. They find ways to minimize an organization's ecological footprint by promoting resource efficiency and adopting innovative sustainable practices through a myriad of chains.

Sustainability and long-term wellness cannot happen if this is not made a priority today.

Prioritizing the well-being (is linked to a state of happiness or life satisfaction) of employees can foster a positive work environment and create an inclusive organizational culture that embraces diversity. Prioritizing the well-being of employees is a key aspect of sustainable leadership. This includes promoting work-life balance and providing opportunities for professional development. To make a point here, happiness is not a destination or goal. If you have pockets of time where you feel happy, then you have succeeded.

The importance of creating strategic alliances to leverage a diversity of strengths can yield strong cooperations and efforts in environment, economic, and social issues that favorable impact all members. Global perspectives allow for information-sharing and knowledge-transfer that can lead to suitable decision-making and problem-solving. This commitment can guide organizations to make great strides in the UN SDGs for 2030.

Embodying these qualities can propel sustainable leaders to build resilient, responsible, and thriving organizations that make positive contributions to the world. Considering how their decisions have a broad or far-reaching impact can bring about discussions regarding mission, vision, innovation, strategic planning, risk-taking, and service orientation.

Sustainable leadership includes a commitment to social responsibility. Leaders actively engage in activities that benefit society, such as community development, philanthropy, and fair labor practices.

Sustainable leaders embrace a mindset of continuous improvement. They regularly assess and reassess their organization's practices, seeking ways to reduce environmental impact, enhance social responsibility, and improve overall sustainability performance.

Sustainable leadership is not just about minimizing negative impacts but actively contributing to a better and more sustainable future. It requires a holistic and integrated approach that considers the interconnectedness of environmental, social, and economic factors in decision-making and organizational strategy.

Can you think of national and international leaders that were sustainable?

Your examples can illustrate that sustainability leaders can emerge in various fields and contexts. Whether in business, politics, social justice, or technology, these leaders share the ability to articulate a compelling vision, inspire others, and drive positive change.

You never know who is watching you. You may be a role model for someone in the sidelines.

Change Management Insight

If you feel like a string cheese being pulled apart in different directions, then that's a sure sign that demands through pressure are being placed on you, which can rapidly lead to burnout in the long run. If you fail to self-care, then you will not be able to take care of your people.

Leaders do not have time for themselves but must make time for wellness. You give 100% of yourself at work and personal life. You navigate the many roles you have in life while keeping yourself in emotional solid composure. There comes a day when you must realize that you are pouring too much of yourself into others, so it's time to take a breather before you hit burnout.

First, prioritize. Make a list of things that must get done in the short term and a list of things that can wait. Second, make a list of things that make you happy. Life will go on after you pass, and things will still get done, so understand that you deserve the break. Some people believe that they can wait until the afterlife to be happy, while others do not. Third, learn to delegate tasks and find support at work and in life. Fourth, be able to distinguish any guilt or shame that you may be implicitly carrying in your heart brain.

Seek out a spouse, good friend, or a trusted colleague to confer with. Someone you trust. Speculate the memories that you feel prevent you from self-care and discuss those with your trusted friend. Your brain's hippocampus is the brain's librarian and remembers everything that has happened in your life, and that's why you implicitly carry memories around with you that cause certain feelings to come up into your conscious state of mind.

Wellness and self-care are intentional acts, so make then a priority this week. A change in your work routine does not have to be immense; small changes can create a huge payoff for your biology and psychology.

There are plenty of career mistakes to avoid, too, so that you can keep your wellness intact.

Try not to put your career ahead of your personal life, because your family and friends matter. This is all part of the work-life balance that allows you to be centered and grounded in your values. Do not blur the line between professional and personal life. Try not to follow someone else's career path; you can assess what is best for you and your family. Be honest with your boss if you have re-evaluated your career goals and want to reorient to a place that best fits your values and new goals. We must make mental health a priority as it spearheads our work and personal lives.

Become a mentor to ensure that emerging leaders are cared about and model the behaviors you wish to pass down to future generations. We must create emerging leaders that are mentally healthy. We will be known by what we create, and what we refuse to eradicate. We must educate for social, environmental, and economic sustainability. We must care for the planet and the people in it.

The wealth of all nations resides in air, water, soil, biodiversity, empathy, and hope. These are the sustaining wealth of the world.

Effective Communication & Conflict Resolution

Sustainable Leader Values

Administration, policies, procedures, resources, sustainability, details, data, dispatching, evaluating, managing, leading, planning, regulating, supervising, long-range planning, SDGs.

Sustainable Leader Stressors

Not following rules, untidiness, lack of records, haphazardness, lack of goals, lack of preparation, no sustainability, zero goals, no regulations.

What does this mean?

This means that when there is a breach of something that you value, then that will cause you a great deal of stress. Stress will lead to an imbalance in the biology of you and manifest into negative symptoms in one or two of your twelve biological systems. That, in turn, will affect the psychology, social, and spirit of you as well.

How can you talk to people that breach something that you value?

Resolution

BE composed and be administrative in the language you use. DO not say, "Why are you so detail-oriented?". The word "you" will signal blame and shame for the Sustainable leader. DO use the "I" statement and say, "I feel disappointed when you do not allow me to lead meetings".

HAVE progress, training, learning, regulating, standards.

👁 **Insight #7:** Make certain that you have the knowledge that gives you the credibility and empathy to conduct effective conversations and meetings:

1. I am knowledgeable about the United Nations Sustainable Development Goals (SDGs) 2030.
2. I know how to integrate the SDGs into what we do here at this company.
3. I am focused and clear on how to embed those goals on the individual, group, and company level.
4. Through empathy, we can make this world a better place for the next generation.
5. I appreciate diversity because I have found the missing link and have connected it with culture.

👍 **Tip #7:** Read Richard D. Lewis' "When Cultures Collide". And "Community-Based Global Learning" by Eric Hartman, Richard Kiely, Christopher Boettcher, and Jessica Friedrichs

🔭 **Tool #10:** Dr. Darla Deardorff, Founder of World Council on Intercultural & Global Competency and UNESCO Chair through Stellenbosch University, has published numerous works on global, sustainable, intercultural, and peaceable actions.
https://sites.duke.edu/darladeardorff/

Dr. Christa Olson has a framework that defines global as both a local and international phenomenon.
https://global-in-circle.org/our-framework/

YOUR TURN

1. Why is the Sustainable Leadership style important?
2. How can you incorporate it in the workplace?
3. How can you use it as a leader for strategic planning and succession?
4. How can you use it to create future leaders?
5. How does the list of sustainable goals make you more grateful?

"

We do not inherit the Earth from our ancestors, we borrow it from our children.

~Indigenous People's Proverb~

"

Chapter 12

Hands-Off Leadership
Activators: Observation & Reflection

Have you experienced these barriers to success? Lack of communication, disengagement, aloofness, detachment, coldness, disconnection, and disinterest.

This chapter discusses Hands-Off Leadership style, personality, preferences, and the environment in which to apply this approach. Hands-Off leadership is often referred to as Laissez-Faire in literature and is a topic of intense debate in many companies. For our intent and purpose, we refer to the Hands-Off leader more positively as one that is aware of work activities and events but does not directly wish to be involved. They trust and observe others to perform their job duties from the periphery. You will find that the Hands-Off leaders tend to have an Introversion personality trait.

Laissez-faire is a French word that translates into English as "leave alone". This implies allowing things to come and go as they like, so a laissez-faire leader would be someone with a "Hands-Off" approach to managing and leading but gets a bad reputation because the word 'laissez' is very close to the word 'lazy' in the brain. Depending on your schema, your bias can dictate a preference towards using and leading with the Hands-Off leadership style or accepting it from other leaders that demonstrate it.

What is your preference?

There are three distinct variables to consider in understanding the Hands-Off leadership style: personality, preference, and environment to ensure your readiness to work with and utilize this leadership style. While all three variables can be fluid and change over time, temperament (nature and disposition) does not. In earlier chapters, we discussed temperament as the nonchanging feature of personality. Therefore, a Hands-Off leader falls in the category of having the 'slow-to-warm-up' temperament, that develops into an introverted adult that does not require vast amounts of energy from the environment. They know this preference to be true and rely on their managers to work closely in achievement. You have come far in the book and can Connect The Dots to the fact that leaders come in all types, shapes, and sizes, to apply their traits and skills towards high performance, results, and success.

If you happen to work for a quiet leader, it is up to you to use your communication skills and ensure that your needs are met. You cannot change others, especially who your boss is, but you can undoubtedly change yourself in how you respond and adapt. Managers will be present and Hands-On to help you to adapt and perform. Here is a good adage: *My reaction to an event determines the outcome*! Now, say that three times in a row to allow it to sink in. Upskilling for adaptability is an important talent to work with all types of leadership styles.

The back brain will want to blame the leadership style, because your perception is that you feel you understand "everything". But there is more information that you are not privy to, therefore your perception will be solely based upon the information you have. It is you who will be held responsible for your comments and actions. So, we highly suggest you speak your truth, not necessarily your mind. Know the difference and learn the difference through self-discovery.

If your brain judges that leadership style which is not congruent with your preference, then you will be stuck with that label thru the back brain. But when you seek to understand and bring about a solution (the rational Frontal Lobe), the situation becomes much better. Be aware of your back brain that loves to complain; this is the default, so train your brain to reorient and bring about metacognition. This habit will work wonderfully for workplace communication. It will show your leader that you are not wasting their time complaining but are aware of your preferences and furthermore have the solutions to mitigate if there is an absence of communication.

The same goes for blaming, limiting thoughts, staying stuck in the past, resisting change, placing an unhealthy emphasis on impressing others, always needing to be right, and constantly needing other people's approval. Through awareness and intention, you can move away from the fixed mindset that wants to react and into the solution-oriented growth one that can help you to respond more realistically to the quiet leadership style. Again, your reaction to the circumstances will determine the outcome in activating success for yourself.

Depending on your perception of this leadership style, we invite you to look upon this quiet leadership style without bias. Be open to looking for the benefits of being and having a quiet leader. Their quiet approach is based on the belief that employees are capable and motivated to complete their tasks without constant guidance. Extroverts may need to learn to recognize their needs and ask for more guidance and involvement, while introverts may joyfully embrace this quiet style.

Here are some key characteristics and considerations associated with a Hands-Off leadership style, that comes from Kurt Lewin's research, that will help you to understand or adopt. As you read this list, think about a few that you can integrate in your work.

Autonomy: Leaders following a Hands-Off approach encourage autonomy among team members. They trust their team to make decisions and handle responsibilities independently.

Flexibility: Hands-Off leaders are often flexible and open to various working styles. They recognize that individuals may have different approaches to solving problems and completing tasks.

Communication: While Hands-Off leaders provide autonomy, they should maintain open lines of communication. Regular check-ins, feedback sessions, and updates ensure that everyone is on the same page and any issues can be addressed promptly.

Team Configuration: A Hands-Off approach may be more effective with a team of experienced and self-motivated individuals who can thrive with minimal guidance.

Decision-making: Leaders using this style may delegate decision-making authority to team members, trusting them to make appropriate choices within their areas of expertise.

Time Management: Hands-Off leaders should be mindful of time management and deadlines. While autonomy is encouraged, it's essential to ensure that tasks are completed within the required timeframe. Therefore, being completely Hands-Off is not an option.

Monitoring and Support: Periodic monitoring and support are crucial. Leaders should be available to provide guidance, resources, experience, and assistance when needed.

Risk of Miscommunication: One challenge of a Hands-Off style is the potential for miscommunication. Another is if team members misinterpret the lack of guidance as a lack of interest.

Empowerment: This leadership style aims to empower employees by giving them more freedom to use their skills and judgment to achieve goals. It can lead to increased job satisfaction and a sense of ownership among team members; especially for those who do not fair well with micromanaging, but just because people do not care for micromanaging does not mean that they are free from communicating. If you dislike micromanagement, then be sure that you are an excellent communicator.

Upskilling: This leadership style can foster skill development and growth as team members take on more responsibilities and challenges. It provides opportunities for learning, building expertise, and capacity, for the individual and also for the group.

What are the pros and cons of the Hands-Off leadership style?

It would be prudent to consider the pros and cons of Hands-Off leadership because it is common for highly motivated leaders with experience who focus on task completion to have intricate knowledge of what their team is working on, without being present and Hands-On.

The Hands-Off leader gives people more freedom to make choices and conduct their daily work. They trust that their people know what they are doing and have the capacity to meet deadlines.

Delegation can be ideal for people who are resourceful, creative, intelligent, innovative, dependable, and confident in their skill sets. Hands-Off leaders who use effective delegation can delegate tasks to the most qualified employee who has the right skills for that particular task. When you do this, it can help the team and improve efficiency. This means you will have to spend the time, initially, to get to know the skills and interests of your people! It always boils down to the people.

As long as teams efficiently complete tasks, those working with Hands-Off leadership can choose *how* they wish to accomplish their duties. This can help develop autonomy, self-confidence, and productivity, and is especially evidenced through remote work. Even though teams can make their own decisions, the Hands-Off leaders ensure that managers are present and prepared to provide feedback. And *this* is where you will have to become an active learner, encourage dialogue, and ensure understanding.

Every person has a distinct personality with traits and preferences. It takes the active development of an open mindset to be comfortable with a Hands-Off leadership style. Therefore, leaders should employ a personality assessment to ascertain which individuals on their teams would be satisfied with autonomy, self-monitoring, and minimal guidance. The system we use is True Colors at www. truecolors.com

You are self-leading all the time, even when you are leading others and being led. Self-leading is a process that occurs inside of you as you develop and grow, and as you help others to develop, grow, and change. Know who you are and what you are achieving within yourself. Comprehend how effective communication can affect your team's emotions and behaviors.

This type of leader is more common than most would like to admit. Introverts may prefer the quiet leader because they do not require a high amount of energy, but extroverts may automatically judge them because they fail to bring about much energy. Whatever your preference, a Hands-Off or Hands-On leader, remember to go back to the pillars of self-discovery, change readiness, and impact.

Change Management Insight

Your interpretation of the Quiet and Hands-Off style translates in through your Schema in the back brain as "they do not care." There are a hundred billion neurons in your brain and ~74K thoughts that come in and out of your brain each day. Some make sense, others are extraneous, and those thoughts can prevent you from staying in the present and in the rational frontal lobe. Your mind automatically drifts off to the past or to the future. Realize that thoughts are not facts.

Emotional self-regulation and intentional self-awareness can help you to gain control of your thoughts. Failure to control your thoughts can turn into negative feelings, anger, and regrettable actions. Tend to your thoughts and regulate them through the Frontal Lobe. Intentionally bring them from the emotional Limbic center to the rational frontal part of your brain. This will take much practice, where practice makes progress.

Recall that you are a product of your past schema. You are never a victim of your past. What you believe and assume becomes your biases that become your lived experience habitually. Your brain tends to remember things you have not accomplished versus those you have accomplished, which is called the Zeigarnik Effect. As heard on many deathbeds, your neurons wire together to pay more attention to what has not been done. The Zeigarnik Effect is subconscious and can creep in slowly and surely in your behaviors and actions. What you can do about this effect is to bring intention and focus to the things you have accomplished!

There will always be a list of things to do, so learn not to stress about getting things done all in one day. Planning, prioritizing, and communication are great skills that can help you to high performance. And let go of the thinking that does not serve you. Don't get stuck. Remember the Beatles song, "Let It Be," and play it now.

You have incredible power to activate success at work and life through what you give attention to!

Effective Communication & Conflict Resolution

Hands-Off Leader Values

Independence, time away, when you bring them some good news, when you don't bother them with the little things, decorum, modesty

Hands-Off Leader Stressors

Clinginess, interdependence, bad news, little things that don't matter in the long run, crazy behaviors that belong on the dance floor, party atmosphere

What does this mean?

This means that when there is a breach of something that you value, then that will cause you a great deal of stress and ill feelings to come up. Stress will lead to an imbalance in the biology of you and manifest into negative symptoms in one or two of your twelve biological systems. That, in turn, will affect the psychology, social, and spirit of you as well.

How can you talk to people that breach something that you value?

Resolution

BE low in your tone of voice and speak slowly. DO not say, "You never pay attention to me!". When you use the word "you" to a Quiet leader, they will misinterpret you as being reliant on, insecure, and controlling. Instead, a better way is to use "I" statements. Say, "I feel _____ when you _____". For example, "I feel discounted, overlooked, and disregarded when you ignore my emails".

HAVE freedom, time to contemplate, check individual and teamwork, creativity.

👁 **Insight #8:** Take time to contemplate and reflect:

1. I check myself to make sure my behavior is appropriate for the situation.
2. I know how to motivate myself to help myself grow and allow others to teach themselves to do the same.
3. I am never apathetic; I show more patience than others.
4. At times, I am a macro-manager who allows others time to come to their conclusions.
5. There is great power in being calm and collected.

Tip #8 Make a list of all the things you have accomplished since you were born. You will notice that you have accomplished a vast number of things. Be proud of yourself and have the confidence to know that if you were successful in the past, then you will be successful in the future.

Neuro Tip #5: Your brain reflects what you eat, think, and do. The brain eats 25% of your daily intake, because it has to keep up the energy it takes ~74 thousand thoughts to weave in and out of the brain. Your brain needs fat for neurons to go through their action potential communication that occurs from one neuron to another. The degradation of the fat that is on the neuron is called Multiple Sclerosis. Eat plenty of nuts and get plenty of sunshine.

Tool #11: Create an activity where the team can analyze their individual accomplishments, then compare and contrast similarities, differences, and patterns. You can use the Dictionary of Occupational Titles (DOT) or O*NET to view the relationships between tasks and skills. These sources come from the national Department of Labor (DOL) www.dol.gov

YOUR TURN

1. Are you a Quiet, Hands-Off leader?
2. What are the benefits of being a Hands-Off leader?
3. Think of a situation where this style can be particularly useful.
4. Think of a situation where this style would not be a good choice.

"

Invisible threads are the strongest ties.

~Friedrich Nietzsche~

"

Chapter 13

Co-Elevation Leadership
Activators: Team Unity & Empathy

Have you experienced these barriers to success? Uncooperative culture, inflexibility, stubbornness, rigidity, one-track-mindedness, lack of team empathy and unity, misunderstandings, struggles, errors, confusion, uncertainty, and disconnectedness.

This chapter discusses the strong suits of the Co-Elevation Leader who is highly cooperative and loves to collaborate and empower teams. Have you noticed how much the world is plagued in finding normalcy in the workplace? The "New Normal Phenomenon", compounded by war and destruction, has created a rise in turf issues as individuals, teams, organizations, and genders begin protecting their professional and philosophical (values)"turf".

The innovative approach of Co-Elevation may be a challenge for traditional systems have created departmental silos; working on and managing only the tasks that are in their domain. There were many times where we were told to "stay in your lane", but we would like to encourage a shift in interdepartmental communication to utilize all human and AI resources available to create cohesiveness and trust.

Turf wars can cause competition among departments for prestige, credibility with a target population, or - worst of all - with funding, and can result in fragmented workplaces.

This can mean individuals asserting "ownership" of information, ideas, equipment, or administrative procedures, and it can cause disastrous splits among staff, ineffectiveness, and inefficient operations, especially in virtual and hybrid work situations.

In resolving these issues, Keith Ferrazzi (2017), presented his Co-Elevation Theory as a set of behaviors that emphasizes collaboration, teamwork, and shared decision-making among group members that encourage each other to elevate their performance and results.

His approach is rooted in the belief that a collective effort is more effective than individual contributions alone. Co-Elevation leaders strive to create an inclusive and supportive environment where team members feel empowered and motivated to work together toward common goals and is initiated by the C-suite as reported by Forbes.

In supporting this relevant Co-Elevation Theory, we found it to be even more effective to couple it with our construct of *Empathy-Ethic* to create a highly operative Co-Elevation leadership style. Based upon the current condition of transitions, we invite you to apply this approach to build teams and create cohesive groups in your organization.

Our Co-Elevation leadership style encompasses features that can help a leader to co-elevate without the use of powerful hierarchies and ego assertion. Our foundational elements to accomplish this style are:

Communication: Co-Elevation leaders encourage open communication among team members. They promote an atmosphere where ideas are shared, and everyone's input is valued. Effective communication is a cornerstone of peaceful workplaces. The use of appropriate language through words and tone.

Recognition of Team Strengths: Cooperative leaders recognize and leverage the unique strengths and skills of each team member.

They encourage individuals to contribute their expertise to the overall success of the team. Allowing people to contribute through their interests. Be mindful when and where people want to stretch and grow.

Focus on Team Goals: Co-Elevation leaders help the team, as a unit, understand the bigger picture and how each member contributes to the overall success of the group by achieving collective goals. They help support individuals to storm, norm, and form.

Flexibility: Co-Elevation leaders are adaptable and open to new ideas. They understand that situations may change, and flexibility is essential to navigate challenges and capitalize on opportunities. Here, the leader will be mindful to individual, and team change readiness.

Conflict Resolution: In a Co-Elevation leadership style, conflicts are addressed constructively. Leaders encourage open dialogue to resolve issues and promote a positive team dynamic. Co-Elevation leadership ensures that information flows freely within the team, and they are skilled at active listening, providing feedback, and fostering a positive communication culture through an Empathy-Ethic.

Building Trust in Teams: Trust is a crucial element of cooperation. Leaders in this style work to build and maintain trust among team members by being transparent, reliable, and demonstrating a commitment to the team's success. You cannot show empathy without building trust.

Continuous Improvement: Co-Elevation leaders encourage a culture of continuous improvement. They seek feedback, analyze performance, and are open to making adjustments to enhance team effectiveness, towards sustainable impact. Allow Co-Elevation leadership to be a practice where team members work together across departments and sectors to make decisions and keep their organization thriving. We encourage this leadership style, especially post-pandemic, to replace the standard top-down leadership method of the past that can reassure the "we" mindset.

Empowerment: Co-Elevation leaders empower team members by providing them with the necessary resources, support, and autonomy to accomplish their tasks. This helps boost confidence and motivation within the team. You cannot empower people without showing empathy.

Co-Elevation leadership approach offers many benefits to employees and leaders. In the C-suite, it can foster a sense of unity among executives, allowing them to make effective business decisions, maintain core values, and strategically address relevant issues.

We would love to see this leadership style in practice through the *Empathy-Ethic* that allows for consideration and compassion. Empathy is the marker that defines psychopathy, because a lack of empathy is the assessor for socio and psychopathy. CEO's that lack empathy will be unable to gather a set of behaviors required to perform a Co-Elevation style. Most people have the capacity to cultivate a certain set of behaviors and skills to achieve camaraderie between human-to-human interactions as well as human to machine interactions.

Workplaces must embrace the Co-Elevation leadership style now more than ever before due to the interconnectedness of humans and machines. We want you to view AI as a team member that can help you to achieve team goals. An AI team member may look like "Apps, digital tools, and big data" that can be used for team decision-making and cross-functional efficiency.

Video conferencing, instant messaging, digital project management, time management, and customized operational programs allow employees in different departments—and even in different physical locations—to actively engage with one another. Products like Google's G-Suite—which allows files to be easily created, edited, and distributed among teams—allow employees to share ideas and opinions virtually.

These products help embrace remote working and the gig economy. Research shows that employees seek ways to stay connected whether or not they are co-located. As a result, organizations that offer such digital communication tools will be in high demand.

For example, a Deloitte study reported that workers were 17 percent "more satisfied with their workplace culture when they had access to effective digital collaboration tools." Similarly, the study found that 46 percent of professionals found that such tools created a sense of transparency within their organization for collaborative communication.

Studies show that professionals today are acquiring many strengths in the workplace that have applications beyond their everyday tasks. Co-Elevation leaders embrace these strengths— from durable skills like strategic thinking, *Empathy-Ethic*, and communication to job-specific skills such as coding, project management, or analytics to apply them cross-departmentally. The Empathy-Ethic is our social responsibility. We are responsible for developing dynamic and agile teams, with humans and AI.

We believe Co-Elevation leadership becomes most critical in organizations that are further in their digital transformation, including those that have digitized most of their operations using technology such as artificial intelligence and machine learning.

AI and machine learning software are commonly used to collect, organize, and present business-related data to industry leadership teams. This results in vast information from which executives must draw conclusions and make impactful, data-based decisions.

In these scenarios, leadership teams that do not act collaboratively risk making choices that might not align with their overall mission or might otherwise not consider the needs of every department within the organization.

Recognize the potential impact of human-machine interconnectedness and cooperative methods in the workplace (Carl Zangerl, 2019), Northeastern Lab for Inclusive Entrepreneurship.

Do Your Research: One of the best ways to learn about interconnectedness is to observe a leader that uses the Co-Elevation style. Comb through your professional network to try and identify a connection who might work under this type of manager or who is one themselves. Depending on your relationship, you might ask to meet up and discuss their experience with collaboration, focusing most specifically on how this practice has impacted their sense of unity as an organization, their personal and team productivity, and their overall workplace culture.

If you don't feel you have anyone in your network who can provide this insight, try tackling your research from a broader angle. Use LinkedIn to search for executives that embrace modernization to further benefit individuals, teams, and organizations.

Practice Empathy in Your Workplace: Although it may take time for people to transition from another leadership method to one of collaboration, there are a few key steps that Zangerl outlines that can set you on the path to success.

Articulate a Clear Vision: Zangerl explains it is up to an organization's leaders to set "a clear vision that collaboration is going to be part of the organization's culture." Without that standard, professionals will have difficulty knowing what they're working toward in collaboration and will lack the inspiration to break boundaries.

Lead by example: To inspire your team to operate collaboratively, it's important to demonstrate what you'd like to see at the executive level. "People within an organization model their behavior on what they see leaders doing," he says. "So, if they see leaders setting and modeling collaborative behavior, then it's more likely they're going to expect that from members of their teams."

Create the right environment: Collaborative leaders are team-oriented, good listeners, and, perhaps most significantly, able to create a collaborative environment in their workplace. This environment should be filled with trust, transparency, and a focus on relationship-building—a combination that will naturally set the tone for shared ideas and perspectives.

Never stop learning: Enrolling in degree and certificate programs is an excellent way for any professional to gain skills and advance in their career. Recall that the brain learns. That's what it does best! So, always ask yourself how you manage your learning and how you manage your learning in teams.

Use the pillars of *Self-Discovery, Change Readiness, and Sustainable Impact* to activate success, because change takes time through logical, incremental steps.

Co-Elevation leaders can support training programs for younger generations of emerging leaders, thus assuring continuity and commitment to pertinent issues the younger generations are addressing. This is a helpful suggestion that can increase self and situational awareness, especially when there are rotating professionals, as in professional associations and committees.

In our experience, emerging leaders are enthusiastic to take on leadership roles. They see the status and money as a great achievement; however, it has been our experience that they have the unconscious tendency to be impatient in climbing the ladder and look around for an escalator to the top. We encourage emerging leaders to observe and learn to build capacity; ask questions; and better assess how and where they can serve. We cannot emphasize how important our Essential Questions are for everyone to become conscious of their behaviors and how they affect the people around them. We also encourage human resource managers to create leadership opportunities that do not require five years or more of experience, thereby creating opportunities for young professionals who have the natural talent to lead.

Empowerment requires the inclusion of all stakeholders - anyone with an interest or involvement in problem-solving and decision-making not only prepares potential and capacity-building but leads to people taking more responsibility to care about what they do. It leads to better functioning in every sphere. If you value relationships, go one step further and ask yourself how you build them without getting disappointed. Cultivate a great vocabulary for emotional self-expression; the inability to express the precise feeling and value will result in zero collaboration.

Co-Elevation leadership breeds elevated leadership, resulting in performance success. This, in turn, creates more willingness to find common ground, tackle new issues, find more effective wide-reaching solutions, and do much more than is required by an individual or team.

The Co-Elevation leader helps disproportionate groups (females and elders) to make authentic connections with one another. Sometimes, leaders get jealous of the people that they have hired, but we have not witnessed any leader with a Co-Elevation style to display jealousy. Anyway, please do not become a jealous leader. You do not want people to view you as a competitor or enemy. You want to create a psychologically safe space where all genders, ages, and races feel valued.

Female leadership refers to the presence, influence, and impact of women in positions of leadership within various domains, including business, politics, academia, and non-profit organizations. Historically, women have faced barriers and challenges in attaining leadership roles, but there has been a growing recognition of the importance of female perspectives in leadership. Only 15% of the Fortune 500 leaders are female; and is up from 7% back in 2002.

Here are some key points and considerations related to female leadership:

Inclusion: Having women in leadership positions contributes to a variety of perspectives, skills, and ideas, which can enhance decision-making, problem-solving, innovation, and creativity. You can still have the "old boys' network" from the past, but we suggest having three groups that are termed: Male think tank; Female think tank; Bicultural think tank; and All-inclusive think tank. You get the idea.

Break Stereotypes: Female leaders can challenge traditional gender stereotypes and serve as mentors and role models for emerging leaders, especially in the Eastern Hemisphere. Their success can inspire other women and girls to pursue leadership roles in different fields. There are more females enrolled in college degrees than males at this time (according to PewResearch. org), so we need to use their talents. We are all for diversity in leadership roles, but make sure that the diversity is also coupled with competence. Boards that insist on hiring diversity to meet company requirements are missing out on the most important factor of all: are they capable, through knowledge/experience/ skills for the leadership role?

Did you know that there are positive and negative stereotypes? Some cultures are viewed as negative and others as positive. For example: "Indians are good at math", is a positive stereotype. Be aware of stereotyping and bias; especially in the boardroom.

Leadership Styles: Research suggests that women may bring different leadership styles to the table, often emphasizing authenticity. However, it is essential to recognize that leadership styles can vary widely among individual personalities, regardless of gender. Be cautious of a double standard. For example, "he is assertive – she is aggressive"; "he has good strategy – she is has tactics". You get the picture.

Barriers and Challenges: Despite progress, women still face barriers and challenges in reaching leadership positions and equal salaries. These can include gender bias, confirmation bias, fixed thinking, stereotypes, lack of or unequal opportunities, and work-life balance issues. Ensure that there is appropriate training in these areas so that people feel supported and valued.

Advocacy and Support: Advocacy for gender equality is in the SDG 2030 goals list. We want you to be supportive of implementing policies that are crucial for promoting female leadership. This includes initiatives such as: mentorship programs, leadership training, and policies that address work-life balance and workplace wellness. The obvious here is that females have the reproductive system that can carry a baby, and males do not, therefore this fact should not be held against them when they need to take time to birth and bond with their baby.

Measuring Progress: Organizations and societies often measure progress in terms of gender diversity at all levels, including leadership. Metrics such as the representation of women in leadership roles, pay equity, and career advancement opportunities are important indicators. The File Drawer Phenomenon" is unethical and cannot serve this world in the manner by which the scientific method was ethically created (sciencedirect.com).

Legal and Policy Frameworks: Legal and policy frameworks play a significant role in promoting gender equality. Legislation and organizational policies that address discrimination, harassment, and provide equal opportunities are essential for fostering female leadership. This is where career developers, employment counselors, and human resource managers need to come together for dialogue! To create viable policies that benefit the individual, team, and organization, and all genders, colors, and cultures.

Global Perspectives: The status of female leadership varies across different cultures and regions of the world. In some countries, there has been significant progress, while in others, challenges persist. For example, Indira Gandhi was a peaceful leader that believed in M. Gandi's (same name, but not her father) philosophy of passive resistance to non-violence. She was assassinated for her beliefs. Understanding and addressing cultural factors is crucial for promoting gender equality on a global scale.

Intersectionality: It's important to consider the intersectionality of gender with other factors such as race, ethnicity, sexual orientation, and socio-economic background. Women's experiences in leadership are diverse, and efforts to promote equality should be inclusive of all identities and biculturality as well.

We cannot emphasize that the antecedent to equality, diversity, and inclusion is always competency and capability, first, for a leadership role!

Promoting Co-Elevation with humans, AI, disproportionate groups, and female leadership is not just about increasing the number of women in leadership positions but also creating environments that are accepting and free from gender-based discrimination. Achieving equity in leadership is a complex and ongoing process that involves an Empathy-Ethic on all three levels of individual-team-organization.

Change Management Insight

Co-elevators want to ensure that everyone is heard, a virtue of moral excellence. Make sure you distinguish between wanting the best and people giving their best. There is a marketable difference; the former refers to perfection, and the latter relates to individual ability at their optimal level of capability. We're connecting the dots here between capability and needs theories.

This is precisely why performance evaluations are biased. Because while you give your very best, it may be compared to someone else's best, and this comparison is not fair or impartial.

Make the change by: looking at all sides; getting comfortable with contradictions; understanding that two conflicting things can co-exist; attempting to find a balanced solution; viewing things as a whole and connected through points.

The "New Normal Phenomenon" is not exclusively about the individual, team, system, strategic planning, or succession. It is about showing genuine concern for people and implementing mutualistic policies that benefit everyone.

Effective Communication & Conflict Resolution

Co-Elevation Leader Values

Acknowledgement, compassion, democracy, belongingness, co-hesiveness, commonality, integrity, listening, mentoring, moti-vating, supporting

Co-Elevation Leader Stressors

Confrontation, conflict, rudeness, dictatorships, inequality, unfairness, disrespect

What does this mean?

This means that when there is a breach of something that you value, then that will cause you a great deal of stress. Stress will lead to an imbalance in the biology of you and manifest into negative symptoms in one or two of your twelve biological systems. That, in turn, will affect the psychology, social, and spirit of you as well.

How can you talk to people that breach something that you value?

Resolution

BE inclusive in the language you use. When you say "you do this and you do that", it sounds accusatory and harsh to a Conscious leader. *DO* use "I" statements. Say, "I feel _____ when you _____". For example, "I feel picked on and singled out when you throw a barrage of 'why' questions at me in meetings".

HAVE cooperation, teamwork, communication, coordination.

👁 **Insight #9:** Here are a few things to think about:

1. If I do not allow my team to re-do the work, then I would be denying a growth mindset that is imperative for them to create.
2. Improvement and change are processes that are necessary to add value to the work that people do daily.
3. Through discussion and reflection, I convey that it is important to learn, upskill, and micro-credential for professional development.
4. Asking the team for clarity builds trust.
5. We can create team traditions through a shared responsibility to celebrate our achievements.

🖐 **Tip #9:** As you work together to understand each other on a team, work to build trust and help each one to win. Show respect to everyone and engage them to get to know each other so you can work hard and have fun in the process. Believe in yourself, but also believe in your teammates.

The workplace is changing. You may find that the skills that you have been working for are no longer needed or have been replaced by AI. This is a good reason to get micro-credentials (certificates in a particular niche).

You may find a situation arise where you will have to help the person that you have labeled as 'the bad guy'. You may find that 'the bad guy' ends up helping you in some way. You may find that the star in your narrative is always you.

🖐 **Neuro Tip #6:** Your brain learns through games and music. Put on a favorite playlist while you are working: the first song can be a song that lifts your spirits, the second song can be one that motivates you, the third song can be one that looks at the world positively, the fourth song can be one that helps you concentrate. You can put these on a loop and enjoy.

Tool #12: Co-Elevation tools for hybrid teams by Keith Ferrazzi at www.coelevation.com

University of Berkeley tools and techniques for team building. https://hr.berkeley.edu/sites/default/files/bpm_team_building_toolkit_2019.pdf

Forbes magazine: https://www.forbes.com/sites/kathycaprino/2020/05/22/co-elevation-how-to-achieve-positive-leadership-impact-without-pre-established-authority/?sh=80fa81e5f932

YOUR TURN

1. Where would you decide to use the Co-Elevation leadership style?
2. Why don't people cooperate in the workplace?
3. How would you enhance cooperation?
4. Have you had a collaborative leader before? Provide an example of their leadership. What did you like or dislike about that style?
5. What is the importance of collaborative leadership, and how would cooperation lead to success for everyone?
6. Think of a time when you were uncooperative. How did that serve you?

"

Someone who feels appreciated will always do much more than what is expected of them.

~Lao Tzu~

"

Chapter 14

Evaluative Leadership
Activators: Measurement & Improvement

Have you experienced these barriers to success? Closed-mindedness, lack of improvement, flexibility, and effort, rigidity, system inefficiency, work-life balance, ineffectiveness, lack of quantitative or qualitative data, no learning.

This chapter discusses the Evaluative leader that is adroit in assessment and measurement of data collection and data interpretation. It is the evaluation that allows for change readiness, change management, and continuous improvement through training and development.

Perhaps you have found yourself reflecting and evaluating while driving; sometimes, your brain goes into autopilot where muscle memory takes over and allows you to wander inward. Recall when you drove and arrived at your destination, but you didn't remember how you got there. Just as this autopilot example, organizational leaders can fall into certain processes and practices that become habits, bringing them undesired results. Just like driving, consider the meetings that you lead or attend. Are you on business autopilot?

If you are on autopilot, then things need to change, because the results that you are getting are the same. Begin by thinking of a leader that led you in a team. Did they value emotional intelligence through self-awareness, positive self-talk, openness, and active listening skills? A thoughtful slant can help you naturally develop a keen understanding of the people in your team through knowledge, theories, and experience. You will need to learn and unlearn for the sake of the individual, the team, and the organization, because leadership is also about human improvement and flourishing.

Let's explore how Evaluative Leadership style takes into account these principles by evaluating behaviors that affect interactions. When you take the time to ask yourself questions such as "What worked, what did not work, what can I do differently next time, etc." then you can have a continuous improvement mindset. These are keys to reducing internal and external barriers regarding change as improvement.

You can create a mindset of evaluation and especially metacognitive examination by asking yourself: How do I think? Why do I think the way I do? Why do I react? How can I respond? The purpose of metacognition for an evaluative leader is to assess *how* you think and why, as well as the link to the **Four Essential Questions** (as stated in the 'how do I stay there?'). When you think about it, evaluation is about learning where learning is akin to measuring and building capacity.

Evaluative leadership involves assessment of performance and outcomes of individuals or teams. This leader emphasizes evaluation, feedback, and decision-making based on assessments.

Quantitative assessment and measurement can look like this:

Performance Assessment: Leaders using an evaluative style regularly assess the performance of their team members. This involves setting clear expectations, monitoring progress, and providing feedback on individual and team accomplishments.

Constructive Criticism: Relevant feedback is the basis of evaluative leadership. Leaders using this style are likely to offer constructive criticism on both strengths and weaknesses. Their feedback is specific, timely, and focused on helping individuals and/or teams enhance their work performance.

Data-Driven Decision-Making: An evaluative leader relies on quantitative data and metrics to make informed decisions. They analyze information to decide on strategies, evaluate the effectiveness of strategies, and identify trends to create a game plan and guide future actions.

Goal Setting: Clear and measurable goals are set by evaluative leaders. These goals serve as benchmarks for performance evaluation and progress that can be regularly reviewed against these objectives.

Accountability: There is a strong sense of accountability within an evaluative leadership framework. Team members are held responsible for meeting expectations and consequences that are tied to high performance outcomes.

Continuous Improvement: Leaders employing an evaluative style encourage a culture of continuous improvement. They seek ways to enhance processes, foster innovation, and drive efficiency based on the evaluations and feedback received. Do not be afraid of evaluation. Be open to receive constructive feedback and ask how you can improve if your performance evaluation is not to your liking. In research, self-report is always skewed by our brain, so it is important to listen to your leaders, managers, and mentors. When you are in a team, please ask for help instead of doing nothing at all!

Decision-Making Authority: Evaluative leaders often retain decision-making authority, as their decisions are informed by assessments and evaluations. This style may not involve as much delegation of decision-making power compared to other leadership styles. We want to interject a word here about internal and external customers: of course, you are providing excellent customer service to your external (outside the organization) customers, however a really good answer to memorize is "I do not have the authority to make that decision. But I will put you in touch with someone who does or can help you for this issue". It's a life-saver, believe us!

Adaptability: An evaluative leader is adaptable and open to adjusting strategies based on the results of evaluations. If a particular approach is not yielding the desired outcomes, they are willing to make changes to improve results. What a breath of fresh air! Be willing to reorient, reset, and reassess change at any time in the process.

It's important to note that while an evaluative leadership style can be effective in promoting accountability and driving performance improvements, it may also be perceived as demanding. The activation of success for this style depends on the leader's ability to balance critiques and evaluations with support and fostering a positive and growth-oriented environment. Additionally, different situations and contexts may require leaders to employ a variety of leadership styles based on the needs and composure of a team. Especially when it comes to performance reviews.

Why do people fear performance reviews?

Let's face it, people need their jobs. They need income to pay their bills. They come to work to do the best job that they can. Not a single client of ours has ever wanted to go into a workplace to mess up. People want to find a job that has meaning and purpose for a myriad of reasons (family, honor, student loans, actualization). People understand that performance evaluation is a necessary element of business. However, they are also aware that evaluation programs are built with inherent bias. Bias through the observations of the manager, and bias through the AI program that has a certain rule embedded into the program. As a leader, you must be fair and check your bias. Check yourself through all the tools in this book for self-discovery and if you have the power to change systems, please think about it.

Some people have a fear or a phobia of evaluation but are doing exceptionally well. They have been conditioned in a negative manner through childhood experiences to view evaluations as punishment and not information for reflection.

Most leaders can attribute their growth and success to both internal and external factors. The inability to attribute success internally is the crux of the **Impostor Phenomenon** or IP. Nowadays, it's been popularized by social media as being "impostor syndrome". The original researchers and psychologists were doctors Pauline Clance and Suzanne Imes (1978) who coined the term "Impostor Phenomenon" when they noticed their graduate students doubting and hesitating to attribute their success. It is important to denote that this is not a diagnosis but rather an occurrence in one's life. "Impostors" secretly feel fraudulent despite ample evidence on the contrary. People that experience such feelings will often attribute their success to external factors such as: right place-right time, certain people, luck, or other external things.

IP is a big deal because it is about self-doubt and the inability to attribute success to the internal self. Famous leaders and celebrities (Sheryl Sandberg, Tom Hanks, Tina Fey) have admitted their impostor feelings. As a leader, you must become aware of feelings of doubt. If doubt creeps in, through the back brain, your anxiety will increase, and your self-efficacy will decrease (Ives Dissertation, 2012). Through awareness and intention, positive self-talk and slow breathing, you can take control of the doubtful thoughts that sneak in through the back brain. Question them and try to bring them to the front brain where rational thinking can help you gain better insights on why, where, and when doubt insists on taking over your brain. You can, then, slowly and surely, condition yourself to raise your self-efficacy and lower your anxiety through replacing the negative with the positive.

Evaluation, reflection, and intention can help you move away from doubt and uncertainty to trust and a more realistic attribution of and activation of success. These can help you design a work and life action plan for moving forward from where you are, and not someone else. Do not compare yourself to someone else. Everyone is in a different chapter in their lives. The good part is that not everyone has the same limitations, so defining self-limitations should not be viewed as a weakness to give up on but as information for growth, change, and improvement.

Improvement requires observation over reaction. As you observe yourself, interrupt negative habits and patterns that cause you to become reactive. You will gain so much insight from carefully deciphering (and journaling) what you see, hear, and feel, what you give attention to, and the meaning that you attach to these things.

Feelings of self-doubt can be debilitating and can easily lead to stress, so ask yourself:

1. What did I see?
2. What did I hear?
3. How did it make me feel?
4. What values breach did you experience?
5. Does it make a difference?

You can certainly reduce the bias you have against yourself. Through awareness and intentionally bring yourself from the back to the front brain to have greater locus of control to regain certainty and self-efficacy. Your willingness to change can lead to growth, which is much better than judgment in the happenstance of life.

View evaluation as an opportunity for growth and change:

1. What brings out your potential?
2. Where do you notice your potential being utilized the most?

3. Where and when are most motivated?
4. How do you learn by yourself?
5. How do you learn in the presence of others?
6. What mode of communication do you prefer?
7. What personality traits help or hinder your success?

As you evaluate yourself, also gauge others through their happenstance. Understanding where others are coming from, their lifespan stages, and how they think and feel can help you adapt your responses to meet their needs. Individuals will immediately sense mutual respect and civility, thereby trusting you.

Symbiosis can benefit cooperation and understanding diversity and cultural humility. You may think you have no time to evaluate, but skipping this step would increase risk liability. Make it a habit to evaluate yourself and reflect daily, monthly, and yearly. Write down what worked (the pluses) and what didn't (the deltas). What would you do differently next time? Once you get into the habit of evaluating, reflecting, and measuring, it will become second-hand and have much value to how you do things at work.

As leaders, we have conducted hundreds of training courses to show people how to incorporate Reflective Evaluation into their current leadership style, approach, and in performance reviews. We accomplish this through three success *activators*: impartiality, no judgment, and confidentiality.

Reflection training as a part of your professional development workshops, roundtables, and discussions will allow people to express themselves authentically and build reflective workplace cultures by fostering reflective learning communities that encompass the appropriate organizational culture that you desire to sustain.

You can further explore models of continuous improvement that include:

Kaizen: Kaizen is a Japanese term that means "change for better" or "continuous improvement." It is often associated with continuous improvement efforts and involves making small, incremental changes to processes or systems.

Plan-Do-Check-Act (PDCA) Cycle: The PDCA cycle, also known as the Deming Cycle or Shewhart Cycle, is a four-step management method used for continuous improvement. It involves planning a change, implementing it, monitoring its effects, and then adjusting the plan accordingly.

Plan: Identify and analyze the problem or opportunity for improvement.
Do: Implement the plan on a small scale.
Check: Evaluate the results of the change to determine its effectiveness.
Act: If successful, implement the change on a larger scale. If not, adjust the plan and repeat the cycle.

Employee Involvement: When employees are engaged, they become encouraged and motivated to work together. Teams are often the ones closest to the processes and short-term tasks and can provide valuable insights into potential improvements along timelines.

Data-Driven Decision-Making: Organizations use data and metrics to measure performance, identify areas for improvement, and track the impact of changes. Data-driven decision-making is crucial for assessing the effectiveness of continuous improvement initiatives.

Standardization: While continuous improvement involves making changes, it also emphasizes the importance of standardizing successful processes. Standardization helps maintain and replicate improvements across the organization.

Training and Development: Providing employees with the necessary skills and knowledge is essential for successful continuous improvement. Training programs can empower employees to contribute to and lead improvement initiatives

They say values start in the home; and we say that values for respect start within the company. It is our belief that the single best way to improve an organization is how people talk to each other internally. We encourage companies to adopt an internal customer philosophy, just as they have for external customers. Measurement of success begins valuing people, but also encouraging people to show value to each other through respect. Success is often driven by and assessed through a commitment to meeting and exceeding customer expectations. If understanding external customer needs is essential for identifying improvement opportunities, then it should begin internally first.

We believe that both internal and external customers require excellent customer service. When you receive a phone call or email from an internal customer, respond as you would for the external customer. There is a value here: respect everyone regardless of who they are and treat each person professionally. People are not an interruption; we are interdependent at work and life.

Improvement, measurement, and assessment is not a one-time event but rather an ongoing, ingrained aspect of organizational culture. By fostering a culture of evaluation, individuals, teams, and organizations can adapt to changing circumstances, increase efficiency, and achieve sustained success, through cross-functional, top-down, and down-top respect.

Change Management Insight

According to Pew Research, Millennials surpassed Generation Xers in 2015 as the largest generational cohort in American workplaces. Millennials look closely at the quality and candor of leadership and management they will work for and are quite vocal about that.

They are unlike their parents, who had a fearful loyalty to a company, sacrificing their needs and values only to get a gold watch at the end of three decades. Gen Z want leaders who can inspire and support them and help to shape their career path. Hence, the company must also have career developers and employment counselors on staff! Gen Z will lose respect for a leader who solely checks boxes; they want someone who measures *and* cares.

Every generation can benefit from an evaluative and reflective leader who can role-model behaviors with depth and meaning that comes from a place of genuine interest and altruism.

Effective Communication & Conflict Resolution

Evaluative Leader Values

Reflection, evaluation, contemplation, observation, appraisal, review, change

Evaluative Leader Stressors

Lack of reflection, no evaluation, no contemplation, no assessment, no reviews, procrastination, lack of organization, inefficiency

What does this mean?

This means that when there is a breach of something that you value, then that will cause you a great deal of stress. Stress will lead to an imbalance in the biology of you and manifest into negative symptoms in one or two of your twelve biological systems. That, in turn, will affect the psychology, social, and spirit of you as well.

How can you talk to people that breach something that you value?

Resolution

BE observant and listen. *DO* not use the word "you", because it will make the Reflective leader feel that you are inefficient. Instead, a better way is to use "I" statements. Say, "I feel _____ when you _____". For example, "I feel confused and hurt when you evaluate me so harshly!".

Create an atmosphere of respect and consideration, so this is what you can also HAVE.

👁 **Insight #10:** Here are a few items for self-leading and leading others:

1. Can we spend a larger portion of the budget for cultural humility and interculturalism trainings?
2. We all tell ourselves stories that we genuinely believe to be true; that's why listening to other people's stories is so important so we can disrupt our habitual patterns of thinking.
3. Putting opinions aside while listening to another person can allow you to alleviate bias.
4. We cannot rescue people because they are not powerless. You can motivate them to realize that they can help themselves and help them to achieve their goals and dreams.
5. A person who has experienced injustice feels the same as someone who has been physically beaten. Therefore, even if your opinion may be that it is trivial, you must be cognizant that it is certainly not trivial to them.
6. Meet people where they are, not where you are.
7. Everyone you meet knows something you don't. It's your job to become interested enough to ask the right questions to prompt their knowledge.

👆 **Tip #10:** Be careful of the power you have as a leader when you conduct performance evaluations. Be aware of how you are thinking and what you are believing about the person. Think about your intention in how you want to mark the evaluation without bias and fear.

👆 **Neuro Tip #7:** Thinking entails many things: logic, clarity, significance, accuracy, and relevance. Your brain needs for things to make sense through clarification, meaning, and importance. When you cultivate Critical Thinking Skills, your brain begins to analyze, understand, evaluate, apply, and create. When you delve into Metacognition, you begin to think about how and why you think the way you do.

Tool #13: Use the True Colors inventory that can help you in assessing your personality and preferences. You can find out if you are a Green, Blue, Gold, or Orange personality at www. trucolorsintl.com.

YOUR TURN

1. Do you believe that you are fulfilling your potential? Why or why not?
2. Are you intrinsically or extrinsically motivated?
3. How do you prefer to learn new things?
4. Do you like learning new things with others?
5. How often are you seeking input?
6. Do you ask for help? Why or why not?
7. Have you ever experienced the Impostor Phenomenon? Where and why? What did you do to alleviate your self-doubt?

❝

Have a bias toward action –
let's see something happen now.
You can break that big plan into small steps
and take the first step right away.

~ Indira Gandhi ~

❞

Chapter 15

Hope Leadership
Activators: Optimism & Strength

Have you experienced these barriers to success? Lack of empathy, lack of vision, pessimism, cynicism, negativity, distrust, disrespect, doubt, hopelessness, and discouragement.

Through our past shared world crisis experiences, we were brought together through fragile bonds of vulnerability that never existed in the workplace before. The traumatic experiences have remained strong in our workplaces and psyches. This chapter supports optimism for the future where the Hope-Centered Leader can embrace empathy, shared vision, and trust to move us forward. We emphasize Hope Theory by Drs. Spencer Niles and Norm Amundsen (2019).

The definition of hope is personal and unique to every leader but has some common elements between all leadership styles and behaviors. According to Merriam-Webster's definition, hope is best expressed by individuals who "cherish a desire with anticipation: to want something to happen or be true." Therefore, it is based upon a person's perspective, and we know that perspectives can differ from one person to another, from one leader to another. Hope is something you create for yourself, team, and company culture. A Hope-Centered Leader focuses on awareness and intention to build hope as the foundation for this leadership style.

Hope is a feeling that can be accessed during crisis and noncrisis times, where negative feelings cause stress. It is one of the greatest durable skills that you will need to bring to the forefront as we move to a new normal. This skill will help catapult you to a new level of durability in work and life, because hope protects the true self from continuing to experience chronic doubt and uncertainty. Once brought into awareness, intention can cultivate optimism that something positive will occur in the future.

Do you need hope to activate success?

Yes! There are cross-applications and overlaps of hope leadership across other leadership styles that want to achieve success. It is in how we choose to look at hope that becomes the signature of a leader.

Hope-Centered leaders can inspire themselves, their teams, and the organization through their vision and positive communication, and through integral actions that can overcome barriers. Where, when, and how hope is applied is a choice through free will. Here are some key aspects that leaders can use to instill hope, and can build hopeful teams and organizational culture:

Empathy: Leaders who understand and acknowledge the feelings and values of their team members can build a sense of trust and hope. An Empathy-Ethic can help create a supportive environment.

Vision: Leaders with a hope-oriented approach typically have a clear and inspiring vision for the future. They communicate this vision in a way that motivates and energizes their team.

Positive Communication: Hopeful leaders use positive and optimistic language. They emphasize the potential for success via a solution-focus, even in challenging contexts.

Resilience: Leaders need to demonstrate resilience in the face of setbacks. By showing that challenges can be overcome, they inspire hope in their team members and foster a culture of determination for the future.

Collaboration and Inclusion: Encouraging teamwork and collaboration can create a sense of collective hope. Leaders who promote inclusivity and value diverse perspectives contribute to a positive and hopeful workplace culture for all members.

Trust Building: Building trust is fundamental to fostering hope. When team members trust their leader and each other, it creates a sense of security and confidence in the team's ability to achieve collective goals.

Recognition: Recognizing and celebrating achievements, both big and small, reinforces a positive atmosphere. It signals progress and success, contributing to a hopeful outlook on work.

Adaptability: Leaders who are adaptable and open to change inspire hope by demonstrating a willingness to navigate challenges and seize opportunities for growth.

We believe that hope and action are necessary to gain positive results when you want to activate success for the future. The more we discover ourselves and become self-aware the closer we are in activating success. When you believe that you can change (through thinking and metacognition) and have success, then you become more hopeful for the future. As you move through the levels of Maslow's Hierarchy of Needs, hope is sustained and propels you to action to give you the momentum you desire to be successful.

How you define success is completely up to you and the life you desire. Take ownership of your definition of success, believe in it and allow hope to fill your heart brain, so you can move towards it. Hope replaces doubt and uncertainty and replaces it with courage, optimism, and strength. Our belief in the activation of success is hope personified.

Spencer Niles, Norm Amundson, Roberta Neault, and Hyung Joon, wrote (Career Recovery, 2022) that the level of hope that a person naturally embraces directly impacts their potential and effectiveness in leading and implementing a positive and hope-focused change.

https://marcr.net/marcr-for-career-professionals/career-theory/career-theories-and-theorists/hope-action-theory/

Hope requires emotional rationality which states that what you believe is at the core of hope, therefore, successful leaders who are hopeful believers can empower others through hope-inspired actions.

There is a natural bridge between hope and leadership, which can be seen in how a leader demonstrates the power of hope to evoke positive emotions in people to get them into inspired action. Strengthening the hoping self, minimizing hope inhibitors, and create a vision of hope in others can lead you into creating a "new normal".

You can build hope by:

1. Utilizing inspired words to motivate
2. Showing a gratitude mindset

3. Accepting change as a learning event
4. Pursuing purpose and meaning
5. Encouraging positivity
6. Holding true to universal values

Undertaking such actions can help to mitigate limiting beliefs and negative self-talk at the individual and team levels. A hopeful leader can also introspect and increase hopefulness through:

- Powerful words.
- New projects or roles.
- Active listening.
- Effective communication in using our Feelings, Values, and Stressors model.
- Environmental cues.
- Attention and Intention.

You made it to the last chapter, so let's Connect The Dots!

You've learned that theories matter and each leadership style is rooted in theory and practice; then you learned the significance of self-discovery through a deep dive into your leadership story; then you learned that any change however great or small requires effective communication and conflict resolution; then you jumped into a myriad of leadership styles that can benefit the context that you find yourself in; and now we intentionally end with hope so you can have sustainability at work and personal life.

Bring hope to the table through **Self-Discovery**:

1. What am I feeling at this moment that is causing such feelings to erupt?
2. What am I observing or focusing on?
3. What am I hearing through my bias?
4. Who should I communicate with first to resolve my cognitive dissonance?

5. What effect is this having on my leadership style?
6. Has this happened to me before? Where and when? And how was it managed through hope?

Generate hope by adapting yourself by intentionally bringing more encouragement, reassurance, and inspiration to the table for the purpose of **Change Readiness**:

Observe yourself in work and life relationships.

- What are you focusing on?
- Are you aware of your Schema (beliefs, assumptions, biases, and values), and how it affects others?
- What are you learning about yourself?
- What are you learning about others?
- Do you care about other people?
- Are you aware that people can show symptoms of a greater emotional challenge?

Maintain success for **Sustainable Impact**:

- Are putting in the time and effort to sustain work and life relationships?
- Are you cultivating the strengths and talents of others?
- Are you consistent in words and actions?
- Do you commit and follow through?
- Are you working with integrity?
- Do you seek opportunities to partner with others?
- Are you mindful of and instilling trust and hope into your work culture?
- What three habits are you improving upon?

You have power, so use that power to help others to flourish.

This gives meaning to the field of leadership.

Change Management Insight

The opposite of hope is pessimism and resistance. Resistance shows up in many different forms of symptomology, just as trauma can. It can be the person who shows up late, takes breaks from the meeting, or doesn't participate. Nonverbally their body posture will indicate resistance, and verbally they may give you ten reasons why something will not work.

This is a chance for you to change.

This is when you will have to upskill your empathetic communication and inclusion skills so you can reframe your relationship to help them understand that they are a part of the change process. Show them you care by asking them what they need to become part of the team. Remember, the feelings, values, and stressors formula to build trust and support hope.

Effective Communication & Conflict Resolution

Hope-Centered Leader Values

Empathy, hope, optimism, peace, understanding, communication, compromise, truth, purpose, helpfulness, growth mindset

Hope-Centered Leader Stressors

Lack of empathy, lack of hope, cynicism, aggression, liars, yellers, egotism, callousness, people who have a fixed mindset and refuse to grow, untrustworthiness

What does this mean?

This means that when there is a breach of something that you value, then that will cause you a great deal of stress. Stress will lead to an imbalance in the biology of you and manifest into negative symptoms in one or two of your twelve biological systems. That, in turn, will affect the psychology, social, and spirit of you as well.

How can you talk to people that breach something that you value? Be honest with your *feelings*.

Resolution

BE the listener. Do not say, "You're giving people too much consideration!". When the other person hears the word "You", it will heighten the empathetic leader's confusion. DO use "I" statements. Say, "I feel _____ when you _____". For example, "I feel apprehensive and worried when you give people too much freedom and latitude".

HAVE harmony, understanding, communication, homeostasis, and equilibrium.

👁 **Insight #11:** When you are at an interview, insert the following information:

1. I have learned that two people can be correct and also that two things can be correct at the same time because _____.

2. I understand that people want to be understood. This is an example of how I show people that I understand them _____.

3. I intentionally work hard to create healthy work relationships by _____.

4. I speak kindly to people and about people because _____.

🔖 **Tip #11:** Go for progress, not perfection. Progress is a significant result.

🔖 **Neuro Tip #8:** Whatever you are not changing, remains the same in the brain.

🔭 **Tool #14:** The Hope-Action Inventory (HAI) provides hope-action competencies, and can be found at www.hopecenteredcareer. com/hai

You can use these questions to get you into a hope-filled stance:

1. Live as a role model to inspire action. Compare your role model with others?

2. Communicate often and in a variety of ways so that your followers understand the path forward (Howard Gardner's Multiple Intelligences). What are the multiple intelligences on our team?

3. Build Conscious Leadership practices into your organizational culture. How can we embed our values into the mission and vision? Creating a strong individual mission statement can help guide you through work and personal life.

4. Show vulnerability as a leader to build trust and connection. Can we have our meeting at a nearby restaurant? Or at the nearby gym?

5. Allow effective flow of vertical information in an organization. How can we talk to each other authentically without anger or retaliation?

Hope mimics motivation for high work and life performance. It shows itself as both a belief and an action. It is fundamental to leadership, crises, and life circumstances. Hope in action propels leaders and their teams through difficulties. Are you ready for the next crisis? Hopeful leaders encourage other leaders to inspire. Hope begets hope. It is intentional that we end this book with hope.

YOUR TURN

1. Why is Hope-centeredness important?
2. How can you incorporate hope in the workplace?
3. How can you become more hopeful towards yourself and others?
4. What would you have to do to cultivate more hope within teams?
5. Create a strong mission statement for yourself. Ask: What do I do well? How do I do it? Who do I do this for? How am I able to help people?

"

Hope is a function of struggle –
we develop hope not during the
easy or comfortable times,
but through adversity and discomfort.

~ Brene Brown ~

"

Parting Thoughts

As you embrace the values in this book, we want you to:

Apply an Empathy-Ethic to positively self-
lead and lead others to success.

Focus on activating success, not accumulating
excess. Make sure you know the difference.

Success will follow self-discipline and altruism.

Activate tremendous success through self-awareness.

Learn to love yourself so you can love others.

Prepare your mind and heart for the next crisis.

Observe the world and challenge your worldview.

Develop cultural humility.

Perfect your elevator pitch to include interculturalism.

Become the best version of yourself by believing
in your capability and capacity.

Focus on that which is an existential threat
against *all* of us and not just against you.

We wish you great success!

Now that you've finished reading this book, please open the workbook and begin those exercises for your change journey.

Please write to us and tell us your success stories.

www.activate-success.com
www.drsujataives.com
www.sandrahorton.com

Author Biographies

Sujata Ives, PhD, GCDFI, OWDSI

Dr. Sujata Ives earned her Doctor of Philosophy in Educational Psychology from Walden University, her Master's degree in Educational Communications & Technology from New York University, and her Bachelor's degree in Biological Sciences from Goucher College.

In addition, she has a Post-graduate Certificate in Administration and Supervision from Johns Hopkins University, and a certificate in Mediation from Harvard University, School of Law, Program on Negotiation. She has national and international certification in employment counseling, career developing, and correctional education.

Dr. Ives was awarded the Best Research Paper award in 2022 by Jain University, India, and created professional assessments for the Chief of Party, University Centers for Career Development, The American University in Cairo, Egypt; for the Fulcrum Performance Lab; Spiritual Assessment; and for this 'Activate Success' book.

Society for Human Resource Managers (SHRM) published her article on common sense leadership at:
www.shrm.org.resourcesandtools.hr-topics.behavioral-competencies.pages.post-crisis-common-sense-global-leadership.aspx?linktext=post-crisis-common-sense-global-leadership

National Career Development Association (NCDA) published her Leadership Academy paper on Interculturalism and Leadership Responsibility at: www.ncda.org

Her article in Counseling Today magazine, a publication of the American Counseling Association, can be found at: https://ct.counseling.org/2023/03/expanding-the-conversation-on-international-perspectives-and-practice-in-counseling/

Her co-authored article on *"Soft Skills as Currency: Perspectives of Policymakers on Pertinent Global Labor Market Issues MEET Industry 5.0,"* through APCDA can be found at: https://asiapacificcda.org/career-trends/#SoftCurrency

Her PhD *dissertation "The Impact of an Online Orientation Program on the Impostor Phenomenon, Self-efficacy, and Anxiety"* By Sujata Kolhatkar Ives can be found at www.ProQuest.com

Dr. Ives has twenty-five years of experience in the fields of education, corrections, and business. Her nineteen global moves through her work and military gave her expertise in interculturalism, cultural humility, and leadership styles. She activates success by eliminating psychological barriers through her 'Ives Neuro-dots Theory™'

Dr. Ives has published and presented research to national and international audiences for the National Career Development Association, where she received the 2022 Diversity Initiative award; Asia Pacific Career Development Association, American Counseling Association, Society for Human Resource Management, Maryland Career Development Association, Maryland Counseling Association, World Council on Intercultural & Global Competency, OtroMundo Congress, where she received the designation of 'Global Visionary 2023', and is on the Board of the Fulcrum Performance Lab.

Learn more about her at:
www.drsujataives.com
www.activate-success.com

Sandra J. Horton, M.A.

Sandra J. Horton, known as the Success Change Catalyst, brings a compelling and authentic voice to the realm of positive transformation. Her mantra is, "activate success first through your own change that leads others to unlock theirs". She supports leaders and organizations to create new pathways of change that ends bully cultures, builds conscious leaders, and enables sustainable impact for future generations.

Drawing from a rich background of over 25 years in healthcare sales and leadership, Sandra made a bold shift towards her passion for leadership and change management. Armed with a Master of Arts in Leadership, she established her own consultancy (2014) focused on empowering leaders and organizations to embrace change with boldness. As a certified Prosci Change Management practitioner, a member of the Association of Change Management Professionals, Sandra has spearheaded impactful change initiatives across the Provinces of Canada.

In her role as a Success Change Catalyst, Sandra leverages a systems' thinking approach to drive change and foster high-performance organizational cultures through strategic planning, team development, and company culture. Through her customized EQ-I 2.0 leader activation and assessment sessions, she guides leaders to unlock their full potential, prevent burnout, and enhance their emotional intelligence.

Beyond her consultancy endeavors, Sandra is a best-selling author and an inspiring motivational speaker. Her contributions to acclaimed books "Voices of the 21st Century" and "Growth Strategies for the Hungry Entrepreneur" showcases her commitment to activate success and catalyze transformation in individuals and organizations worldwide.

Reach me at:

LinkedIn: www.linkedin.com/in/sandra-j-horton
Facebook: https://www.facebook.com/sandra.j.horton
Instagram: https://www.instagram.com/sandrajanehorton/
Learn more at www.activate-success.com

References for Four Waves of Psychology

First Wave: Psychodynamics

Sigmund Freud

https://psychoanalysis.org.uk/our-authors-and-theorists/sigmund-freud

Freud, S. (1915). The Unconscious. Vol. XIV (2nd ed.). Hogarth Press, 1955.

Watson, J.B. & Rayner, R. (2002). "Conditioned emotional responses", Journal of Experimental Psychology 3, 1920; in Hock, Forty Studies (2002), pp. 70–76.

https://www.ncbi.nlm.nih.gov/books/NBK559106/

https://www.simplypsychology.org/defense-mechanisms.html

https://www.verywellmind.com/defense-mechanisms-2795960

https://www.cambridge.org/core/books/cambridge-guide-to-psychodynamic-psychotherapy/F4C4DE6BC604B41B585A78227012CC93

Second Wave: Behaviorism

B.F. Skinner

www.bfskinner.org

Ferster, C. B. & Skinner, B. F. (1957). Schedules of reinforcement. New York: Appleton-Century-Crofts.

Rutherford, A. (2009) Beyond the box: B. F. Skinner's technology of behavior from laboratory to life, 1950s-1970s, Toronto: University of Toronto Press.

Sagal, P. T. (1981) Skinner's Philosophy. Washington, DC: University Press of America.

Wolfgang, C.H. and Glickman, Carl D. (1986) Solving Discipline Problems Allyn and Bacon, Inc.

https://www.ncbi.nlm.nih.gov/pmc/articles/PMC6194517/

https://psycnet.apa.org/record/2023-80647-000

https://study.com/academy/lesson/principle-of-conditioning-definition-lesson-quiz.html

https://positivepsychology.com/cbt-cognitive-behavioral-therapy-books/

https://www.simplypsychology.org/behaviorism.html

Third Wave: Humanism

https://www.ncbi.nlm.nih.gov/pmc/articles/PMC8429332/

https://onlinelibrary.wiley.com/doi/abs/10.1002/johc.12086

https://link.springer.com/chapter/10.1007/978-3-031-11677-3_6

https://www.thoughtco.com/carl-rogers-4588296

https://www.verywellmind.com/what-is-humanistic-psychology-2795242

https://positivepsychology.com/jungian-psychology/

https://exploringyourmind.com/carl-jungs-11-best-books/

Piaget, Jean

https://positivepsychology.com/piaget-stages-theory/

Tzu, Lao (18th Century), The Tao Te Ching, Taoism.

Abraham Maslow

Deckers, Lambert (2018). Motivation: Biological, Psychological, and Environmental. Routledge Press. ISBN 9781138036338.

Maslow, Abraham H. (1996). "Critique of self-actualization theory". In Hoffman, Edward (ed.). Future visions: The unpublished papers of Abraham Maslow. Thousand Oaks, CA: Sage. pp. 26–32. ISBN 978-0761900511.

Maslow, Abraham H. (1971). The farther reaches of human nature. New York: The Viking Press.

Maslow, A. H. (1970). Motivation and personality (2nd ed.). New York: HarperCollins.

Maslow, Abraham H. (1969). "The farther reaches of human nature". Journal of Transpersonal Psychology. 1 (1): 1–9.

Maslow, A. (1962). Toward a psychology of being. D Van Nostrand. https:,,doi.org,10.1037,10793-000

McLeod, Saul (December 29, 2021). "Maslow's Hierarchy of Needs". Simply Psychology. Retrieved January 2, 2022

Urie Bronfenbrenner

https://bctr.cornell.edu/about-us/urie-bronfenbrenner

Bronfenbrenner, U. (1979). The ecology of human development. Cambridge, MA: Harvard University Press.

Bronfenbrenner, Urie (1977). "Toward an experimental ecology of human development". American Psychologist. 32 (7): 513–531.

Ceci, Stephen J. (2006). "Urie Bronfenbrenner (1917-2005)". American Psychologist. 61 (2): 173–174.

Urie Bronfenbrenner. (2009). The Ecology of Human Development: Experiments by Nature and Design. Cambridge, Massachusetts: Harvard University Press. ISBN 0-674-22457-4.

Fourth Wave: Positive Psychology

Csikzentmihalyi, M. (1995). Finding Flow, Basic Books Publishing

Seligman, M.E.P. (1995). "The effectiveness of psychotherapy: The Consumer Reports study" (PDF). American Psychologist. 50 (12): 965–974.

https://www.psychologytoday.com/us/blog/finding-new-home/201804/the-fourth-wave-psychotherapies

https://psycnet.apa.org/record/2018-11766-005

https://www.ncbi.nlm.nih.gov/pmc/articles/PMC9810337/

https://www.semanticscholar.org/paper/A-Fourth-Wave-of-Psychotherapies%3A-Moving-Beyond-Peteet/6563038cea27ca73da78baef31d0cd07db02dc17

https://www.tandfonline.com/doi/full/10.1080/09638288.2019.1602674

https://www.researchgate.net/publication/322904672_A_Fourth_Wave_of_Psychotherapies_Moving_Beyond_Recovery_Toward_Well-Being

https://www.simplypsychology.org/four-waves-feminism.html

https://link.springer.com/book/10.1007/978-3-319-53682-8

Zinn, Jon-Kabat

https://jonkabat-zinn.com/

https://www.mindful.org/jon-kabat-zinn-defining-mindfulness/

https://www.npr.org/sections/health-shots/2024/03/10/1236802998/mindfulness-mbsr-jon-kabat-zinn-public-health

https://medium.com/@sorapazer/the-psychology-of-self-improvement-mastering-personal-development-skills-0dac7b291acb

https://positivepsychology.com/self-discovery/

https://www.healthline.com/health/self-discovery

https://www.forbes.com/sites/tracybrower/2024/04/23/how-to-increase-change-readiness/?sh=2ca5131b70b4

https://hbr.org/2021/11/how-to-become-more-comfortable-with-change

https://www.prosci.com/blog/when-should-you-use-a-change-management-readiness-assessment

https://www.unsustainablemagazine.com/authors/

https://www.weforum.org/agenda/2020/02/unesco-cities-of-literature-recommended-books-sustainable-development-goals/

https://www.un.org/sustainabledevelopment/goal-of-the-month/

https://positivepsychology.com/empathy-books/

https://www.joincake.com/blog/books-on-empathy/

PSYCHOLOGY REFERENCES

www.counseling.org

https://asiapacificcda.org/

https://iccglobal.org/

https://www.truecolorsintl.com/about

https:www.scientificamerican.com,article,do-the-eyes-have-it/

REFERENCES

https:qz.com,1213768,the-forgetting-curve-explains-why-humans-struggle-to-memorize

https:www.growthengineering.co.uk,what-is-the-forgetting-curve

American Psychological Association (2023). Glossary of psychological terms. https://www.apa.org/

Allport, G. W (1985). "The Historical Background of Social Psychology". In G. Lindzey and E. Aronson (ed.). The Handbook of Social Psychology. New York: McGraw Hill. p. 5.

Arnett, J. J. (2008). "The neglected 95%: Why American psychology needs to become less American". American Psychologist. 63 (7): 602–614.

Badcock, Christopher R. (2015). "Nature-Nurture Controversy, History of". International Encyclopedia of the Social & Behavioral Sciences. pp. 340–344.

Baddeley, A. D. (1992). Is working memory working? Quarterly Journal of Experimental Psychology, 44A, 1-31.

Bandura, A. (1973). Aggression: A social learning analysis. Englewood Cliffs, NJ: Prentice-Hall.

Baumeister, Roy (September 2016), "Charting the future of social psychology on stormy seas: Winners, losers, and recommendations", Journal of Experimental Social Psychology, 66: 153–158.

Beus, J. M., McCord, M. A., & Zohar, D. (2016). Workplace safety: A review and research synthesis. Organizational Psychology Review, 6, 352-381.

Boyle, Gregory J. (1995). "Myers-Briggs Type Indicator (MBTI): Some Psychometric Limitations". Australian Psychologist. 30: 71–74.

Brain, Christine. (2002). Advanced psychology: applications, issues and perspectives. Cheltenham: Nelson Thornes. ISBN 0-17-490058-9.

Bureau of Labor Statistics, U.S. Department of Labor, Occupational Outlook Handbook. 2023.

Carol, Bobby (2013). "The Evolution of Specialties in the CACREP Standards: CACREP's Role in Unifying the Profession". Journal of Counseling & Development. 91: 35–43.

Carver, C., & Scheier, M. (2004). Perspectives on Personality (5th ed.). Boston: Pearson.

Cascio, Wayne F. (2015). "Industrial–Organizational Psychology: Science and Practice". International Encyclopedia of the Social & Behavioral Sciences. pp. 879–884.

Centers for Disease Control and Prevention. Occupational Health Psychology (OHP). 2022.

Chrisman, S. M., Pieper, W. A., Clance, P. R., Holland, C. L., & Glickauf-Hughs, C. (1995). Validation of the Clance impostor phenomenon scale. Journal of Personality Assessment, 65, 456–467.

Chryssochoou, Xenia (2015). "Social Psychology". International Encyclopedia of the Social & Behavioral Sciences. pp. 532–537.

Clance, P. R., & Imes, S. A. (1978). The impostor phenomenon in high achieving women: Dynamics and therapeutic intervention. Psychotherapy: Theory, Research and Practice, 15, 241–247.

Costa, Paul T., McCrae, Robert R. (1978). "Objective Personality Assessment". The Clinical Psychology of Aging. Springer US. pp. 119–143. ISBN 978-1-4684-3342-5.

Costa, Paul T.; McCrae, Robert R. (1985). "The NEO personality inventory manual". Odessa, FL: Psychological Assessment Resources.

Costa, P. T., Jr., & McCrae, R. R. (1992). NEO PI-R professional manual. Odessa, FL: Psychological Assessment Resources, Inc.

Costa PT, Terracciano A, & McCrae RR (August 2001). "Gender differences in personality traits across cultures: robust and surprising findings". Journal of Personality and Social Psychology. 81 (2): 322–31.

Cowan, S. E., & Ferrari, J. R. (2002). Am I for real? Predicting impostor tendencies from self-handicapping and affective components. Social Behavior and Personality, 30, 119–126.

Crain, W. (2014). Theories of development: Concepts and applications. 6th ed. Edinburgh: Pearson. ISBN 978-0205810468.

Damásio, A. (1999). The feeling of what happens: Body and emotion in the making of consciousness.

Deakin, Nicholas (2015). "Philosophy, Psychiatry, and Psychology". International Encyclopedia of the Social & Behavioral Sciences. pp. 31–36.

Demetriou, Andreas (2015). "Intelligence in Cultural, Social and Educational Context". International Encyclopedia of the Social & Behavioral Sciences. pp. 313–322.

Developmental Psychology | Simply Psychology. www.simplypsychology.org.

Ebbinghaus, Hermann (1913). Memory: A Contribution to Experimental Psychology. Translated by Ruger, Henry; Bussenius, Clara. New York city, Teachers college, Columbia University.

Everett, J. J., Smith, R. E., & Williams, K. D. (1992). Effects of team cohesion and identifiability on social loafing in relay swimming performance. International Journal of Sport Psychology, 23, 311-324.

Frankl, V.E. (1984). Man's search for meaning (rev. ed.). New York: Washington Square Press. p. 86.

Frankel, Richard, Quill, Timothy, McDaniel, Susan (2003). The Biopsychosocial Approach: Past, Present, Future. Boydell & Brewer. ISBN 978-1-58046-102-3.

Gardner, H. (1985). The mind's new science: A history of the cognitive revolution. New York: Basic Books. ISBN 0-465-04635-5.

Gelso, Charles J. (2015). "Counseling Psychology". International Encyclopedia of the Social & Behavioral Sciences. pp. 69–72.

Green, C.D. & Groff, P.R. (2003). Early psychological thought: Ancient accounts of mind and soul. Westport, Connecticut: Praeger.

Guthrie, Robert. Even the Rat was White: A Historical View of Psychology. Second edition. Boston, Allyn and Bacon (Viacon), 1998. ISBN 0-205-14993-6.

Haggbloom S.J. (2002). The 100 most eminent psychologists of the 20th century, Review of General Psychology, 6 (2). 139–152.

Harris, B. (1979). Whatever happened to Little Albert? American Psychologist, 34, 151-160.

Harris, Judith Rich (2006). No Two Alike: Human Nature and Human Individuality. New York: W. W. Norton & Company. ISBN 978-0393329711.

Harris, Judith Rich (2009) [1998]. The Nurture Assumption: Why Children Turn Out the Way They Do (2nd ed.). New York: Free Press. ISBN 978-1439101650.

Henrich, Joseph; Heine, Steven J.; Norenzayan, Ara (2010). "The weirdest people in the world?" (PDF). Behavioral and Brain Sciences. 33 (2–3): 61–83.

Hergenhahn, B.R. (2005). An introduction to the history of psychology. Belmont, California: Thomson Wadsworth. pp. 528–536.

Hochschild, A. (2011). To End All Wars: A Story of Loyalty and Rebellion, 1914–1918. ISBN 978-0-547-75031-6.

Houdmont, J., & Leka, S. (2010). An introduction to occupational health psychology. In S. Leka & J. Houdmont (Eds.). Occupational health psychology (pp. 1–30). John Wiley: Hoboken, NJ.

Hunt, Earl B. (2011). Human Intelligence. New York: Cambridge University Press. p. 94. ISBN 978-0521707817.

Ives, Sujata Kolhatkar (2012). "The Impact of an Online Orientation on the Impostor Phenomenon, Anxiety, and Self-efficacy", Walden University, ProQuest.

Janis, I. L. (1972). Victims of groupthink. Boston: Houghton Mifflin.

Joshua N. Friedlander, "Military Psychology: An Army Clinical Psychologist" in Morgan et al. (ed.), Life After Graduate School in Psychology (2005).

Kamenetz, Anya (19 March 2020). "'Panic-gogy': Teaching Online Classes During the Coronavirus Pandemic". NPR.

Kentnor, H. (2015). "Distance education and the evolution of online learning in the United States". *Curriculum and Teaching Dialogue*. 17: 21–34.

Kohlberg, L. (1973). Continuities in childhood and adult moral development revisited. In P. Baltes & K. W. Schaie (Eds.), Life-span development psychology: Personality and socialization. San Diego, CA: Academic Press.

Kwiatkowski, R., Duncan, D. C., & Shimmin, S. (2006). What have we forgotten - and why? *Journal of Occupational and Organizational Psychology*, 79(2), 183-201.

LeDoux, J.E. (1998). The emotional brain: The mysterious underpinnings of emotional life (Touchstone ed.). Simon & Schuster. ISBN 0-684-83659-9.

Leary, M. R., Patton, K. M., Orlando, A. E., & Funk, W. W. (2000). The impostor phenomenon: self-perceptions, reflected appraisals, and interpersonal strategies. Journal of Personality, 68, 725–756.

Leslie C. Morey, "Measuring Personality and Psychopathology" in Weiner (ed.), Handbook of Psychology (2003), Volume 2: Research Methods in Psychology.

Lucas, Richard E.; Baird, Brendan M. (2004). "Extraversion and Emotional Reactivity". *Journal of Personality and Social Psychology*. 86 (3): 473–485.

Luria, A. R. (1973). The working brain: an introduction to neuropsychology. Translated by Haigh, Basil. New York: Basic Books. ISBN 0-465-09208-X. OCLC 832187.

Mandler, G. (2007). A history of modern experimental psychology: From James and Wundt to cognitive science. Cambridge, MA: MIT Press.

Mayer, J. D., & Salovey, P. (1997). What is emotional intelligence? In P. Salovey & D. J. Sluyter (Eds.), Emotional development and emotional intelligence: Educational implications (pp. 3–34). Basic Books.

McGue M, Gottesman II (2015). "Behavior Genetics". The Encyclopedia of Clinical Psychology. pp. 1–11.

McCrae, Robert R., Costa, Jr., Paul T., Martin, Thomas A. (June 2005). "The NEO–PI–3: A More Readable Revised NEO Personality Inventory". Journal of Personality Assessment. 84 (3): 261–270.

McKee, Connor, and Ntokos, Konstantinos (2022). "Online microlearning and student engagement in computer games higher education". Research in Learning Technology. 30: 2680.

McWilliams, Spencer A. (2015). "Psychology, History of (Twentieth Century)". International Encyclopedia of the Social & Behavioral Sciences. pp. 412–417.

Milgram, Stanley (1963). "Behavioral Study of Obedience". Journal of Abnormal and Social Psychology. 67 (4): 371–378.

Miller, G. A. (1956). The magical number seven, plus or minus two: Some limits on our capacity for processing information. Psychological Review, 63, 81-97.

Models in Psychology

https://www.verywellmind.com/understanding-the-biopsychosocial-model-7549226

https://www.ncbi.nlm.nih.gov/books/NBK552030/

https://www.physio-pedia.com/Biopsychosocial_Model

https://www.ncbi.nlm.nih.gov/books/NBK552028/

Moorhead, G., & Griffin, R. W. (2017). Organizational behavior: Managing people and organizations, 12th Ed. Boston: Cengage. ISBN 978-1-305-50139-3.

Myers (2004). Motivation and work. New York, NY: Worth Publishers.

Nixon, A. E., Mazzola, J. J., Bauer, J., Krueger, J. R., & Spector, P. E. (2011). Can work make you sick? A meta-analysis of the relationships between job stressors and physical symptoms. Work & Stress, 25, 1-22.

Panksepp, J. (1998). Affective neuroscience: The foundations of human and animal emotions. New York and Oxford: Oxford University Press.

Paranjpe, Anand C. (2006). "From Tradition through Colonialism to Globalization: Reflections on the History of Psychology in India", in Brock (ed.), Internationalizing the History of Psychology (2006).

Parsons, H. M. (1974). "What happened at Hawthorne?: New evidence suggests the Hawthorne effect resulted from operant reinforcement contingencies". Science. 183 (4128): 922–932.

Pe-Pua, Rogelia (2015). "Indigenous Psychology". International Encyclopedia of the Social & Behavioral Sciences. pp. 788–794.

Pinel, John (2010). Biopsychology. New York: Prentice Hall. ISBN 978-0-205-83256-9.

Poortinga, Ype H. (2015). "Cross-Cultural Psychology". International Encyclopedia of the Social & Behavioral Sciences. pp. 311–317.

Ruben Ardila, "Behavior Analysis in an International Context", in Brock (ed.), Internationalizing the History of Psychology (2006).

Schonfeld, I.S., & Chang, C.-H. (2017). Occupational health psychology: Work, stress, and health. New York, NY: Springer Publishing Company.

Selye, Hans

https://www.stress.org/about/hans-selye-birth-of-stress

https://www.ncbi.nlm.nih.gov/pmc/articles/PMC5915631/

https://www.ncbi.nlm.nih.gov/books/NBK349158/

Shackman, Gene; The Global Social Change Research Project (2017). "What is Program Evaluation? A Beginners Guide (Presentation Slides)". SSRN Electronic Journal. Elsevier BV.

Shettleworth, S.J. (2010) Cognition, Evolution and Behavior (2nd Ed), New York: Oxford.

Singal, J. (2021, June 7). Positive psychology goes to war: How the Army adopted an untested, evidence-free approach to fighting PTSD. Chronicle of Higher Education.

Smith, Edward E. (2015). "Cognitive Psychology: History". International Encyclopedia of the Social & Behavioral Sciences. pp. 103–109.

Stanford Encyclopedia of Philosophy. (2006). "Wilhelm Maximilian Wundt".

Steven Williams, "Executive Management: Helping Executives Manage Their Organizations through Organizational and Market Research" in Morgan et al. (ed.), Life After Graduate School in Psychology (2005).

T.L. Brink. (2008) Psychology: A Student Friendly Approach. "Unit One: The Definition and History of Psychology." pp 9.

Truxillo, D. M., Bauer, T. N., & Erdogan, B. (2016). Psychology and work: Perspectives on industrial and organizational psychology. New York: Psychology Press. ISBN 1134705697.

Want, J., & Kleitman, S. (2006). Imposter phenomenon and self-handicapping: Links with parenting styles and self-confidence. Personality and Individual Differences, 40, 961–971.

Windholz, G. (1997). "Ivan P. Pavlov: An overview of his life and psychological work". American Psychologist. 52 (9): 941–946.

Wozniak, R.H. (1999). Introduction to memory: Hermann Ebbinghaus (1885,1913). Classics in the history of psychology.

SOCIOLOGY REFERENCES

Berger, Peter L., and Thomas Luckmann. 1966. The Social Construction of Reality: A Treatise in the Sociology of Knowledge.

Durkheim, Émile. 1895. The Rules of the Sociological Method. Cited in Wacquant (1992).

Latour, Bruno, and Woolgar, Steve (1979). Laboratory Life: The Construction of Scientific Facts.

https://openstax.org/books/introduction-sociology-3e/pages/1-references

https://www.thoughtco.com/famous-sociologists-3026648

https://academicinfluence.com/inflection/study-guides/sociology-influential-books

https://www.readthistwice.com/lists/best-sociology-books

https://bookauthority.org/books/best-sociology-books

https://www.thoughtco.com/
major-sociological-studies-and-publications-3026649

SYSTEMS THINKING REFERENCES

Senge, Peter (1990, 2006). The Fifth Discipline: the art and practice of the learning organization, Doubleday publishing.

Peter Senge and the learning organization. In fed.org. 16 February 2013. Retrieved 12 April 2018.

Senge, Peter (2004) Excerpt Spirituality in Business and Life: Asking the Right Questions.

https://link.springer.com/
referenceworkentry/10.1007/978-3-030-02006-4_538-1

https://www.weforum.org/agenda/2021/01/
what-systems-thinking-actually-means-and-why-it-matters-today/

https://curve.mit.edu/ask-an-mit-professor-what-is-system-thinking-and-why-is-it-important

CAREER DEVELOPMENT REFERENCES

Arnold, Randall; et al. (2016). Work Psychology, 6th edition. Harlow: Pearson. pp. 555–558.

Award for distinguished scientific applications of psychology: John L. Holland." American Psychologist, Vol 63(8), Nov 2008, 672-674.

Barnett, R. C. and Hyde, J. S. 2001. "Women, Men, Work, and Family." American Psychologist 56:781-796.

Brooks, Arthur C. (July 2019). "Your Professional Decline Is Coming (Much) Sooner Than You Think". The Atlantic. ISSN 1072-7825. Archived from the original on 2019-07-04.

Center for Credentialing in Education. (2017). Global Career Development Facilitator.

Gunz and Heslin (2005). "Reconceptualising career success". *Journal of Organizational Behavior*. 26 (2): 105–111.

Hall and Chandler (2005). "Psychological success: When the career is a calling". Journal of Organizational Behavior. 26 (2): 155–176.

Heslin, Peter (2003). "Self and other referent criteria of career success". *Journal of Career Assessment*. 11 (3): 262–286.

Holland, John (1997). Making Vocational Choices: A Theory of Vocational Personalities and Work Environments (Third Edition)'. Florida: PAR. p. 22. ISBN 0-911907-27-0.

Hooley, T. (2012). "How the internet changed career: framing the relationship between career development and online technologies" (PDF). *Journal of the National Institute for Career Education and Counselling* (NICEC). 29: 3.

Hooley, T.; Watts, A. G.; Sultana, R. G.; Neary, S. (2013). "The 'blueprint' framework for career management skills: a critical exploration" (PDF). British Journal of Guidance & Counselling. 41 (2): 117.

Inkson, Dries and Arnold (2014). Understanding Careers, 2nd edition. London: Sage. ISBN 978-1-44628-291-5.

REFERENCES

Jaunarajs, Imants

https://www.ohio.edu/experts/expert/imants-jaunarajs

McDonald., and Hite, Kimberly., and Linda (2016). Career development: a human resource development perspective. New York, New York: Oxfordshire, [England]: Routledge. pp. 2-4. ISBN 9781138786127.

National Career Development Association. (2022). What is a career development facilitator?, www.ncda.org

Ng and Feldman (2014). "Subjective career success: A meta-analytic review". Journal of Vocational Behavior. 85 (2): 169–179.

Niles, Spencer

https://www.amazon.com/Career-Recovery-Creating-Hopeful-Difficult/dp/1793518920

https://education.wm.edu/ourfacultystaff/faculty/niles_s.php

Ott-Holland, C. J.; Huang, J. L.; Ryan, A. M.; Elizondo, F.; Wadlington, P. L. (October 2013). "Culture and Vocational Interests: The Moderating Role of Collectivism and Gender Egalitarianism". Journal of Counseling Psychology. American Psychological Association. 60 (4): 569–581.

Pope, M. (2009). Jesse Buttrick Davis (1871-1955): Pioneer of vocational guidance in the schools. Career Development Quarterly, 57, 278-288.

Schreuder, A. M. G. (2006). Careers: An Organisational Perspective. p. 187. ISBN 9780702171758.

Splete, H. H., & Hoppin, J. (2000). The emergence of career development facilitators. Career Development Quarterly, 48, 340–347.

Sullivan, S (1999). "The changing nature of careers: a review and research agenda". Journal of Management. 25 (3): 457–484.

Sullivan, Sherry E.; Baruch, Yehuda (December 2009). "Advances in Career Theory and Research: A Critical Review and Agenda for Future Exploration". Journal of Management. 35 (6): 1542–1571.

Super, Donald E. (1953). "A theory of vocational development". American Psychologist. 8 (5): 185–190.

Tyrell-Smith, Tim, "How to Choose a Career That's Best for You". U.S. News & World Report. Archived from the original on 2017-09-11.

Zytowski, Donald, "Frank Parsons and the Progressive Movement," The Career Development Quarterly, vol. 50, no. 1 (September 2001), pp. 57–65.

<u>CHANGE MANAGEMENT REFERENCES</u>

Association of Change Management Professionals

https://www.acmpglobal.org/

Bennett, John L., Bush, Mary Wayne (2013). Coaching for Change. Routledge. p. 172. ISBN 9781136496011.

Burnes, Bernard (2019-12-18). "The Origins of Lewin's Three-Step Model of Change". The Journal of Applied Behavioral Science. 56 (1): 32–59.

Calish, Irving; Gamache, Donald. "How to overcome organizational resistance to change". Management Review. 70 – via Business Source Premier EBSCO Host.

Cameron, Esther; Green, Mike (2020). Making Sense of Change Management. Kogan Page.

Hansen, Morten T. (2012-09-21). "Ten Ways to Get People to Change". Harvard Business Review. ISSN 0017-8012. Archived from the original on 2021-11-08.

Hiatt, J. M. (2006), ADKAR: a model for change in Business, Government and our Community, Prosci Learning Center.

Kotter, John P. (1995-05-01). "Leading Change: Why Transformation Efforts Fail". Harvard Business Review. ISSN 0017-8012.

Levin, Ginger (2012). "Embrace and Exploit Change as a Program Manager: Guidelines for Success". Project Management Institute.

Phillips, Julien R. (1983). "Enhancing the effectiveness of organizational change management". Human Resource Management. 22 (1–2): 183–99.

Raza, Syed Arshad; Standing, Craig (2011-06-01). "A Systemic Model for Managing and Evaluating Conflicts in Organizational Change". Systemic Practice and Action Research. 24 (3): 187–210.

Tisdall, Lewis (2016-02-26). "Why is change management necessary in contemporary organisations?". Lewis Tisdall's Business Blog. Archived from the original on 2017-05-01.

CHANGE THEORY REFERENCES

Austin, J. and Bartunek, J. (2004) Theories and Practice of Organization Development. Handbook of Psychology, Vol.12 309–332.

Chen, H.T., Rossi, P.H. Chen, H.T., & Rossi, P.H. (1980) 'The multi-goal, theory-driven approach to evaluation: A model linking basic and applied social science' in Social Forces, 59, 106–122.

Coryn Chris, Lindsay Noakes, Carl Westine and Daniela Schroter (2011). A Systematic Review of Theory-Driven Evaluation Practice from 1990 to 2009. American Journal of Evaluation 32 (2) 199–226.

Funnell, S. and Rogers, P. (2011). Purposeful Program Theory: Effective Use of Theories of Change and Logic Models. San Francisco, CA: Jossey Bass.

Jackson, E. (2013) Interrogating the theory of change: evaluating impact investing where it matters most. Journal of Sustainable Finance & Investment, 3:2, 95–110.

McLellan, Timothy (2020). "Impact, theory of change, and the horizons of scientific practice". Social Studies of Science. 51 (1): 100–120.

https:,,www.leadershipchallenge.com,Research,Five-Practices.aspx

https://www.success.com/5-practices-of-exemplary-leadership/

https://journals.sagepub.com/doi/full/10.1177/0021886319892685

https://www.sciencedirect.com/science/article/pii/S2444569X16300087

https://www.ncbi.nlm.nih.gov/pmc/articles/PMC9462626/

THOUGHT LEADERSHIP REFERENCES

Kotter, John P. "John P. Kotter – Faculty – Harvard Business School". Hbs.edu. Retrieved 24 August 2014.

Kotter, J., The 8-Step Process for Leading Change, accessed 10 January 2021.

Kotter, John P. (1996). Leading Change. Harvard Business School Press. ISBN 978-0-87584-747-4.

Rating the Management Gurus. Businessweek. 2001-10-14. Archived from the original on August 24, 2012. Retrieved 24 August 2014.

Thinkers 50 | Scanning, ranking and sharing the best management ideas in the world. thinkers50.com. Retrieved 1 January 2015.

https://hbr.org/2012/11/the-gurus-guide-to-creating-th

https://link.springer.com/referenceworkentry/10.1007/978-3-030-39666-4_15-2

HUMAN RESOURCE MANAGEMENT REFERENCES

Armstrong, Michael (2009). Armstrong's handbook of human resource management practice. Armstrong, Michael, 1928- (Eleventh ed.). London: Kogan Page. ISBN 9780749457389.

About SHRM. Society for Human Resource Management. Archived from the original on 16 January 2009. Retrieved 22 December 2011.

Armstrong, Michael (2006). "Human capital management".
A Handbook of Human Resource Management Practice. Gale

virtual reference library. Kogan Page Publishers. p. 29. ISBN 9780749446314.

Cappelli, Peter (July 2015). "Why We Love to Hate HR and What HR Can Do About It". *Harvard Business Review* (July–August 2015).

Conaty, Bill, and Ram Charan (2011). The Talent Masters: Why Smart Leaders Put People Before Numbers. Crown Publishing Group. ISBN 978-0-307-46026-4.

Doran, G. T. (1981). "There's a S.M.A.R.T. way to write management's goals and objectives" (PDF). Management Review. 70 (11): 35–36.

Gladwell, Malcolm (4 May 2009). "How David Beats Goliath". newyorker.com.

Storey, John (2014). New Perspectives on Human Resource Management (Routledge Revivals). ISBN 9781315740560.

Ulrich, Dave; Younger, Jon; Brockbank, Wayne (September 2008). "The twenty-first-century HR organization". Human Resource Management. 47 (4): 829–850.

Jonathan E. DeGraff (21 February 2010). "The Changing Environment of Professional HR Associations". Cornell HR Review. Archived from the original on 11 February 2012.

Locke, Edwin A. & Latham, Gary P. (2002). "Building a practically useful theory of goal setting and task motivation: A 35-year odyssey". American Psychologist. 57 (9): 705–717.

Obedgiu, Vincent (2017-01-01). "Human resource management, historical perspectives, evolution and professional development". Journal of Management Development. 36 (8): 986–990.

LEADERSHIP REFERENCES

Acton, Q. Ashton, ed. (10 January 2013). Issues in Culture, Rights, and Governance Research. Atlanta, Georgia: ScholarlyEditions (published 2013). ISBN 9781481649261.

Ames, Daniel R., Flynn, Francis J. (2007). "What breaks a leader: The curvilinear relation between assertiveness and leadership". Journal of Personality and Social Psychology. 92 (2): 307–324.

Bass, B. M.,Riggio, R. E. (2006). Transformational leadership (2nd ed.). Mahwah, New Jersey: Lawrence Erlbaum Associates Publishers.

Bass, B. M., Riggio, R. E., eds. (2006). Transformational Leadership (2nd ed.). Mahwah, N.J.: Lawrence Erlbaum Associates. p. 47.

Baumeister, R. F., Senders, P. S., Chesner, S. C., Tice, D. M. (1988). "Who's in charge here? Group leaders do lend help in emergencies". Personality and Social Psychology Bulletin. 14 (1): 17–22.

Bennis, W. G. (1975). Where have all the leaders gone?. Washington, D.C.: Federal Executive Institute.

Berdahl, J. L., Anderson, C. (2005). "Men, women, and leadership centralization in groups over time". Group Dynamics: Theory, Research, and Practice. 9: 45–57.

Berkowitz, L (1953). "Sharing leadership in small, decision-making groups". Journal of Abnormal and Social Psychology. 48 (2): 231–238.

Bono, J. E., Ilies, R. (2006). "Charisma, positive emotions and mood contagion". The Leadership Quarterly. 17 (4): 317–334.

Browning, Michelle (2018). "Self-Leadership: Why It Matters" (PDF). International Journal of Business and Social Science. 9 (2).

Burns, James Macgregor (2004). Transformational Leadership. Grove Press. ISBN 9780802141187.

Cano, Librado F. (2010). Transformation Of An Individual Family Community Nation And The World. Trafford Publishing. p. 134. ISBN 9781426947667.

Chan, K., Drasgow, F. (2001). "Toward a theory of individual differences and leadership: Understanding the motivation to lead". Journal of Applied Psychology. 86 (3): 481–498.

Dannhauser, Zani (2007). The Relationship between Servant Leadership, Follower Trust, Team Commitment and Unit Effectiveness (PhD thesis). Stellenbosch University.

Dasborough, M. T. (2006). "Cognitive asymmetry in employee emotional reactions to leadership behaviors". The Leadership Quarterly. 17 (2): 163–178.

Evans, Jules (2012-05-04). "What can business leaders learn from ancient philosophers?". The Guardian.

Forsyth, D. R. (2009). Group dynamics (5th ed.). Pacific Grove, Calif.: Brooks,Cole.

Forsyth, Donelson (2010). Group Dynamics. Belmont, California: Wadsworth.

Gardner, J. W. (1965). Self-Renewal: The Individual and the Innovative Society. New York: Harper and Row.

George, J. M. (2000). "Emotions and leadership: The role of emotional intelligence". *Human Relations*. 53 (8): 1027–1055.

George, J. M. (2006). "Leader Positive Mood and Group Performance: The Case of Customer Service". *Journal of Applied Social Psychology*. 25 (9): 778–794.

Gershenoff, A. G.; Foti, R. J. (2003). "Leader emergence and gender roles in all-female groups: A contextual examination". Small Group Research. 34 (2): 170–196.

Goleman, D.; Boyatzis, R.E.; McKee, A. (2003). The New Leaders: Transforming the art of leadership. London: Sphere. Sphere. ISBN 9780751533811.

Goleman, Daniel; Boyatzis, Richard E.; McKee, Annie (2003). New leaders. Sphere. ISBN 9780751533811.

Greenleaf, Robert K. (2002) [1977]. Servant Leadership: A Journey Into the Nature of Legitimate Power and Greatness. Mahwah, New Jersey: Paulist Press. ISBN 9780809105540.

Gregory, Scott (2018-03-30). "The Most Common Type of Incompetent Leader". *Harvard Business Review*. ISSN 0017-8012. Retrieved 2020-09-23.

Griffin, Ronald J. Ebert, Ricky W. (2010). Business essentials (8th ed.). Upper Saddle River, New Jersey: Prentice Hall. pp. 135–136. ISBN 978-0-13-705349-0.

Hackman, M., Johnson, C. (2009). Leadership: A communication perspective. Long Grove, Ill.: Waveland Press, Inc.

Henry P. Knowles, Borje O. Saxberg (1971). Personality and Leadership Behavior. Reading, Mass.: Addison-Wesley. pp. 884–89. ISBN 9780140805178.

Hoyt, C. L., Blascovich, J. (2016-07-26). "Leadership Efficacy and Women Leaders' Responses to Stereotype Activation". Group Processes & Intergroup Relations. 10 (4): 595–616.

Ingrid Bens (2006). Facilitating to Lead. Jossey-Bass. ISBN 978-0-7879-7731-3.

Jones, Eric E.; Kelly, Janice R. (2007). "Contributions to a group discussion and perceptions of leadership: Does quantity always count more than quality?". *Group Dynamics: Theory, Research, and Practice*. 11 (1): 15–30.

Jung, D.; Wu, A.; Chow, C. W. (2008). "Towards understanding the direct and indirect effects of CEOs transformational leadership on firm innovation". The Leadership Quarterly. 19 (5): 582–594.

Jung, Dong I., Sosik, John J. (2002). "Transformational Leadership in Work Groups: The Role of Empowerment, Cohesiveness, and Collective-Efficacy on Perceived Group Performance". *Small Group Research*. 33 (3): 313–336.

Kaiser, Robert B., Hogan, Robert, Craig, S. Bartholomew (2008). "Leadership and the fate of organizations". American Psychologist. 63 (2): 96–110.

Leadership Styles

https://reedsy.com/discovery/blog/leadership-books

https://teambuildingworld.com/leadership-styles-books/

https://hbr.org/2024/04/6-common-leadership-styles-and-how-to-decide-which-to-use-when

https://www.indeed.com/career-advice/career-development/10-common-leadership-styles

https://positivepsychology.com/leadership-styles/

https://www.betterup.com/blog/types-of-leadership-styles

Levi-Sanchez, Suzanne (2018). "Civil Society in an Uncivil State". Journal of International Affairs. 71 (2): 50–72.

Lipman-Blumen, J. (2005). The Allure of Toxic Leaders. New York: Oxford University Press Inc.

Magnusson, D. (1995). "Holistic interactionism: A perspective for research on personality development". In Pervin, L. A.; John, O. P. (eds.). Handbook of personality: Theory and research. New York: Guilford Press. pp. 219–247.

Mast, Marianne Schmid Hall, Judith A. (2004). "Who Is the Boss and Who Is Not? Accuracy of Judging Status". *Journal of Nonverbal Behavior*. 28 (3): 145–165.

Matthews, Michael D., Eid, Jarle, Kelly, Dennis, Bailey, Jennifer K. S., Peterson, Christopher (2006). "Character strengths and virtues of developing military leaders: An international comparison". *Military Psychology*. 18 (Suppl): S57–S68.

Mumford, M. D., Zaccaro, S. J., Harding, F. D.; Jacobs, T. O., Fleishman, E. A. (2000). "Leadership skills for a changing world solving complex social problems". The Leadership Quarterly. 11: 11–35.

Northouse, Peter G. (2018). Leadership: Theory and Practice (8 ed.). California: Sage Publication. ISBN 9781506362298.

Palmer, Michael A. (1988). "Lord Nelson: Master of Command". Naval War College Review. 41 (1): 105–116. JSTOR 44636707.

Rosenthal, Seth A.; Pittinsky, Todd L. (2006). "Narcissistic Leadership". The Leadership Quarterly. 17 (6): 617–633.

Saffold, Guy (2005). "Leadership Through Vision". Strategic Planning: Leadership through Vision. Nairobi: Evangel Publishing House. p. 137. ISBN 9789966201225.

Salovey P, Mayer JD (1989). "Emotional intelligence". Imagination, Cognition, and Personality. 9 (3): 185–211.

Saxena, P.K. (2009). Principles of Management, A Modern Approach. New Delhi: Global India Publications PVT LTD. p. 30. ISBN 978-81-907941-5-2.

Schmid Mast, M (2002). "Female dominance hierarchies: Are they any different from males'?". Personality and Social Psychology Bulletin. 28: 29–39.

Schyns, B. (2006). "The role of implicit leadership theories in the performance appraisals and promotion recommendations of leaders". Equal Opportunities International. 25 (3): 188–199.

Scouller, James (2011). The Three Levels of Leadership: How to Develop Your Leadership Presence, Knowhow and Skill. Cirencester: Management Books 2000. ISBN 9781852526818.

See Donald Markwell (2013). "Instincts to lead": on leadership, peace, and education. Australia: Connor Court Publishing. ISBN 978-1-922168-70-2.

Sergent, Kayla (2020). "Women's Leadership Is Associated With Fewer Deaths During the COVID-19 Crisis: Quantitative and Qualitative Analyses of United States Governors". Journal of Applied Psychology. 105 (8): 771–783.

Singh, Ravinder, Rani, Ajita (2017). Human Behaviour. Notion Press. ISBN 978-1-946983-31-2.

Sivunen, Anu (2006). "Strengthening Identification with the Team in Virtual Teams: The Leaders' Perspective". Group Decision and Negotiation. 15 (4): 345–366.

Spillane, James P., Halverson, Richard, Diamond, John B. (2004). "Towards a theory of leadership practice". *Journal of Curriculum Studies*. 36 (1): 3–34.

Sun Tzu (2003). The Art of War: Complete Texts and Commentaries. Translated by Cleary, Thomas. Shambhala. ISBN 9781590300541.

Sy, T., Cote, S., Saavedra, R. (2005). "The contagious leader: Impact of the leader's mood on the mood of group members, group affective tone, and group processes" (PDF). Journal of Applied Psychology. 90 (2): 295–305.

Tsui; Nifadkar; Ou (2007). "Cross-Cultural Organizational Behavior Research: Advances, Gaps, and Recommendations". Journal of Management. 33 (3): 426–478.

Veldsman, Theo (14 January 2016). "How Toxic Leaders Destroy People as Well as Organisations". The Huffington Post. BuzzFeed, Inc.

Vinkenberg, Engen, Eagly; Johannesen-Schmidt (2011). "An exploration of stereotypical beliefs about leadership styles: Is transformational leadership a route to women's promotion?" (PDF). *The Leadership Quarterly*. 22 (1): 10–21.

Vroom, Victor H., Yetton, Phillip W. (1973). Leadership and Decision-Making. Pittsburgh: University of Pittsburgh Press. ISBN 978-0-8229-3266-6.

Yadav, Jyoti, Singh, Karan (2015). "Gender and Politics of Culture". Political Science: 77.

Zaccaro, S. J. (2007). "Trait-based perspectives of leadership". American Psychologist. 62 (1): 6–16. CiteSeerX 10.1.1.475.9808.

Zaccaro, S. J., Banks, D. J. (2001). "Leadership, vision, and organizational effectiveness". In Zaccaro, S. J.; Klimoski, R. J. (eds.). The Nature of Organizational Leadership: Understanding the Performance Imperatives Confronting Today's Leaders. San Francisco: Jossey-Bass.

Zangerl, Carl

https://inspireandinfluence.cps.northeastern.edu/2019/10/24/collaborative-leadership-what-it-is-and-why-its-important/

INTERCULTURALISM REFERENCES

Deardorff, D. K. (2009). The SAGE Handbook of Intercultural Competence. Thousand Oaks, CA: Sage.

Deardorff, D.K. (2012). International Student Success: The Missing Piece. Academic Impressions. https://www.academicimpressions.com/trainings/?_domains=student-success

Fennes, H., & Hapgood, K. (1997). Intercultural Learning in the Classroom. London, United Kingdom: Cassell.

Hofstede, G.J., Pederson, P. B., & Hofstede, G. (2002). Exploring Culture: Exercises, Stories and Synthetic Cultures. Boston: Intercultural Press.

Kubokawa, Amanda (2009). "Positive Psychology and Cultural Sensitivity: A Review of the Literature". *Graduate Journal of Counseling Psychology*. 1: 2. Archived from the original on 20 June 2018. Retrieved 20 June 2018.

Lederach, J. P. (2011). Building Peace: Sustainable Reconciliation in Divided Societies. United States Institute of Peace.

REFERENCES

NAFSA: Association of International Educators
https://www.nafsa.org/

PISA Global Competence Results
https://www.oecd.org/pisa/publications/pisa-2018-results-volume-vi-d5f68679-en.htm

Rasmussen, Louise J., Sieck, Winston R. (1 September 2015). "Culture-general competence: Evidence from a cognitive field study of professionals who work in many cultures". *International Journal of Intercultural Relations*. Intercultural Competence. 48: 75–90.

Sternberg, R. J. (Ed.). (2005). The Psychology of Hate. Washington, DC: American Psychological Association.

Storti, C. (2001). The Art of Crossing Cultures (2nd ed.). Yarmouth, ME: Intercultural Press.

Storti, C. (2017). Understanding the World's Cultures: 20th Anniversary Edition of the Classic, Figuring Foreigners Out, A Practical Guide. Yarmouth, ME: Intercultural Press (Nicholas Brealey).

Stringer, D. M., & Cassiday, P. A. (2009). 52 Activities for Improving Cross-cultural Communication. Yarmouth, ME: Intercultural Press.

UNESCO (2013). Intercultural Competences. Paris: UNESCO.

Universal Declaration of Human Rights, United Nations.

Universal Declaration on cultural diversity, United Nations.

Veerasamy, Y.S. (2021). Emerging Direction of U.S. National Higher Education Internationalization Policy Efforts between

2000 and 2019. Retrieved from https://www.ojed.org/index.php/
jcihe/issue/view/243

CRISIS REFERENCES

Aristovnik A, Keržič D, Ravšelj D, Tomaževič N, Umek L
(October 2020). "Impacts of the COVID-19 Pandemic on Life of
Higher Education Students: A Global Perspective". Sustainability.
12 (20): 8438.

Bush, George (September 20, 2001). "Text: President Bush
Addresses the Nation". *The Washington Post*. Retrieved July 4,
2015.

Davis, Mark (August 24, 2022). "The Impact of 9,11 on Business".
Investopedia. Retrieved July 23, 2023.

Dolfman, Michael L., & Wasser, Solidelle F. (2004). "9,11 and the
New York City Economy". Monthly Labor Review. 127.

Fernandez, Bob (September 22, 2001). "U.S. Markets Decline
Again". KRTBN Knight Ridder Tribune Business News.

"How much did the September 11 terrorist attack cost America?".
Institute for the Analysis of Global Security. Retrieved April 30,
2014.

Kubler-Ross, Elisabeth (1981). Living with Death and Dying.
MacMillan. ISBN 0025671103.

https://www.psycom.net/stages-of-grief

Makinen, Gail (September 27, 2002). "The Economic Effects
of 9,11: A Retrospective Assessment" (PDF). Congressional
Research Service, Library of Congress. p. 5. Retrieved September
4, 2011.

Morgan, Matthew J. (August 4, 2009). The Impact of 9,11 on Politics and War: The Day that Changed Everything?. Palgrave Macmillan. p. 222. ISBN 978-0-230-60763-7.

https://www.npr.org/2022/02/24/1079823095/are-we-ready-for-covid-19-as-a-central-theme-in-literature

https://www.nytimes.com/2021/08/12/books/review/covid-pandemic-books.html

https://bookauthority.org/books/best-covid-19-books

https://bookriot.com/6-new-books-about-covid-19/

https://www.ncbi.nlm.nih.gov/pmc/articles/PMC8744451/

The New Normal

https://academic.oup.com/jpubhealth/article/43/2/e344/6158063?login=false

https://www.researchgate.net/publication/342888752_The_New_Normal_-_A_New_Era_Full_of_Inspiration_and_Resilience_after_COVID-19

https://link.springer.com/article/10.1007/s11125-020-09521-x

https://www.ncbi.nlm.nih.gov/pmc/articles/PMC8855221/

https://educationaltechnologyjournal.springeropen.com/articles/10.1186/s41239-017-0087-5

https://jamanetwork.com/journals/jama/fullarticle/2787944

https://educationaltechnologyjournal.springeropen.com/articles/10.1186/s41239-020-00234-x

https://www.nytimes.com/2021/03/15/technology/artificial-intelligence-google-bias.html

https://www.tandfonline.com/doi/full/10.1080/18387357.2020.1792633

https://online.hbs.edu/blog/post/
ethics-and-accountability-in-the-workplace

https://www.unesco.org/en/artificial-intelligence/
recommendation-ethics

https://news.harvard.edu/gazette/story/2020/10/
ethical-concerns-mount-as-ai-takes-bigger-decision-making-role/

https://news.un.org/en/story/2021/11/1106612

https://www.pega.com/unraveling-complexity-human-ai-relation
ships?&msclkid=7051c9bb93df1e89ebe8af92c4ad6ff2&gclid=7
051c9bb93df1e89ebe8af92c4ad6ff2&gclsrc=3p.ds

www.ingramcontent.com/pod-product-compliance
Lightning Source LLC
Chambersburg PA
CBHW062116020426
42335CB00013B/992